AVERY CRAVEN

AN HISTORIAN AND THE CIVIL WAR

THE UNIVERSITY OF CHICAGO PRESS
CHICAGO AND LONDON

Library of Congress Catalog Card Number: 64-15802

The University of Chicago Press, Chicago & London
The University of Toronto Press, Toronto 5, Canada

Published 1964. Printed in the United States of America

CONTENTS

INTRODUCTION

The futility of trying to understand and explain the causes of the American Civil War grows on anyone who gives much time and thought to the subject. Only those who have not fully explored the field are confident in their ability to do so. The more one knows of the American people who got themselves into that war and of the tangled factors which played upon them, the less he is inclined to generalize and to offer simple answers. He is conscious that physical and economic factors, human qualities and reactions, moral and social values and habits, and a hundred and one circumstances entered into the complex picture. Even then, he comes to understand that neither he nor the people of that North and South can or could explain how things drifted beyond the ability of the democratic process to deal with it. He also knows there is a wide gulf between the factors which produced disagreements, engendered fears, guilt, hatred, and complete misunderstanding and the reasons why the people of a whole nation ultimately accepted and took part in bloodshed. Thousands who had no deep feelings for or against issues ultimately went to war and fought gallantly for one side or the other. Robert E. Lee himself, a man who played a considerable part in prolonging the war, defended neither slavery nor secession. His greatest biographer views him as a man "who loved peace" and who fought for reasons not generally included in "causes."

It is for these reasons that one, whom a recent writer calls "the scholar who has wrestled most persistently with the problem of why the American nation broke apart a century ago," has thought that there might be some value in bringing together a group of essays written at various times over a period of thirty-five years. The idea being that such a collection might reveal something of the troubled course which one historian followed in trying to unravel the mysteries of the coming of the Civil War.

In reading these essays, the time element should always be kept in mind. A revised view of the Civil War was begun by American scholars in an age in which changes rapid and drastic made a consistent approach to any problem almost impossible. It began with a great depression which seemed to invalidate most of the economic and social institutions and values by which the American people had ordered their lives since the Civil War. It was followed by the New Deal, whose methods were largely those of trial and error, and then by the disturbing events which led to the Second World War and a long period of postwar reconstruction.

The chaotic conditions of the period in which these historians worked may have been in part the reason for turning back a hundred years to pre–Civil War days, when conditions and problems seem to have been equally chaotic. Perhaps more important was the fact that an older generation of historians, by whom many of these men had been trained, was rapidly moving off the stage. Such outstanding historians as Frederick Jackson Turner, Edward Channing, Charles A. Beard, Ulrich Bonnell Phillips, and Carl Becker, to mention only a few, had already made their contributions. They had revised earlier points of view and given American history a new set of approaches. They had written for their own generation and had done an exceedingly good job.

The generation of scholars which followed these masters naturally retained an understandable reverence for them and for their methods and interpretations. In spite of the fact that the whole order for which these men had written had suddenly gone to pieces, the younger historians could not break away quickly. As a result, I think their work for a time reveals a transition quality, a tangling of the new with the old, and a tendency to state their new positions more sharply than they would have done under other circumstances. Conscious of the fact that they were breaking new ground and differing with revered predecessors, they probably overstressed certain points in order to make their position clear. As I have read some of these early essays I have often wished to change many statements, but I have not done so. That would have destroyed the purpose of republishing.

The essays here presented dealing with Frederick Jackson Turner and the West, and those which were the first to deal with the Civil War show these tendencies. Those which follow show more and more the influence of the 1930's and 1940's and an effort to see the Civil War as representing a stumbling, blundering generation which got itself into what some called a needless war. Such an approach also required a new look at slavery and the part which it played in the struggle. (At least it had to be shown that slavery was not the only factor in producing the war.) This approach stressed the part which unreasoning emotion played and dealt rather severely with the abolitionists who, along with the Southern fire eaters, made war inevitable. Two of my essays illustrate this point.

The redistribution of blame, however, hardly fitted the needs of a day in which the old problem of central-government efficiency versus local freedom was again disturbing the American people. Did not the Civil War reveal the tragic story of the failure of the democratic process in its most dramatic form? Had the built-in conflict between the American dream as set forth in the Declaration of Independence and the legal stability afforded by the Constitution ever come into the open so clearly? Had we ever had such clear and solid defenses of our obligation to the federal system and a strict, literal interpretation of the Constitution as was then offered by John Taylor of Caroline, Robert Turnbull of Charleston, and John C. Calhoun of South Carolina? And had the claims of nationalism and of our moral obligations to the Declaration of Independence ever been so well argued as by Daniel Webster, Theodore Weld, and Abraham Lincoln? Or had the nation ever produced such politicians who avoided troublesome abstractions and insisted on compromise as did Henry Clay and Stephen A. Douglas? Several of the later essays show clearly the attempt to state the problems and the issues which grew out of the conflict between our great American documents.

Finally, as a cold war settled down on the United States in the 1940's as something to be endured yet as something which always threatened a tragic ending, the historian of the Civil War was more impressed with the tragedy involved. He saw it as a case of a people getting themselves into a predicament in which moderate, well-intending men could find no language but that of force. The final essays reproduced here seemingly grew out of this new understanding, and they round out the course which one historian of the period followed in his thinking. Since most of these essays culminated in books, the combination of the two seemed to lend solid support to Edward H. Carr's definition of history as "a continuous process of interaction between the historian and his facts, an unending dialogue between the present and the past." And the historian of the Civil War would certainly also agree with Carr in his confession that "I hope I am sufficiently up to date to recognize that anything written in the 1890's must be nonsense. But I am not yet advanced enough to be committed to the view that anything written in the 1950's necessarily makes sense."[1]

[1] Edward H. Carr, *What Is History?*

I

THE AGRICULTURAL REFORMERS OF THE ANTE-BELLUM SOUTH

The problems which the agricultural reformers of the ante-bellum South faced were the same fundamental problems which their kind have faced in all times and in all places. Stated in simplest form their task was one of introducing methods among those who tended the soil which would give profits without destroying fertility and which, in regions where already the earth's fullness had been spent, would restore lands to fruitfulness. The Old South faced the problems of profits and restoration; the Lower South, the problems of profits and conservation.[1] The difference was merely one of age—the tobacco lands of the one were already badly depleted, the cotton and sugar lands of the other were everywhere being reduced by wasteful practices.[2]

And yet there was nothing unique about the southern situation and the forces that had produced it, nor is there any vital reason why the problems of the Old South and the Lower South should be separated for treatment from those of the North and the Northwest. All sections alike were confronted by the ruins which the destructive methods of frontier days had wrought, and which they were still leaving in their wake as the pioneer passed through the forest and over the farming lands.[3] If the Old South had greater ruins than did the other sections, it was largely because it had been more successful in quickly and cheaply gathering the riches which Nature offered and in spending them in the faraway markets where the com-

Reprinted from the *American Historical Review,* XXXIII, No. 2 (January, 1928), 302–14. A paper read at the meeting of the American Historical Association, at Rochester, December 28, 1926.

1 The Kentucky-Tennessee region and Texas have not been included in this study. Both had their reform leaders and deserve separate study.

2 See A. O. Craven, *Soil Exhaustion as a Factor in the Agricultural History of Virginia and Maryland, 1606–1860* (Urbana, Ill., 1925).

3 It should be noticed that the so-called "soil exhaustion" was but the agricultural side of frontier exploitation of natural resources, which was matched in the treatment accorded the forest, mineral resources, etc.

forts and luxuries of a more advanced life might be secured. Thus, while the settlers of Massachusetts yielded their English standards of living under the scanty returns of a stingy Nature, the Old South, with its destructive tobacco culture, went on to the reproduction of an English gentry order which seemed to give adequate compensation for the ruined soils. And if the Lower South in the ante-bellum period was in like manner exploiting its soils in extensive, single-crop cotton production, it was doing no more than the frontier farmer of the Northwest was attempting to do with his wheat and corn, with results that differed largely according to the hunger of the markets found for the crops produced. The frontier everywhere created problems of restoration and varied the degree of ruin which it left only by the speed with which it gave way to a more complex and diversified economic-social order.[4]

Other factors, however, had a hand in creating southern agricultural problems. In the colonial period, tobacco not only bore the burden of quickly lifting a frontier to a complex life, but it long carried the added load of British regulations and taxation and that of an indirect and expensive marketing system.[5] In the ante-bellum period the frontier cotton planter of the Lower South likewise struggled against the action of government in the form of tariffs, which many students of the South still believe to have been harmful, and sold his crops in distant markets through the hands of northern factors that were as greedy as their predecessors of Scottish and English origin. Under such conditions the planters of both periods were forced to center their efforts upon the most profitable single crop, produced by those methods most economical of capital and labor, but which could draw most heavily upon the virgin soils as the planter's one advantage in production. If profits were to be made which were capable of maintaining the social standards established, then soil-conserving agriculture was out of the question.

Nor were these factors peculiarly Southern or limited to this time and place. Agriculture as a more primitive economic effort seldom gains the political favors freely given to the industrial interests which represent the rise of a more complex social-economic or-

[4] B. H. Hibbard, *The History of Agriculture in Dane County, Wisconsin,* pp. 125–31; J. G. Thompson, *The Rise and Decline of the Wheat Growing Industry in Wisconsin,* pp. 20–23; J. F. W. Johnston, *Notes on North America,* I, 163, 172, 355; *Genesee Farmer,* VI, 108; R. H. Holt, "History of Wheat Growing in Illinois, 1840–1870" (master's thesis, University of Illinois, 1926).

[5] Craven, *op. cit.,* pp. 40–50.

der. Manufacturing means the development of an advanced stage of progress, and it inevitably secures favors in any society rising from primitive foundations. It has usually been considered decidedly "American" to give aid to industry; it has as often been considered "un-American" even to suggest aid by legislation for agriculture. Furthermore, the scattered character of rural society and the peculiar individualism developed by a life lived apart in constant contact with a wilful Nature places the marketing of the farmer's crops in the hands of middlemen who need seldom fear any sustained combination or co-operation in resistance to prices paid for produce. The farmer usually gains from the sale of his crops just enough to keep him going at his task and plunders his soils for any additional returns. Little wealth has probably ever been acquired from American agriculture except that which has come from exploiting the natural fertility of the soil and from the so-called unearned increment which has arisen from the constantly increasing values of land. And there is no reason to hope, unless decided changes come, that, with the ending of these two sources of profit, the American farmer will not follow the course of farmers in all lands, in all periods of time, in accepting the status of a peasant as his lot.[6]

Only one factor belongs to the South as a unique force in the creation of ante-bellum problems. That problem arose from the peculiar character of her geographic and climatic conditions. Southern rainfall was always heavy and concentrated. The annual precipitation ranged from forty to eighty inches, and showers yielding as much as fifteen inches of water in the course of three days were known to have fallen. Such rainfall, even under the most favorable conditions, would present serious problems; but in the South—where the sod-formation was always poor, many of the soils were loose or their subsoils compact, and much of the land was rolling or even badly broken—the losses from leaching and erosion were always serious.[7] Added to this, the warm climate caused the soils to teem

[6] Prices, of course, are not fixed by the local middleman. The term is used here to indicate the whole indirect process by which the farmer's crops are handled and to indicate the failure of the farmer, either by control of production or by organization in selling, to have a hand in determining the selling price of his produce.

The statement regarding the failure of agriculture to produce wealth is based upon a comparison of the wealth in certain typical regions with the increased values of land and the rather uncertain matter of soil deterioration. The problem is highly involved and definite conclusions impossible. The statement made here, however, seems to the writer to be warranted by his studies. (This, of course, was written before the New Deal.)

[7] W. W. Ashe, in *Review of Reviews,* XXXIX, 439–43; R. O. E. Davis, "Soil Erosion in the South," *Bulletin of the United States Department of Agriculture;* Bennett, *The Soils and Agriculture of the South.*

with life, and soil diseases and harmful micro-organisms were given a wider play than in any other part of the country.[8] In these features the problems of the South were in degree greater and the losses permitted by poor methods more extensive than elsewhere. But in all else little can be found that belonged distinctly to this section. In the main the problems presented were the normal and universal problems of the American farmer.

Reduced to practical terms, the reformers of the South had first to arouse a will to improve and then to indicate the steps by which profitable changes might be made; the old monoculture had to come to an end and a wider diversification of crops be adopted; the widest use of fertilizers, both natural and artificial, was imperative; better plowing, which would not only reach new soil but also check the losses from erosion, had to be introduced; and everywhere, both on low and on higher lands, better drainage systems had to be developed. If these improvements could be made and profits still maintained, then the South might go on to power and prosperity.

The first great reformer of the period was John Taylor of Caroline. Writing to Thomas Jefferson in an early day, he declared: "There is a spice of fanaticism in my nature upon two subjects—agriculture and republicanism, which all who set it in motion, are sure to suffer by."[9] Fortunately for Virginia and the entire South there was much to keep in motion the "fanaticism" of this keen intellect, and through his efforts the whole region awakened to a realization of serious dangers which threatened, and started upon the road toward reform. His agricultural work perhaps reached its fullest expression in the publication of his book, *Arator*, which brought together the ideas he had stated earlier in private correspondence, in public addresses, or even in scattered newspaper articles. This book made its appearance in 1813, and, as Edmund Ruffin later said, "opened the eyes of many in this part of the country to see that agriculture ought to be and did embrace more than simply cutting down trees, grubbing and plowing land."[10] "It was . . . throughout a trumpet-tongued exposure" of the "general impoverishment and ruinous progress" which everywhere held sway.[11]

[8] E. J. Russell, *Soil Conditions and Plant Growth*, pp. 150–51.

[9] John Taylor to Thomas Jefferson, March 5, 1795, Papers of Thomas Jefferson, Library of Congress. For sketch of John Taylor, see W. E. Dodd, "John Taylor of Caroline, Prophet of Secession," *John P. Branch Historical Papers of Randolph-Macon College*, II (June, 1908), 214–353.

[10] *Farmer's Register*, II, 12–14.

[11] *Southern Planter*, XII, 258.

John Taylor saw clearly the great agricultural problem of the Old South. "Our land has diminished in fertility," he declared as he pointed to whole counties where once tobacco grew in great quantities but which were now "too sterile to grow any of moment," or to keep the wheat crops, which had been substituted, up to the level of profits.[12] "No profit . . . can be made by tilling poor land," he said, ". . . to make it rich, therefore, ought to be the first object of our efforts."[13]

The only practical way to a restored fertility, as Taylor saw it, lay in the creation and use of all kinds of manure—animal and vegetable.[14] The atmosphere was the great source of life, and plants alone could draw upon it and reduce its creative substances to a form in which they could be given to the earth, either directly by plowing under the plants themselves or indirectly by the application of animal manure. Plants, like animals, feed upon each other, he thought, and organic material alone could return the capital so lavishly spent by the harvests of earlier days. The first step, therefore, from which Taylor advanced to all others was summed up in what he called "enclosing."[15] This was his way of practicing his doctrine that "the best system of practical agriculture" was the one offering "the best mode of raising manure."[16] By this he meant the exclusion of all stock from the arable and grass lands and the production of those crops which afforded the greatest amount of offal for conversion into manure by plowing under, penning, bedding, or feeding.

The one crop which seemed to him to give greatest advantage both for profit and improvement was the then despised Indian corn. Corn furnished a maximum of food for both man and beast, and its generous stocks, blades, shucks, and cobs could be used for barnyard litter or could be plowed under in the fields as direct vegetable manure. "We seek after a vegetable proper for poor ground," he writes; "it is found in corn."[17]

But corn as a single crop was not to be tolerated. Clover was to be grown on every spot where it could be "prevailed upon to exist," and field peas together with every kind of grass were commended

[12] John Taylor, *Arator,* pp. 11–12, 14.

[13] John Taylor to Thomas Jefferson, March 5, 1795, Jefferson MSS.; *Arator,* pp. 68–71.

[14] *Niles' Weekly Register,* XV, 177–81.

[15] *Arator,* pp. 72–86; *Farmer's Register,* VII, 561–64.

[16] *Arator,* p. 87.

[17] John Taylor to Thomas Jefferson, March 5, 1795, Jefferson MSS.

for widest use in improving rotation.[18] Deep and horizontal plowing to check erosion was to accompany these crops, and artificial fertilizers, such as gypsum, lime, and marl, were heartily approved. In fact there was scarcely a thing along the line of advancement, from the use of better machinery to the selection of better seed, that escaped his eager eye or was left out of his constructive programme.[19]

But Taylor was as keen a critic as he was a builder, and his sharp attack upon the ills and enemies of agriculture was as telling as were his suggestions for reform. Tobacco was rejected; the overseer system was condemned; the drawing of capital and ability from agriculture to industry was bitterly noted; the folly of too many slaves for personal supervision was pointed out; and the neglect of agriculture by the government as contrasted to the tariffs given to manufacturing was denounced as a burden thrust upon the one for the benefit of the other.[20] In fact, it is a question whether Taylor's greatest contribution lies in improvements preached or in attacks launched against the shortcomings of the old order. Viewed from either angle—as a force in awakening men to the realization of a bad situation or as a leader in new things—John Taylor of Caroline must be placed at the head of the list of early ante-bellum agricultural reformers.

A few other men of the earlier period deserve some attention. James M. Garnett of Fredericksburg in Virginia was early urging reform through the medium of the Agricultural Society and the public press.[21] He advocated the selection of seed corn from the larger and more prolific stocks; he condemned the extravagances in living which consumed the capital so necessary for improvements; he urged men to adopt better methods of plowing and took his stand alongside John Taylor in uncompromising opposition to protective tariffs; he worked unceasingly for the organization and extension of the agricultural society, local, state, and national, and no voice was lifted more untiringly in the effort to arouse men to the realization of their shortcomings or in pointing out the ways for improvement.

Thomas Mann Randolph should be noticed for his work with

[18] Richmond *Enquirer,* June 16, 1818; *Memoirs of the Philadelphia Agricultural Society,* II, 100; *American Farmer,* I, 257 ff.

[19] *Arator,* pp. 150–52, 111–13; *American Farmer,* II, 31; Taylor to Jefferson, November 19, 1797, Jefferson MSS.

[20] *Arator,* pp. 41–52, 232, 260.

[21] *American Farmer,* II, 89, III, 114, IV, 41, 290–91; *Farmer's Register,* IV, 541–44; Richmond *Enquirer,* November 3, 1818, August 20, 24, 27, 1819.

horizontal plowing;[22] Stephen McCormick for his improved plows;[23] Fielding Lewis for the early use of lime on soils;[24] Philip Tabb, John Singleton, William Meriwether, and W. C. Nicholas for the extensive use of manure, deep plowing, and grass crops in improving rotations.[25] Nor can the work of George Jefferys of North Carolina be passed by. He corresponded with improvement-minded farmers all over the Old South, sent out questionnaires dealing with the subjects of fertilizers, plowing, and crop rotation, and then by letter and printed article scattered the knowledge gained to every corner of the section.[26] To these men credit is due for their teachings, but there were many others who practiced but did not preach because, as one of them said: "I have been too negligent in my profession, and have ploughed the old farm up and down hill so long, that its soil has followed the plough furrows, branches, and creeks, until it has in all probability reached the Atlantic, leaving me in my fifty-second year, to renovate the sub-soil . . . instead of writing in my parlour for your periodical. . . ."[27]

Little of permanent success came to these early reformers, but the fault was not their own. Markets and ways to market were poor, and improved farming requires profits in order to succeed. The whole law and gospel of agricultural improvement, for all times, is expressed in the words of the Virginia farmer who wrote in 1821: "It is not worth while to make crops, we can get nothing for them. . . . Neither is it any object to improve lands. . . ."

The second group of agricultural reformers, whose efforts run well down to the War between the States, may well be headed by the energetic John Skinner of Baltimore.[28] Trained for the law and admitted to the bar, he early turned aside to accept Madison's appointment as postmaster at Baltimore, in which position he found

[22] American Historical Association, *Annual Report* for 1918, I, 299–300; *American Farmer,* II, 94–95.

[23] Richmond *Enquirer,* January 5, 1826; Stephen McCormick Papers (Herbert Kellar of the McCormick Library, Chicago, kindly placed at my disposal papers showing the importance of McCormick's plows to this section); *American Farmer,* IV, 189; Richmond *Enquirer,* August 13, 1819.

[24] *Southern Planter,* XIV, 19–20; *Farmer's Register,* I, 18.

[25] *American Farmer,* II, 28, 115; Richmond *Enquirer,* October 27, 1818, June 8, 1819, August 13, 1819, June 9, 1820; *Farmer's Register,* X, 94; *Southern Planter,* LXXV, 757. (These references are typical of many that might be given to show the work of these men.)

[26] *American Farmer,* II, 5, 14, 28, 59, 374, etc.

[27] *Farmer's Register,* IV, 577–79. Other names, such as John Wickham, Thomas Marshall, F. Tilghman, and J. H. Roy, might be added, but the purpose here has been only to list the outstanding leaders.

[28] For a sketch of John Skinner's life, see *American Farmer,* 4th ser., VII, 325.

time in 1819 to begin the publication of the *American Farmer.* It was the *Farmer*'s "great aim and chief pride to collect information from every source, on every branch of Husbandry," in order that the readers by comparisons might discover "the best system" for "all circumstances."[29] Almost from its first issue it became the organ through which individual reformers conveyed their ideas to the public and in which the agricultural societies ordered their papers and proceedings published. From its office the first guano used in the South was distributed;[30] in its pages the editor described improved methods observed in his travels; its editorial columns urged reform and advocated the establishment of agricultural schools, the employment of agricultural chemists, and the wider organization of farmers for co-operation and exchange of ideas. From 1819 throughout the period, under different editors and even under different names, it continued to preach the gospel of reform.[31]

Skinner himself left the *American Farmer* in the late twenties, edited the *Turf Register* for a time, acted as assistant postmaster general under Harrison, then returned to agricultural work as editor of the *Farmer's Library and Agricultural Journal* in New York City and later of *The Plough, the Loom, and the Anvil* in Philadelphia. The name of John Skinner became associated with agricultural advancement throughout the South, and, though the *American Farmer* constituted his greatest single contribution, southern men followed him to his other papers and continued to profit by his efforts. He was a pioneer among the agricultural editors who strove to awaken and advance the South. He heads a list that can be mentioned here only by name and paper: David Wiley of the *Agricultural Museum* (Georgetown, D.C.); Theoderick McRoberts of the *Virginia Farmer* (Scottsville, Va.); E. P. Roberts and Samuel Sands of the *Farmer and Gardener* and *American Farmer* (Baltimore, Md.); J. D. Legaré and G. R. Carroll of the early *Southern Agriculturist* (Charleston, S.C.) and A. G. Summer and William Summer of the later one (Laurensville, S.C.); J. W. Jones, James Camak, Daniel Lee, and D. Redmond of the *Southern Cultivator* (Augusta, Ga.); John Sherwood of the *Farmer's Advocate* (Jamestown, N.C.); N. B. Cloud and Charles A. Peabody of the

[29] *American Farmer,* I, 5.

[30] *Ibid.,* VI, 316.

[31] This paper was known as the *Farmere and Gardener* for a time but resumed its original name when Skinner returned as editor in 1839. It kept the name when Samuel Sands assumed control to allow Skinner to become assistant postmaster general in 1841.

American Cotton Planter (Montgomery, Ala.); T. C. Botts, J. M. Daniels, R. B. Gooch, and F. G. Ruffin of the *Southern Planter* (Richmond, Va.); and last, but far from least, J. D. B. De Bow of the *Commercial Review* (New Orleans, La.).[32]

But the greatest name of the new period was that of Edmund Ruffin of Virginia. Improved farmer, scientific investigator, editor of the greatest agricultural paper of the time, reformer by virtue of intense agricultural interests and unbounded southern patriotism, he belonged to the South as a whole rather than to any single state, and did a work for agriculture that reached almost to the dignity of statesmanship.[33] At a time when men were fleeing the older sections of the South or sinking into direst poverty, Ruffin began his work at Coggin's Point with a trial of John Taylor's methods. They failed him, and in desperation he struck out on new lines in an effort to rebuild his depleted soils. His investigations led him to the conclusion that the great trouble lay in an increasing acidity of soil produced by the excessive and unscientific cropping of the past. He noticed that where lands abounded in calcareous materials to the destruction of acidity, there fertility remained, and sedge, sorrel, and pine were absent. He reasoned that if a neutralizer could be applied to the so-called "exhausted soils" then their latent fertility would assert itself and manures become truly effective.[34] He put his ideas to test by the use of marl, and increased yields of from 40 to 50 per cent proved to his satisfaction that his theories were correct. He early presented the results of his experiments, together with his plans for reform, to the local agricultural society and later developed them into his famed book called *Essay on Calcareous Manures* —a work which, at the end of the century, an expert in the United

32 It is not the intention to give a complete list of the editors of all the agricultural papers started in the South in this period. There were perhaps others who deserve mention, but the writer has not been able personally to inspect and evaluate such papers as *The Soil of the South* (Macon, Ga.), the *North Carolina Farmer* (Raleigh, n.c.), the *Farmer's Gazette* (Sparta, Ga.), the *Planter's Banner* (La.), the *Alabama Planter* (Tuscaloosa, Ala.), and the *Valley Farmer* (Winchester, Va.), and has hesitated to include their editors among a list that, after a rather close study, seems to merit attention. The *Agricultural Museum* antedates Skinner's *American Farmer,* and is, I believe, the first agricultural paper established in the United States. The *Museum* began publication in 1810, and while it was able to continue only for a few years, it maintained a high standard. The *Farmer's Register* has been intentionally omitted from this list, because of its treatment later under Edmund Ruffin's work.

33 H. G. Ellis, in *John P. Branch Historical Papers of Randolph-Macon College,* Vol. III, No. 2, pp. 99–123; De Bow's *Commercial Review,* XI, 431–36; Diary of Edmund Ruffin, Library of Congress.

34 *Farmer's Register,* VII, 659–67; *American Farmer,* 4th ser., VII, 293; 1st ser., III, 313–19; *Essay on Calcareous Manures, passim.*

States Department of Agriculture declared to be the most thorough piece of writing on an agricultural subject ever published in the English language.[35]

In 1832 he founded the *Farmer's Register*, which John Skinner called "the best publication on agriculture which this country or Europe has ever produced," and which, in De Bow's quaint wording, "exhibited" in all its attractions "the noble science of agriculture" and by its diffusion "of rich stores of scientific and practical information" aroused "the energies and dispelled the lethargy" of the Old South.[36]

Opposition to the editor's attitude on the bank question combined with financial losses to bring the *Register* to an end in 1842, but Ruffin continued his reforms as a member of Virginia's first state Board of Agriculture and later as agricultural commissioner for the state Agricultural Society.[37] In the meantime he became agricultural surveyor of South Carolina and found time to bring out new editions of his *Essay on Calcareous Manures* and to publish in 1855 a new volume called *Essays and Notes on Agriculture*.[38] His reports from official positions together with his addresses to the various agricultural societies round out a full statement of his theories and practices.[39]

The use of marl on worn lands was ever the first step in Ruffin's system. But the wider application of manures, the continued growing of legumes, such as clover and field peas, the rotation of crops, the laying of covered drains, and better plowing of all kinds were held in equal esteem when once the first step had been taken.[40] His

[35] W. P. Cutter, in *Yearbook of the United States Department of Agriculture, 1895*, p. 493.

[36] Richmond *Enquirer*, June 18 and August 2, 1833, November 11, 1834; De Bow's *Commercial Review*, XI, 435.

[37] *American Farmer*, 4th ser., VII, 293; *Farmer's Register*, IX, 618–19, 163–66, X, 155.

[38] Five editions of the *Essay on Calcareous Manures* were issued January, 1832; April, 1835, December, 1842 (supplement to Vol. X of *Farmer's Register*), 1844, 1853. *Essays and Notes on Agriculture* published in 1855.

[39] *An Address on the Opposite Results of Exhausting and Fertilizing Systems of Agriculture, read before the South Carolina Institute at Its Fourth Annual Fair*, November 18, 1853 (Charleston, 1853); "Report to State Board of Agriculture on the Most Important Recent Improvements of Agriculture in Lower Virginia," *Farmer's Register*, X, 656–66; "Sketch of the Progress of Agriculture in Virginia and Causes of Depression," *ibid.*, III, 748–60; "Rotation of Crops," *Southern Planter*, XII, 289–305 (commissioner's communication); *Agricultural Survey of South Carolina* (Columbia, 1843). These are but a few of the most important writings which were issued in pamphlet form or printed in agricultural papers. He was a frequent contributor to the press throughout his life.

[40] *Southern Planter*, VI, 135–42; *Farmer's Register*, VII, 609–10; Diary of Edmund Ruffin; *Southern Planter*, XII, 329.

understanding of soil fertility and soil depletion was startingly modern. He rejected the static notion of exhaustion by the removal of elements in plant growth and insisted that the absence of organic matter, the physical condition of the soil, and the increase of acidity were far more important.[41] He was familiar with De Candolle's idea of toxicity from continued growth of like crops and urged objections that compel respect even today. So keenly did he diagnose the soil problems of his section and so wisely did he prescribe remedies that, where his teachings were heeded, decline ceased, emigration was checked, and, even though not one-twentieth of the lands had been touched, their values in lower Virginia increased by over $30,000,000 in the twenty years before 1850. Wheat and corn yields tripled and quadrupled, and fields once "galled and gullied" were described as growing rank with clover.[42] Ruffin had, indeed, as a contemporary said, erected to himself a monument in the restored soils of his state.[43]

But Ruffin's aim was not mere material prosperity. He was primarily interested in the upbuilding of the South as a section. The declining soils had limited southern population, had lessened southern political power in the national councils, and had put the South at the mercy of the industrial North in tariff and slavery conflicts. To restore his beloved section to power or to fit her for prosperous independence was his goal. The way lay through a restored fertility that would hold her population at home and enable her to keep pace with her rival in the contest for power. It was this ideal that led the great agricultural reformer to scatter the John Brown pikes to the southern legislatures; to originate the "League of United Southerners" which Yancey adopted as his own; to become, as *Leslie's Weekly* said, "a political Peter the Hermit" going "about from Convention to Convention . . . preaching secession wherever he goes"; and, in the end, to fire the first gun at Sumter. It steeled an old man of seventy to fight through four long years of bitter warfare and to take his own life in grief at Lee's surrender. Edmund Ruffin, agriculturist, was also Edmund Ruffin, southern patriot.[44]

[41] *An Address on the Opposite Results of Exhausting and Fertilizing Systems of Agriculture;* Diary of Edmund Ruffin; *Farmer's Register,* VII, 609–10.

[42] *Southern Planter,* XIV, 104, IX, 226–37; Diary of Edmund Ruffin (especially years 1858–59); *Farmer's Register,* I, 606, VII, 114, VIII, 415–18, 484–97, X, 40.

[43] *American Farmer,* 4th ser., VII, 297.

[44] The Diary of Edmund Ruffin furnished the material from which this paragraph has been written. Day-by-day accounts are given of events and clippings from newspapers, etc.

A few other reformers of the period can be noticed only briefly. James H. Hammond of South Carolina, who occupies the almost unique position among farmers of not liking "what is old" and of knowing "hardly . . . anything old in corn or cotton planting but what is wrong," advocated and practiced better plowing and drainage, the use of fertilizers, and especially the diversification of husbandry by grain and stock, leaving cotton to the newer West.[45]

N. B. Cloud of Alabama was a specialist in fertilizing;[46] Jethro V. Jones and David Dickson of Georgia, H. W. Vick and R. Abbey together with the "Petit Gulf" group of Hunt, MacGruder, and Freeland in Mississippi, all acquired justly high reputations for the breeding of improved strains of cotton;[47] Dr. M. W. Phillips of Mississippi, Vardry McBee and William Elliott of South Carolina, R. Peters, J. V. and J. B. Jones of Georgia were advocates of all-round better farming and wider diversification of production;[48] Robert F. W. Allston of South Carolina did much for rice and P. A. Wilkinson, Valcour Aime, and Judge P. Rost labored to advance sugar methods in Louisiana.[49] These men, with those who have been named before, constituted a leadership in an agricultural reformation that by 1860 had taken advantage of improved markets to place southern agriculture on the road toward sound development. The older regions had done most. They had overcome difficulties greater than those faced in any other part of the nation and, with an agricultural intelligence unequaled, had solved the problem of restoration.[50] The leaders in the newer sections had done less, but they had been forced to combat the unbending purpose of the frontier to

[45] Elizabeth Merritt, *James H. Hammond,* "Johns Hopkins University Studies in Historical and Political Science," Vol. XLI; James H. Hammond, *An Address delivered before the South Carolina Institute, at the First Annual Fair, on the 20th November, 1849* (Charleston, 1849); Hammond Papers, Library of Congress, especially diary. The words quoted here are given in U. B. Phillips, *American Negro Slavery,* p. 216. See also *De Bow's Review,* pp. 24, 501–22.

[46] *Ibid.,* XIV, 194; Phillips, *American Negro Slavery,* p. 215.

[47] *De Bow's Review,* XII, 192–93, 75, III, 1–7; L. H. Bailey, *Cyclopedia of American Agriculture,* IV, 567.

[48] F. L. Riley, "Diary of a Mississippi Planter," *Mississippi Historical Society Publications,* X, 305–481; *De Bow's Review,* XIII, 314–18, XII, 192–93.

[49] *Plantation Diary of the Late Mr. Valcour Aime* (New Orleans, 1878); *De Bow's Review,* III, 223–34, 417–28, 383–85, VI, 55–57, XII, 574, XVI, 535, XXIV, 321–24; *Oration delivered before the Agricultural and Mechanics Association of Louisiana on the 12th of May, 1845* (Philadelphia, 1845; copy in Howard Memorial Library, New Orleans). The names of Cyrus H. McCormick, Obed Hussy, John A. Seldon, Hill Carter, P. H. Steinbergen, W. W. Bowie, Col. Capron, and others might be included in a more detailed study of improvements.

[50] Craven, *op. cit.,* pp. 122–61.

spend its natural wealth for immediate returns. They had, at least on the larger estates and in the better portions, done enough toward checking destructive practices and introducing a wider diversification of crops, to render the long-held notion of complete dependence upon the Northwest for food supplies the worst of myths.[51]

Yet too much should not be claimed. Reform, as yet, had been confined largely to the production end of agriculture—a natural consequence of exploitive frontier beginnings—and many more complicated problems lay yet ahead. In a few places the problem of organization, division, and supervision of well-considered quantities of labor had been attacked and substantial progress made,[52] but the final step necessary in converting agriculture into a mature, well-established business undertaking, that is, the adjustment to and control of profitable markets through sound marketing methods, then as now, awaited the complete breakdown of returns from soil exploitation and increasing land values. The agricultural reformer of the ante-bellum South, like his kind in other times, gave his attention largely to the problems causing immediate discomfort.

51 C. M. Thompson, "Southern Food Supply—1859–1860." A paper read at the meeting of the American Economic Association at St. Louis, December 28, 1926. Dean Thompson, after subtracting the exports, found that the per capita value of food crops for the nation as a whole was $45. Compared to this, the lower Mississippi group of states averaged $44; the middle Mississippi group (all slave) averaged $72; and the upper Mississippi group $74. Florida averaged $38; South Carolina (excluding rice), $38; North Carolina, $53; and Virginia, $48. The slave states taken as a whole showed a value average of $53.

The per capita value of corn for the nation as a whole was just under $24. In Louisiana it was $21; in Georgia, $26; Mississippi, $33; Arkansas, $37; Tennessee, $42; Kentucky, $50; Missouri, $56; South Carolina, $19; North Carolina, $27; and Virginia, $22.

In slaughtered animals the national per capita value was $6.77. Only three slave states—Louisiana, Florida, and Maryland—fell below this average.

The South as a whole fell slightly below the average in wheat production per capita, but if whites alone are counted, the difference is not great. In peas, beans, and potatoes the South again showed an advantage, if sweet potatoes are included.

Professor Thompson finds that in four of the five most important cotton-growing counties in Mississippi the per capita value of food crops exceeded the national average; in one it reached $78; in another, $63; and in another, $60.

52 Especially on the larger plantations in Virginia and Maryland.

II

JOHN TAYLOR AND SOUTHERN AGRICULTURE

The way of the farmer, like that of the transgressor, is hard. He must ever plant and await his harvest amid the uncertainties of weather, pests, and markets. Hope must ever be tempered with fear. The brightest prospects may at any moment turn to utter ruin. Heat and cold, rain and sun are both his fickle friends and his brutal enemies. One can well sympathize with the beaten tiller of stubborn soils who quit farming with the declaration that he was going to get into some business with which the Lord had less to do.

But the farmer's troubles are not all with a willful nature. The very character of his tasks renders him a rugged individualist—a man capable of standing on his own feet and quite determined to do so. Constant experience with the fixed ways of nature of the rule of thumb methods necessary to circumvent or co-operate with her make him both conservative and backward in his tendencies. He is, regardless of time and place and changing conditions, always more or less a frontiersman in his outlook.

Such characteristics may serve well in simple rural-pioneer days; they become stumbling blocks when urban-industrial developments crowd the rural-agricultural order and institute conflict of interest and complexity of relationships. Then co-operation, efficiency, and capacity for rapid readjustment are essential to dominance. The farmer lags behind. He loses social standing. The richer economic rewards go to others. In time the farmer sinks to the level of serf or peasant while the men of commerce, finance, and industry rule the day. Such is the story which history has to tell of those who have fed mankind through the years.

The Virginia planter of Colonial days began his course at one of the few periods favorable to farmers in the history of the Western world. He was heir to the station and prestige of the English country

Reprinted from the *Journal of Southern History,* IV, No. 2 (May, 1938), 137–47.

gentleman. He came at a time when modern capitalism was ingrafting a new acquisitive individualism onto that older ideal and making it possible for a rural man to speculate in lands, to exploit the natural resources of a raw continent, and to enslave black men for his benefit. Profits were no longer below a gentlemen's purposes. He could defend without loss of dignity the laissez faire theory in economics and politics and insist that natural laws, if allowed free play, would give the greatest human happiness. He could measure happiness in terms of property and believe that the democratic form of government was the best political expression of all these things. Democracy gave more freedom and more of equality and more of material opportunity.

In like vein he could proclaim with wide approval the superiority of agriculture over any other economic endeavor. It gave the basic products of food and raw materials for fabrication. It added something to character and it encouraged virtue. The farmer might even envisage himself as the chief factor in God's own great experiment in human well-being. John Taylor of Caroline once boasted that "the divine intelligence which selected an agricultural state as a paradise for his first favourites, has here again prescribed the agricultural virtues as the means for the admission of their posterity into heaven."[1] He further insisted that on the maintenance of republican institutions, partial to farmers, depended "whether the United States [should] . . . establish a new era in the world, or [should] . . . follow the inglorious track marked by the career of other nations."[2]

However fair the prospect for the realization of a rural paradise may have been in the beginning, times had changed sharply for the worse with the American Revolution and the establishment of a new national government. For many decades profits had been uncertain and an air of poverty and despair had fallen on this embryo Eden. Tobacco, the great staple of Colonial days, had long languished under British regulations, the heavy burdens of indirect marketing, and the wasteful practices of frontier farming methods. Soils had depleted as crop after crop had been taken from the lands and as destructive rainfall had carried surface materials out to the

[1] John Taylor, *Arator, Being a Series of Agricultural Essays, Practical and Political* (4th ed.; Petersburg, Va., 1818), pp. 188–89; *id., Tyranny Unmasked* (Washington, 1822), pp. 129, 345–47.

[2] *Id., An Enquiry into the Principles and Tendency of Certain Public Measures* (Philadelphia, 1794), p. 110.

ocean.[3] By the end of the Revolution, a traveler through the section where once William Fitzhugh boasted of his 54,000 acres, of good debts lying out to about 250,000 pounds, and of Negroes whose increase would keep the stock good forever, found "the inhabitants betraying strong symptoms of poverty" and their houses "uniformly" of "a mean appearance."[4]

A decade later another described the landowners of Virginia as generally "in low circumstances, the inferior rank of them wretched in the extreme"; agriculture there, according to him, "had arrived at its lowest state of degradation." The price of land in most neighborhoods had fallen sharply, as thousands, despairing of profits, offered their lands for sale so that they might seek new homes in the more fertile West. Some actually abandoned their fields and left their dilapidated houses to fall into desolate ruin. Others shifted from one kind of crop to another. Plantations were divided into farms where subsistence farming took the place of staples.[5]

Some said the soils were completely worn out and could no longer support a decent standard of living. Some grumbled at the middleman who still took more than his share of the returns. Some saw that markets were unsatisfactory. A few criticized the methods used in agriculture. They pointed out the lack of crop rotation, of good plowing, of sufficient stock to give manure for the hungry lands. A smaller number called attention to the wastefulness of slavery. All agreed that unless something was done, and done soon, the Old Dominion would lose the best of her inhabitants and the greater part of her prestige.[6]

To material conditions a more alarming factor was soon added. The formation of the Constitution and the triumph of federal policies under the leadership of Alexander Hamilton brought new interests forward to contend with agriculture for control in a government of majorities. In quick succession came the creation of a great national funded debt, the establishment of a national bank with its accompanying extension of credit, and the possibilities of enlarged issues of paper money. Then came the demand for protective tariffs uniting what one alarmed citizen called the "monied

[3] Avery Craven, *Soil Exhaustion as a Factor in the Agricultural History of Virginia and Maryland, 1606–1860* (Urbana, 1925), pp. 81–85.

[4] Duc de la Rochefoucauld-Laincourt, *Travels in North America* (2 vols; London, 1799), II, 23.

[5] William Strickland, *Observations on the Agriculture of the United States of America* (London, 1801), p. 49.

[6] Craven, *Soil Exhaustion,* pp. 86–121.

aristocracy" with the industrial privileged and requiring a "consolidation of government" well beyond what agrarian philosophers thought the Constitution permitted. Thus both agriculture and local democracy were being endangered.

Such was the situation that stirred John Taylor of Caroline to inaugurate a movement which, when revived in later days, was designated by the title, *I'll Take My Stand.* With courage and clear insight he began that lavish shedding of ink which has characterized the movement. Pamphlets and books flowed from his pen, and the glories and the soundness of a rural-agricultural way of life were unfolded to an unreceptive world.

In sound seventeenth-century fashion Taylor struck first at the "legal factions" which, through an enlarged activity of central government and legislation favoring industrial and financial groups, were threatening to become an American aristocracy. He bitterly contrasted this "order of stock-jobbers in loans, banks, manufactories, contracts, rivers, roads, houses, ships, lotteries, and an infinite number of inferior tricks to get money," with the "honest, virtuous, patriotic and bold" landed gentry whom they were replacing. He asserted: "Monarchies and arstocracies, being founded in the principle of distributing wealth by law, can only subsist by frauds and deceptions to dupe ignorance into an opinion, that such distributions are intended for its benefit; but in genuine republics, founded on the principle of leaving wealth to be distributed by merit and industry, these treacheries of government are treasons against nations."[7]

He thus implied that in a true republic the majority of the citizens would always be farmers and the mass of wealth would always be in the hands of those who tilled the soil. On their backs would rest the burdens of both the legitimate and the illegitimate creations of legislation. "Agriculture," he said, "pays and must forever pay most of whatever is collected by taxes, by charters, by protecting duties, by paper systems of every kind, for armies, for navies, and though last, not the least of its losses, of whatever the nation is defrauded by a treasury system operating in darkness."[8]

This being the case, one could assume that where officeholders, speculators, and industrialists were prospering above the farming class, they were "filching" wealth from its real producers and setting

[7] Taylor, *Arator,* pp. 31–33.
[8] *Ibid.,* p. 31.

up an artificial social-economic scheme of things. Such a situation had long existed in England and in other countries of the Old World. It was now being established in the United States. Already because wealth "thus filched is made by laws to yield a better profit without labour, than . . . with it," capital was "flying from the fields, to the legal monopolies, banking and manufacturing. The laws [had] . . . established a thousand modes by which capital [would] . . . produce quicker and larger profits, than when employed in the slow improvements of agriculture." He estimated that "forty per centum" of the farmer's earnings were being paid "to a legal faction . . . pretending to no religion, to no morality, to no patriotism, except to the religion, morality and patriotism of making itself daily richer."[9]

The remedy for such evils lay first in a quick return to natural and sound relationships. The dignity and prosperity of agriculture, which once gave it unchallenged economic-social pre-eminence, must be restored. If that had been lost through the growth of "consolidated" government, then the political situation should be changed. "The plough can have very little success," said Taylor, "until the laws are altered which obstruct it. . . . So long as the laws make it more profitable to invest capital in speculations without labour, than in agriculture with labour . . . a love of wealth, and a love of ease" will make agricultural improvement impossible. Farmers, he thought, "had become political slaves" because they were "political fools." They had allowed domination to "those whose object is to monopolize the sweets of life, which [farmers] . . . sweat for." The weight in Congress was "very visably against the agriculturists," not because of "popular folly in elections," as some thought, but because of "the transit of wealth, and of course wisdom, from agriculture to its natural enemies, charter and privilege." In this he saw "the inevitable fate of the agricultural interest."[10]

The significant thing about Taylor's statements is the clear understanding of the importance of the economic factor. He saw that if the farmers were to maintain their station in American life they had to prosper. Unless their share in the national income was commensurate with their proportion of production, they must yield both place and power. The country gentleman ideal, which had given the planter of the South his high social standing, could not survive

[9] *Ibid.,* pp. 36–37.
[10] *Ibid.,* pp. 42–46.

poverty. Gentility rested on firm economic foundations. And economic foundations, in turn, rested on a just government. The surrender of political leadership to urban groups and the acceptance of legislation which augmented their development would ultimately rob the farmer of his political influence, of his economic superiority, and, in the end, of his social status. Urban and rural worlds were inherent enemies. Even in democratic America farmers might become peasants. If lesser interests, dominating legislation to their own benefit, became sectional in character, then the dissolution of the Union might become a necessity for the protection of the rural way of life.[11]

Taylor thus saw the true nature of the "irrepressible conflict" toward which the nation was drifting—the day when the southern agriculturist in the name of constitutional rights might face urban industrial sections in a final struggle to preserve government as it had been established and an economic life free from favoritism.

From such an understanding Taylor shaped his program of resistance and reform. His purpose was to restore democracy in government and society, and to rebuild agricultural prosperity. He had early opposed the adoption of the Constitution on the grounds of insufficient protection afforded individuals and states. He lined up solidly with his friend and fellow planter, Thomas Jefferson, against Hamilton's schemes for "consolidation" through funding, banking, and tariffs. He introduced Jefferson's famous resolutions in the Virginia assembly, insisting that the usurpation "of constitutional principles . . . if allowed to acquire maturity . . . [would] yield to the dreadful remedy of civil war."[12] Throughout the administrations of Adams and Jefferson he kept up his fight and brought it to a grand climax in bitter opposition to protective tariffs and to John Marshall's consolidating court decisions in the teens and early twenties. He was, without question, the most profound and the most persistent champion of individual and local democracy in the period.

[11] John Taylor, *New Views of the Constitution of the United States* (Washington, 1823), pp. 50–83. "If either [section] can acquire local advantages from national supremacy, it will aggravate . . . a perpetual warfare of intrigue and a dissolution of the union will result."

[12] John Taylor, *Construction Construed, and Constitutions Vindicated* (Richmond, 1820), p. 298; Henry H. Simms, *Life of John Taylor* (Richmond, 1932), *passim;* John Taylor, *A Definition of Parties* (Philadelphia, 1794), p. 1; *id., Enquiry into the Principles,* p. 2.

Political scientists have viewed him largely from the angle of "strict construction" doctrine. They have generally missed the fact that in all this fight John Taylor was struggling to preserve a "way of life" which America had brought out of Old England and given firm foundations in the southern plantation. He was trying to hold back government as the creator of urban-industrial groups who by privilege upset the whole natural economy of agricultural dominance. He was attempting to check the flow of capital from farming to industry—for he saw that only through the dignity bestowed by being a capitalist, an entrepreneur, an employer of labor in large-scale effort, could farmers remain gentlemen. He was waging the battle of his own interest against that of another group whose advantages in politics and in financial manipulation for profits were so much greater than his own that they endangered the whole rural way of genteel living. He was taking his stand for a fundamental social conception.

The second part of Taylor's program was thoroughly interwoven with the first. Its purpose was agricultural reform for profits. And here Taylor began by practice followed soon by preaching. On his plantation, "Hazelwood," near the town of Port Royal, he carried on experiments in the use of fertilizers, crop rotation, and improved plowing, creating, in the midst of general decline, "a farm . . . distinguished by the verdure of its fields . . . [and] the abundance of its crops."[13] In 1803 he began a series of articles on agriculture in a Georgetown newspaper, and in 1813 he gathered these together with some additions into a little volume called *Arator*. By 1818 it had gone through five editions and had attracted attention even in New England. John Adams stated that it surpassed any agricultural treatise he had seen from the pen of a northern writer.

The book caused an immediate stir in Virginia. Weary planters, about ready to abandon their lands for the western trek, took new hope. One writer spoke of a new complexion to the face of agriculture in the lower part of the state and called Taylor's book the "*vade-mecum* of almost every cultivator of the soil."[14]

The central idea in his book was that soils were depleted and fertility must be restored. "It is absurd," he said, "to talk of a

[13] *American Farmer* (Baltimore, Washington, 1819–97), II (1820), 198; *Memoirs of the Philadelphia Society for Promoting Agriculture* (Philadelphia, 1808–26), III (1814), 198; *Niles' Weekly Register* (Philadelphia, 1811–48), XV (1822), 177–81; *Farmer's Register* (Shellbanks, Petersburg, Va., 1833–42), II (1835), 612–14.

[14] *American Farmer,* I (1819), 78.

system of agriculture, without having discovered, that every such system good for anything, must be bottomed upon fertility. Before, therefore, we launch into any system, we must learn how to enrich our lands."[15] To do this old methods and old crops must be abandoned. Tobacco had dominated the fields too long.[16] The overseer system had bribed men to "impoverish" lands, not to improve them. Wages, not a share of the crop, must be paid and long-time terms granted to those who were put in charge.[17] Slavery itself, always "a misfortune to agriculture," needed some revision also. The number should be reduced to that in keeping with the ability of the master to personally supervise and profitably use.[18] Regulations should be tightened and the free Negro eliminated from southern society. These were first steps to be taken before positive efforts could hope for success.

Taylor's restorative program began with what he called "inclosing."[19] By this he meant the "exclusion of all stock from the arable lands and the planting of such lands in those crops which would give the greatest quantity of vegetable matter for feeding or for direct return to the soils." The great source of fertility, he thought, was to be found in the atmosphere, and plants alone could draw on this source of supply and make it available for man to return to the earth. Vegetable offal and animal manure would restore depleted soils.

He did not, it will be noticed, understand the use of legumes for the increasing of nitrogen, but he did believe that red clover, together with Indian corn, furnished the best means toward his ends. Clover should be grown on every spot where it could be "prevailed upon to exist"; Indian corn was the "vegetable proper for poor ground."[20] Gypsum, lime, and marl might assist in the work of restoration, and good plowing, both for depth and for checking erosion, were prerequisites to other factors. Crop rotation, especially a three-shift system of corn, wheat, and pasture, if not the only means relied upon, had its value. But when all was said and done the way back to fertility and prosperity lay in the production and use of animal and vegetable manures. As he wrote to Jefferson:

[15] Taylor, *Arator,* p. 56.
[16] *Ibid.,* pp. 181–83.
[17] *Ibid.,* pp. 56–58.
[18] *Ibid.,* pp. 48–55.
[19] *Ibid.,* pp. 59–68.
[20] *Ibid.,* pp. 102–15.

"Manure can come only of great offals, and great offals, only of great crops. These great crops, and great offals then are the desiderium."[21]

It is not necessary for us to discuss in detail the strength and weakness of this program in the light of modern scientific knowledge. There are some observations and some suggested improvements which would pass muster even today. The criticisms of old methods, the insistence on the necessity for vegetable and animal manures in soil fertility, and the encouragement of better plowing are all recognized as valuable and enduring contributions. He erred in some of his theories and in a few of his practices. Failure dogged the footsteps of most of those who attempted to follow his teachings in the years which followed. But it would be quite unsound to determine the place of John Taylor in southern agricultural history on the basis of the success or failure of his agricultural methods. That is to miss the whole point.

The significant thing about Taylor's program was the effort to give a firm and enduring economic foundation from which the farmer might wage his battle for the preservation of the country gentleman ideal. Agricultural reform was a part of the struggle against Alexander Hamilton and John Marshall. Democracy was worth preserving only because it gave the practical result of domination by honest and intelligent planters. Planters could remain the force behind true democracy only by being economically strong. Taylor quite frankly spoke of "the fallacy of form" and declared that any form of government was good which "produces the happiness . . . of a nation." The colonies did not revolt from England "for nothing but forms."[22] They revolted to set up a more perfect social order in which happiness, as comprehended in the rural way of life which the seventeenth century praised, could be maintained. "Cupidity, avarice, or monoploy," as represented in the urban-industrial classes, could bring misery under a democractic system or form as well as under any other. Save as these "artificial aristocrats" were restrained by a written constitution, strictly interpreted, they would become rulers. Unless the sovereignty of the state could dissolve geographic majorities, and unless the farmers could enjoy prosperity which would enable them to keep their numbers and their prestige, consolidation and resulting favors

[21] Taylor to Thomas Jefferson, March 5, 1795, Jefferson MSS., Division of Manuscripts, Library of Congress.

[22] Taylor, *Construction Construed,* pp. 13–15.

would bring to an end all that the Fathers had dreamed and had established.

Thus John Taylor forged a single program of political philosophy and agricultural practice. He was preparing the way for John C. Calhoun and Edmund Ruffin. He was providing a section, where old agrarian ideals and practices persisted, with the constitutional and agricultural weapons with which it might better fight for self-preservation. He was trying to prevent American democracy from becoming a means by which the few might plunder the many; he was trying to keep peasantry from American shores.

III

COMING OF THE WAR BETWEEN THE STATES: AN INTERPRETATION

When Lee surrendered at Appomattox a tall gaunt North Carolinian stolidly stacked arms and fell back into line.[1] He was worn, hungry, and dirty. The insistent Yankees had granted him little time during the past weeks for relaxation. Food had been scarce; the opportunities for cleanliness lacking. He had gone on fighting more from habit than purpose. He had quit because the orders were to that effect. Suddenly, with a sharp realization of what was taking place around him, he turned to his neighbor and drawled: "Damn me if I ever love another country!"

In these words the disheartened Tarheel passed judgment on a generation.

Up to 1825 there had been no "United South" nor "self-conscious North." There were some recognizable differences between these larger sections in climate, in economic interests, in ideals, and in those intangible things which go to make "a way of life." But these differences were of long standing and were no more acute than those existing between other geographic regions within the nation. With a population ever on the move toward the West or the city, new and old societies constantly found themselves bound together under the same political organization. With highly diversified natural resources, conflicting types of economic endeavor grew up, side-by-side, to contend for favorable legislation. Social patterns brought into new lands from different sources fought for dominance. The struggle for control in governments, where majorities ruled, forms the central theme in more than one era of the nation's history.

Nor were the sections units. The careful scholar must ever recognize the cleavage between Upper and Lower New England,

Reprinted from the *Journal of Southern History,* II, No. 3 (August, 1936), 1–20.

[1] A paper read at the meeting of the American Historical Association, Chattanooga, Tennessee, December 27, 1935.

between the Ohio Valley and the lake region of the Old Northwest, between the mountains and the bluegrass of Kentucky and Tennessee.[2] He must understand the basic differences between the "tidewater districts" and the "upcountry" in the Old South. He must know that before 1860 every issue which later divided North and South had been fought out and reduced to a workable compromise by southern men struggling against southern men in Virginia and the Carolinas—the rights of minorities, the distribution of power between local and central governments, the relative values of a single economic effort as against diversification secured by tariffs and other legislative aids, even the problem of free and slave labor!

Differences—economic, social, and political—did not then or afterwards portend an "irrepressible conflict" between North and South, to be settled only by bloodshed. The War between the States in 1861–65 did not come simply because one section was agricultural and the other industrial, because one exploited free labor and the other slaves, or because a sectional majority refused to respect the constitutional rights of the minority. The Northwest was as thoroughly agricultural as the South; the Republican party was vigorous in disclaiming abolition tendencies and was willing to leave slavery alone; and no minority has ever found the Constitution of much value in the face of "manifest destinies." The problem of why these sections went to war lies deeper. It is one of emotions, cultivated hostilities, and ultimately of hatred between sections. Bloodshed was "necessary" because men associated their rivals with disliked and dishonorable symbols and crowned their own interests with moral sanctions. Differences were but the materials with which passions worked. Each side, in the end, fought the other for principles and the glory of God, for the preservation of civilizations, for the maintenance of honor. The conflict was the work of politicians and pious cranks! The peoples knew little of each other as realities. They were both fighting mythical devils.

The steps by which sectional differences were emotionalized are highly involved and often obscure. Of one thing only can we be reasonably certain: The first apprehensions and resentments which stirred the people in each section were the product of purely local conditions. We can understand the national situation only when we have grasped the vital forces at work in each locality. Men react to what they know—they create their symbols from such

[2] There are, in fact, three units in each of these states.

experiences. But they shed blood for and against abstractions which carry all the good and all the evils which they imagine possible from their limited experiences. We must begin with everyday affairs in each section.

The general period in American history from 1825 to 1860 was one of vast material growth and expansion. But it was also one in which the wealth and power of the few grew disproportionately to that of the many. Democracy was not functioning properly. *Liberty* was putting an end to *equality*. If some were content, others felt deepest resentments and dreamed of a more perfect society as the political and moral right of an American. It is sometimes difficult to discover whether this claim rested on the Constitution, the Scriptures, or the Declaration of Independence. Perhaps they did not make such unimportant distinctions. At any rate, injustice, lack of material prosperity, loss of equality, or failure to achieve American purposes—all became matters of moral significance and evidence of God's plan thwarted. It was, on the one hand, a day of pulling down aristocrats, fighting devils, saving democractic institutions, acquiring material things as a natural and moral right; and on the other, of checking harebrained movements which threatened social security, private rights, and private property.

In the Northeast, the Industrial Revolution was in full swing. Old commercial centers and fishing villages found themselves overshadowed by a new life which grew up at the fall line. The city became a land of opportunity—the center of a varied and attractive life. Wealth shifted into new hands and new places. Labor became dependent on capital. Dominance in legislative halls passed from farmers, merchants, and fishermen to industrial leaders and the lawyers they sent to do their bidding. Daniel Webster's conversion from free trade to protection was only a larger manifestation of a common phenomenon. The harbor was passing into eclipse.[3]

Alongside of these urban changes went an agricultural revolution as significant in effects. For the first time the farmers of this region had expanding markets of their own. Opportunities for specialized crops which could feed both men and machines brought capital into farming, crowded out the less efficient, and often set sheep, as in

[3] Caroline F. Ware, *Early New England Cotton Manufacture: A Study of Industrial Beginnings* (Boston, 1931); Victor S. Clark, *History of Manufactures in the United States, 1607–1860* (Washington, 1916), pp. 367–68; Arthur B. Darling, *Political Changes in Massachusetts, 1824–1848: A Study of Liberal Movements in Politics* (New [illegible] 1925), pp. 16–17; Raynor G. Wellington, *The Political and Sectional Influence* [illegible] *ublic Lands, 1828–1842* (Boston, 1914), p. 27.

Old England, to "gobbling up" farms and villages. Thousands, unwilling or unable to make the required adjustments, turned cityward or toward the New West from which they soon poured floods of agricultural produce to plague those who remained behind. Every decade held a crisis for those who tilled the soils of New England and Upper New York. The abandoned farm became the symbol of permanent decline.[4]

Meanwhile a series of Wests were rising one after the other in the great region which stretched from New York to the Mississippi —"a greater New England," the Ohio Valley, the Old Northwest. Each began as a frontier but hurried on as rapidly as exploitation of natural resources could accomplish the task toward a more perfect and complex society. Their citizens had sacrificed the present for future returns which depended on easy access to rich lands and open ways to profitable markets. Their hopes ever outran their realizations, but their faith in the dividends of democracy did not decline. They were American pioneers and they had a right to prosper and would do so if democracy functioned properly. But the Panic of '37 spread wreck and ruin among them; land legislation lagged behind their demands; internal improvements came all too slowly; prices slumped as home markets broke and "overproduction" glutted the few outside markets they had developed. Throughout the "middle period" this was a region of half-realized purposes, of extravagant dreams checked by hard raw realities, of plain men who sought consolation and found emotional outlet in evangelical churches, of earnest souls who, here and there, even talked with God. All things, economic as well as social, were either "right" or "wrong." And too many things in this period were "wrong."[5]

The rural North, therefore, throughout the era, was a region of potential and actual unrest. The "average farmer," for whose welfare the American system had been established, resented bitterly the growing importance of the city and the mounting wealth of those engaged in what he considered "minor pursuits." Securing the

4 Perry W. Bidwell, "The Agricultural Revolution in New England," *American Historical Review,* XXVI (1921), 683–98; *New England Farmer,* XVII (1838), 113; II (1823), 122–23; IV (1825), 212–13; Massachusetts State Board of Agriculture, *Annual Report,* 1860; Avery O. Craven, "The Abandoned Farms of New England," American Historical Association, *Annual Report,* 1922, I, 353–54.

5 Frederick J. Turner, *The United States, 1830–1850* (New York, 1935), pp. 253–351; Avery O. Craven, "The Advance of Civilization into the Middle West in the Period of Settlement," in Dixon R. Fox (ed.), *Sources of Culture in the Middle West: Backgrounds versus Frontier* (New York, 1934), pp. 39–71.

support of the lesser folk of the towns, only recently come from nearby farms, he launched his protests in various forms but all in the name of a faltering democracy. The labor movements of the period, says Commons, were "not so much the modern alignment of wage-earner against employer" as they were the revolts of "the poor against the rich, the worker against the owner."[6] Professor Darling has shown that the "Workingmen's Movement" in Massachusetts was almost exclusively a farmers' effort—"a protest against the 'accumulations' in Bostonian society, the assault of 'country folk' on the 'exclusive privileges' of the wealthy."[7] The bitter New England farmer who declared he would "sooner, infinitely sooner, follow [his] daughters to the grave than see them '*go out* to service' " in the kitchens of those "who by successful industry, by good luck, or possibly fraud were in a situation to make hewers of wood and drawers of water of their less fortunate sisters and brethren," was merely expressing a very prevalent attitude.[8]

The Locofoco groups were even more concerned about inequality and privilege. An Upper New York convention in 1836, "appointed by the farmers, mechanics and others friendly in their views," struck at the "Banking System" because it "filled the coffers of the already wealthy and took from the earnings of the poor." It denounced the practices of "the courts of law" for being "aristocratic"; it declared in a form consciously modeled after the Declaration of Independence that "the foundations of Republican Government are in the equal rights of every citizen, in his person and property, and in their management." This group talked much of the "aristocracy of wealth" and "the odious distinctions betwixt the rich and the poor." They would restore democracy by public education and by granting to every man his "inalienable right to a share of the bounties of our Common Father"—meaning the public domain.[9]

It should also be noted that the transcendental protest against materialism took point from the new urban-industrial growth; that Brook Farm, Hopedale, and Fruitlands represented a return to rural-agricultural living; that the well-being of common men in a

6 John R. Commons and Helen L. Sumner (eds.), *Labor Movement, 1820–1840* (*Documentary History of American Industrial Society* [Cleveland, 1910], Vol. V), I, 24.

7 Arthur B. Darling, "The Workingmen's Party in Massachusetts, 1833–1834," *American Historical Review,* XXIX (1924), 81–86; *id., Political Changes in Massachusetts, 1824–1848,* p. 3.

8 *New England Farmer,* X (1831), 18–19.

9 F. Byrdsall, *History of the Loco-Foco or Equal Rights Party* (New York, 1842), pp. 68–69, 71–74, 147–51.

democracy formed a basic argument for temperance, peace, women's rights, and abolition. Both the misfortunes and the hopes of a disgruntled people were moving under the banners of *democracy.*

To this glorification was soon added another. The cause of the oppressed was also the cause of "righteousness." Rural folk, whose one social center was the church and whose great spokesman was the preacher, could hardly have escaped this conclusion. The great revivals which burned through the back country and of which Charles Grandison Finney was the leader, shifted the emphasis in Calvinism from "a painful quest for a safe escape from life" to the transforming of this world into the Kingdom of Heaven. Salvation was no longer the "end of all human desire"; it was but the beginning of "*being useful in the highest degree possible.*"[10] Not only was social reform an obligation, but social evils had to do with morality; and the purposes of religion, society, and democratic politics were one and the same. "It is a departure, in our representatives and judges, from the laws of nature and laws of the Creator, which has produced the derangement in the affairs of our State," declared the Locofoco convention referred to above.[11] "To a Believer who has rejoiced in the light of Locofocoism, as an outward sign of the inward light of Christianity,"[12] was the dedication in F. Byrdsall's history of the movement. The *Democratic Review* echoed this sentiment by insisting that ". . . Democracy is the cause of Humanity. . . . It is essentially involved in Christianity, of which it has been well said that its pervading spirit of democractic equality among men is its highest fact."[13] Gerrit Smith's congregation at Peterboro in December, 1840, resolved among other things, that:[14]

> Whereas there is, ever amongst professors of religion, a prevailing opinion that it is wrong to preach politics on the Sabbath. *Resolved,* That the correctness of this opinion turns wholly on the character of the politics which are preached; for whilst it is clearly wrong to preach anti-Bible or unrighteous politics on the Sabbath or on any other day, nothing can be clearer than that no day is too holy to be used in preaching politics which are inculcated in the Bible.

Smith himself declared that "No man's religion is better than his politics." He believed that righteous civil governments depended

[10] Gilbert H. Barnes, *The Anti-Slavery Impulse, 1830–1844* (New York, 1933), p. 11.
[11] Byrdsall, *History of the Loco-Foco or Equal Rights Party,* pp. 71–74.
[12] *Ibid.*
[13] Quoted in William Trimble, "Diverging Tendencies in New York Democracy in the Period of the Locofocos," *American Historical Review,* XXIV (1919), 396.
[14] Octavius B. Frothingham, *Gerrit Smith, a Biography* (New York, 1909), p. 62.

on "the prevalence of [a] Christianity," which kept from office "anti-abolitionists, and land-monopolists and other enemies of human rights." To leave God out of "a moral reformation" was like enacting "the play of Othello" and leaving out "the part of Othello." To him "Civil Government" was "of God."[15] And Jeffersonian Democracy was God's chosen form of civil government.

In the Northwest the sublimation of local resentments in terms of democracy and morality was even more pronounced. The addition of men and ideas from the Northeast played some part in the formation of attitudes, but the expression was largely native. Western men began with the naïve assumption voiced by the members of the Missouri assembly that: "Our country is peculiarly the asylum of the oppressed, and emphatically the poor man's home."[16] They were certain that: "Every law . . . which opens to the poor man the way to independence . . . not only subserves the cause of Humanity but advances and maintains the fundamental principles of our Government." They believed that "persons . . . disposed to live out of the labors of others" (meaning land speculators) were establishing "a petty aristocracy" which would "choke the tree of Liberty and cause her leaves to wither so that her sons . . . [could] no more recline under her balmy shadows, but . . . [would] be compelled to endure the scorching rays and blasting influences of the slavery making idol of money tyrants."[17] In early days the danger arose from " 'Eastern *millionaires* . . . who like the flies that come upon the borders of Egypt' " caused " 'the land to stink,' " but their resentments were vague enough to be lodged in any direction as occasion required.[18] Senator Lewis Cass of Michigan climaxed the argument in favor of settlers by insisting that "we shut our eyes upon the seven hundred per cent., and look to our duty as a Christian people."[19] And a colleague in the House argued that the public lands should go "as God intended, and as good governments and good men desire they should go, into the hands *of the people*."[20] The significant fact was that here were

[15] *Ibid.*, pp. 72, 148–49, 157.

[16] *American State Papers, Public Lands* (Washington), V (1860), 36.

[17] John R. Commons (ed.), *Labor Movement, 1840–1860* (*Documentary History of American Industrial Society* [Cleveland, 1910], Vol. VIII), II, 44–45.

[18] George M. Stephenson, *The Political History of the Public Lands from 1840 to 1862* (Boston, 1917), p. 102.

[19] *Congressional Globe*, 33 Cong., 1 sess., Appendix (n. s., XXXI), p. 1088 (1854).

[20] *Ibid.*, p. 956 (June 10, 1854).

men who believed in the natural right of settlers to lands and who felt that the failure to secure that right constituted an infringement on democracy and on God's purposes.

The Jacksonian war against "the money power" in an earlier period was "from this same cloth." It represented far more the deep resentments of a "grasping" people than it did a belief in abstract ideals. The same holds, in a degree, for the so-called "free-soil" movement. Historians have largely overlooked the fact that the "liberty groups" with a single human rights appeal failed to gain any great following in the Northwest—but that when Salmon P. Chase, the Democrat, broadened the platform to one in which homesteads, internal improvements at federal expense, and home markets by tariffs were included, the moral indignation against slavery rose to a burning flame.[21] A local convention in Chicago in 1848 resolved that the Wilmot Proviso "is now and ever has been the doctrine of the Whigs of the free States" and added hastily, "the Whig party has ever been the firm, steady, and unchanging friend of harbor and river appropriations."[22] Lincoln himself would keep slavery from the territories because God had intended them "for the homes of free white people."[23] The Wisconsin farmer, whose interest in Negroes was slight, did not further heckle this great Commoner when the assurance was given that the prime purpose behind his program was a 160-acre farm for all interested persons.[24] Thus the halo of democracy and morality, in part borrowed from the abolitionist, was placed upon the brow of all vital Western needs, and its bitterness from unrealized ambitions became a holy sentiment.

The next step in the process was one of transferring the resentment, generated out of local conditions, to the southern planter and fashioning him into the great symbol of aristocracy, of immorality, and of disloyalty to democratic government. It began when the evangelical churches accepted slavery as a sin rather than an evil; it reached its climax in the triumph of a political party, purely

21 Theodore T. Smith, *The Liberty and Free Soil Parties in the Northwest* (New York, 1897).

22 Chicago *Journal,* April 3, 1848.

23 See his speeches at Peoria, October 16, 1854, and at Alton, October 15, 1858, in John G. Nicolay and John Hay (eds.), *Complete Works of Abraham Lincoln* (New York, 1905), II, 190–262; V, 29–71. See also James G. Randall, "Has the Lincoln Theme Been Exhausted?" *American Historical Review,* XLI (1936), 270.

24 Speech at Milwaukee, September 30, 1859, in Nicolay and Hay (eds.), *Complete Works of Abraham Lincoln,* V, 236–56.

sectional and openly hostile on moral grounds to the institutions of another section.

The antislavery movement was, in the beginning, part and parcel of the larger humanitarian impulse which got going in the early nineteenth century and which sought to be rid of injustice and to establish a more wholesome social order. It was closely related to the peace movement, the effort for women's rights, the temperance crusade, prison and Sabbath reforms, the improvement of education, and many other efforts of the kind. It rose to particular dominance only gradually and among certain well-defined groups. It was fortunate in leadership but more fortunate in its appeal. Human slavery more clearly violated democratic institutions than any other evil of the day; it was close enough to be touched now and then, yet far enough removed to give widest scope to the imagination; it violated most completely the moral senses of a people whose ideas of sin were largely in terms of self-indulgence and whose purposes in religious expression were toward the social betterment of the downtrodden; and, what was as important, it constituted the most talked-of feature in the life of a rival section long contending for control in a government of majorities. Garrison, who, if living today, could profitably consult a psychiatrist, early denounced slavery as a crime and the slaveholder as a criminal. But, of more reaching consequences were the teachings of Theodore Weld and his type, who as W. C. Preston said, made "the anti-slavery cause identical with religion" and urged men "by all the high and exciting obligations of duty of man to God, by all that can warm the heart and inflame the imagination, to join the pious work of purging the sin of slavery from the land."

It was but a step from such attitudes to the condemnation of southern men for holding slaves or permitting others to hold them. By 1841 Garrison was speaking of "the desperadoes from the South, in Congress" and declaring: "We would sooner trust the honor of the country . . . in the hands of the inmates of our penitentiaries and prisons, than in their hands. . . . they are the meanest of thieves and the worst of robbers. . . . We do not acknowledge them to be within the pale of Christianity, of republicanism, of humanity."[25] And then finding his hatred not entirely spent, he lamented the poverty of the English language which

[25] Wendell P. and Francis J. Garrison, *William Lloyd Garrison, 1805–1879* (New York, 1889), III, 32–33.

prevented doing full justice to the infamy of the South.[26]

This conception of the slaveholder opened the way for abolition imaginations to create much needed symbols. In a surprisingly short time *all* Southerners, except a few "poor whites," were planters, living in great white-pillared mansions, drinking intemperately, consorting with female slaves, and selling "down river" their own blood without the trace of a civilized blush. "A million and a half slave women, some of them without a tinge of African blood, are given up, a lawful prey to the unbridled lusts of their masters," declared an antislavery tract.[27] A whole section of the nation living upon the toil of a downtrodden race! Here was the aristocrat *par excellence*, the perfection in licentiousness and self-indulgence! Harriet Beecher Stowe in *Uncle Tom's Cabin* pictured a way of life which would have done credit to the romancing of a Thomas Nelson Page; novels, and there were scores of them, like *Our World; or the Slaveholder's Daughter*,[28] pictured a society of licentiousness which must have disturbed the dreams of many an abstemious Puritan. The South had begun to do service for all aristocrats and all sinners in an era of democracy and morality!

Garrison and his kind, of course, were few; his violence was shared by only a handful of antislavery men who, in turn, formed a very, very small minority in the North. His attitudes are important only because they were *extreme* and by their extremeness reveal in clearest fashion something of what was gradually to seep into the subconsciousness of a whole peoole. One day, only a few decades off, the moral weaknesses of slaveholding would form a vital part of the understanding of a whole section and hatred of Southerners be so near the surface that "the shedding of a little blood" would set them savagely at the throats of their neighbors.

The next step in the process was one of directly associating the slaveholding South with the economic and social ills from which men of North and West suffered. The "hard times" of the late 1830's, they said, were due to the fact that northern capital had been loaned to "prodigal" southern planters who could not and would not repay. "Slavery," said the report of the American Anti-Slavery Society in 1837, "is the rule of violence and arbitrary will. . . . It would be quite in character both with its theory and prac-

26 *Ibid.*, II, 57–58.

27 *Revolution the Only Remedy for Slavery* (American Anti-Slavery Society, "Anti-Slavery Tracts," No. 7 [New York, 1855]).

28 Anonymous, New York, 1855.

tice . . . if the slave-drivers should refuse to pay their debts and meet the sheriff with dirk and pistol." Three years later the Society resolved: "That the existence of Slavery is the grand cause of the pecuniary embarrassments of the Country; and that no real permanent relief is to be expected . . . until the total abolition of that execrable system." One writer estimated that within five years the South had taken "more than $100,000,000 by notes which will never be paid."[29]

This period saw also the rise of the idea of a "slave-power" or "slaveocracy" which had seized control of the federal government to shape its policies in the interests of slavery. It had already destroyed "the protective system 'at the hazard, if not with the intention' of breaking up the manufacturing interests of the free states." It had developed and protected markets for cotton "in all parts of the known world, while it studiously avoided doing anything to procure a market for the free products of the grain growing Northwest."[30]

The aggressive opposition of southern leaders to pre-emption and homestead legislation in the period from 1840 to 1860 added to the growing belief that slave interests were hostile to western development. A typical point of view was that of Senator James M. Mason of Virginia who declared that he had "not yet known . . . a bill so fraught with mischief, and mischief of the most demoralizing tendency, as the homestead bill."[31] "*The Columbus* [Mississippi] *Democrat* insisted that settlers on homesteads would be abolitionists" and declared that it would be "better for us that these territories should remain a waste, a howling wilderness, trod only by red hunters than be so settled."[32] Robert Y. Hayne of South Carolina added insult to injury by implying that a homesteader was a "drone," a man unworthy "of protection in a country where every man goes ahead who has any strength of will, or any firmness, or any character."[33]

Northwestern reaction to such attitudes was sharp and direct. "When did the Senator from Georgia ever vote anything for Iowa or the West?" growled Augustus Caesar Dodge at one who opposed

[29] *Free American,* August 19, 1841. See Julian P. Bretz, "The Economic Background of the Liberty Party," *American Historical Review,* XXXIV (1929), 250–64.

[30] *Ibid.* See also G. M. Skinner to Lyman Trumbull, January (?), 1858, W. H. Herndon to Trumbull, February 19, 1858, Trumbull Papers, Library of Congress.

[31] *Cong. Globe,* 35 Cong., 2 sess., Pt. II, p. 1076 (February 17, 1859).

[32] *Ibid.,* 35 Cong., 1 sess., Pt. III, p. 2304 (May 22, 1858).

[33] July 22, 1854.

his measures.[34] "I, sir, have inherited my Democracy," said James M. Cavanaugh, member of the House from Minnesota, "have been attached to the Democratic party from my boyhood. . . . But, sir, when I see southern gentlemen come up . . . and refuse . . . to aid my constituents, refuse to place the actual tiller of the soil, the honest, industrious laborer, beyond the grasp and avarice of the speculator, I tell you, sir, I falter and hesitate."[35] The Dubuque (Iowa) *Herald* revealed the emotional extent reached in 1860 in these words: "Last Saturday the old reprobate, who now sits in the Presidential chair at Washington *vetoed the Homestead Bill. . . .* The slave propagandists demanded that the Bill should be vetoed, and their pliant tool was swift to obey them. Let the pimps and hirelings of the old sinner defend this last act of his, if they dare."[36]

Even more bitter was the complaint against southern opposition to river and harbor improvements. "This harbor question," said the Chicago *Democrat* after Polk's veto of a favorable bill, "is not a political one, but a sectional one. It is one between the North and the South. The iron rod wielded over her [the North] by southern despots must be broken."[37] Another Chicago paper declared:

> The North can and will be no longer hoodwinked. If no measure of protection and improvement of anything North or West are to be suffered by our Southern masters, if we are to be downtrodden and all our cherished interests crushed by them, a signal revolution will eventually ensue. The same spirit and energy that forced emancipation for the whole country from Great Britain will throw off the Southern Yoke. . . . The power to oppress shall not again be entrusted to men who have shown themselves to be slaveholders, but not Americans.[38]

A final charge against the so-called "slaveocracy" was the corruption of the Democratic party. When James K. Polk was elected president in 1844, certain old leaders such as Martin Van Buren, Francis Preston Blair, and Thomas H. Benton were pushed aside. Each in turn blamed John C. Calhoun and the slave interests; each in a different way added to the impression that the party was no longer a fit place for those who followed the immortal Andrew

[34] *Cong. Globe,* 32 Cong., 2 sess., Appendix, pp. 237–38 (March 18, 1853); Louis Pelzer, *Augustus Caesar Dodge: A Study in American Politics* (Iowa City, 1909), p. 168.

[35] *Cong. Globe,* 35 Cong., 2 sess., p. 505 (January 20, 1859).

[36] Quoted by Stephenson, *Political History of the Public Lands,* p. 217. See also resolutions passed by Chicago Germans, January 19, 1858, Trumbull Papers.

[37] Chicago *Democrat,* November 10, 1846.

[38] Chicago *Daily Journal,* August 19, 1846.

Jackson. The antislavery groups darkened the picture, and Whig and Republican partisans completed it. Distrust thus created ended in a widespread belief that the annexation of Texas, the Mexican War, the Kansas-Nebraska Act, and the Dred Scott Decision were steps in a well-worked out scheme for the extension of slavery and the rule of the slaveholder. Scholars have revealed the falsity of such opionions; yet in the years before the war they served all the purposes of fact, and Seward and Lincoln used them as deliberately as did the recognized demagogues. Even John Wentworth, a staunch Northern Democrat, accused his southern colleagues of always acting as slaveholders, never as party men.[39] By 1860 Wyndham Robertson, looking back at the recent Republican victory, could say: "The possession of the power of the Federal Government by the Democratic party . . . furnished the pretext . . . to confound the whole slave-holding interest as identical with democracy, and thus to turn and direct opposition, for whatever cause, to the policy and acts of the Democratic party, into opposition to the slave-holding interests."[40]

Thus by 1860 the apprehensions and resentments of the North had deepened as they had been sanctified by democracy and morality. That section, striving, as it believed, for things truly American, had fallen short of realization because of opposition from aristocratic and ignoble enemies. The time for being firm had arrived. The right to hate had been achieved. And what was as important, the South had been fashioned into the perfect symbol of all they feared and all they despised. The extreme abolition picture of what slaveholders were had been given legal currency by the bombast of politicians in verbal conflict for place and power and favors. They pictured an aggressive interest, wringing great wealth from unwilling and overworked Negroes, bent on extending its system to the ends of the land. They talked of "a house divided against itself"; of "a higher law"; of "the aristocratic lords of slavery." The ends they sought were immediate, but common folk back home, under the sway of unimaginative evangelical clergymen, could think only in terms of the eternal verities. In 1854 they

[39] *Indiana Sentinel*, June 2, 1849.

[40] *Speech of Wyndham Robertson, Esq. of Richmond City, on the State of the Country delivered in the House of Delegates on March 5th and 6th, 1860* (Richmond, 1860).

created the Republican party which in six short years passed from an expression of the moral indignation of a limited group to the position of carrier of all the material aspirations of a section and the political hopes of most of those not under the Democratic roof. It was the party of homestead legislation—the culmination of America's greatest democratic effort, the fruition of God's purpose, as Senator John P. Hale put it, to have His lands inhabited (and it might be added, a policy made more democratic and more holy by relieving poor settlers from competition with slaveholders).[41] It was the party of internal improvements with federal aid—a policy now embracing a Pacific railroad along the central route for the upbuilding of Chicago and St. Louis. Lincoln's railroad support in 1860 rivaled that of Douglas and came from lines better placed for future trends than his.[42] It was the party of protective tariffs—a policy lifted by the logic of William H. Seward into the very cornerstone of democratic society. Free farmers and industrialists at last united for common accomplishment! Satisfactory markets and new prosperity for all, including Pennsylvania and Cameron! Here was a program making the Union worth saving; the experiment in democracy would pay sound dividends.

But this was not all. The great ideals of an evangelistic Calvinistic society had not been sacrificed in the turn toward "respectability." In opposing the extension of slavery, the party skillfully capitalized on all the moral indignation long generating against the institution itself. Its leaders disavowed all the political implications of abolition sentiment yet openly announced their personal abhorrence of slaveholding. They even took profit from the few who went further. Charles Sumner's bitter invectives, aimed "to keep alive that old Puritan hatred of wickedness, which must overthrow slavery," were carefully distributed by the machine throughout the rural North.[43] Seward permitted his "higher law" and "irrepressible conflict" doctrines to become "all things to all men." And Lincoln's "ultimate extinction" policy was used to satisfy all but the most extreme abolitionists. The Republican "stock-in-trade" was indeed, as Caleb Cushing said, "the insolent assumption, in some of them, perhaps, the stupid mental delusion, that whatever

[41] *Cong. Globe,* 35 Cong., 1 sess., Pt. III, p. 2305 (May 22, 1858).

[42] Jacob R. Perkins, *Trails, Rails and War: The Life of General G. M. Dodge* (Indianapolis, 1929), pp. 57–58.

[43] Laura A. White, "Charles Sumner and the Crisis of 1860–1861," in Avery Craven (ed.), *Essays in Honor of William E. Dodd* (Chicago, 1935), pp. 131–93.

view they take of the measures of government *is the only moral side of public questions.*"[44]

It was this situation which produced a crisis in the party when Douglas' squatter sovereignty, in practice, yielded only free territory. The danger of slave extension, on which the party was founded, was over. And by 1858 even Republican leaders understood this fact. Some said the party had fulfilled its mission and should join with Stephen A. Douglas in the formation of a new party for wider sectional and national ends. Some talked of a "broad base" by which the Republicans could attack the old Southern Whigs.[45] But Abraham Lincoln, in his "House Divided" speech, prevented himself and his party from being thrust aside by a desperate appeal to old moral foundations. Though *his* own policy and that of "Judge" Douglas gave identical results, the latter was not born of moral conviction. And until the issue was conceived in terms of "the eternal struggle between two principles—right and wrong—throughout the world," the fight must go on. That is why a man who was willing to save the Union at the cost of a bloody civil war, even with slavery untouched, would not save it by a compromise which yielded party principle but which did not sacrifice a single material thing. The party was one with God and the world's great experiment in Democracy.

The southern side of the story needs only to be suggested.[46] Rural and lacking in means for the easy creation and expression of public opinion, the section was ever peculiarly susceptible to the ideas and oratory of a few leaders. As a result, the focal point of consciousness was, in the beginning, generally an abstract and theoretical right which logic deduced from some traditional source. In the ante-bellum period, when farmers, who lived by staple crops,

[44] Claude M. Fuess, *The Life of Caleb Cushing* (New York, 1923), II, 207–8 n. Italics not in the original.

[45] Horace Greeley to J. Medill, July 24, 1858, in John G. Nicolay and John Hay, *Abraham Lincoln: A History* (New York, 1890), II, 140–41 n.; George A. Nourse to Trumbull, January 1, 1858, J. A. Berdon to Trumbull, March 2, 1858, and William H. Herndon to Trumbull, April 12, 1858, Trumbull Papers; Jacob Marsh to Elihu Washburn, April 28, 1858, Washburn Papers, Library of Congress; L. E. Chittenden to T. H. Dudley, November 1, 1860, Dudley Papers, Huntington Library.

[46] See details as developed in Avery O. Craven, *Edmund Ruffin, Southerner* (New York, 1932). The purpose of this paper is to suggest an approach to the whole problem, and since this has been done here in some detail for the North, and elsewhere by the writer for the South, it has not been thought necessary to suggest more than the larger outline. This should not imply a sectional prejudice.

felt the sting of poverty, these spokesmen, under the influence of Old World agrarian thinking, voiced protest in terms of local government versus a central government made strong by the power to grant economic favors.[47] Specifically, industry and commerce, largely centering in the North, were, by tariffs and centralization, profiting at the expense of the nation's real producers. Before long Southerners were calculating the millions-of-dollars tribute paid to this "Lord North" and were talking of being in a state of colonial dependence.

The remedy was found in a strict adherence to the Constitution. Yankee traits could be controlled and southern rights preserved by a series of phrases, on the meaning of which not even the framers could agree. The section had begun to chop logic; it was the champion of things as they were—a conscious minority in a republican system. Yet in its own eyes, the South was the defender of democratic government against the onslaughts of those who would distort sacred institutions in order to promote their own material interests. All that the Revolution had won, all that "the Fathers" had achieved, was involved in the struggle.

When opposition to slavery developed, a new threat of economic loss, now joined with fear of racial conflict and social unrest, was added. When that drive became a moral attack on the whole southern way of life, the defense broadened in proportion and emotions deepened. The Constitution was not enough against those who would not respect its provisions; the whole South must become unified for political efficiency. The section must have that security which the Constitution guaranteed and an equal right to expand with its institutions *as a matter of principle*. Keen minds set to work to reveal the virtues in slavery and the life it permitted in the South. When they had finished, a stratified society, with Negro "mudsills" at the bottom, permitted genuine republican government, escaped the ills of labor and race conflict, gave widest opportunity for ability and culture, and truly forwarded the cause of civilization.[48] The stability and quiet under such a system were contrasted with the restless strife of the North which was developing socialism and threatening the destruction of security in person

[47] John Taylor, *Tyranny Unmasked* (Washington, 1822), and *Construction Construed and Constitutions Vindicated* (Richmond, 1820); Jesse T. Carpenter, *The South as a Conscious Minority, 1789–1861* (New York, 1930).

[48] William S. Jenkins, *Pro-Slavery Thought in the Old South* (Chapel Hill, 1935).

and in property. The southern way of life was the way of order and progress.

Here was something else worth fighting to preserve. The old struggle against "King Numbers," which in large part had been won at home, must go on. But the field had broadened, and the struggle was against a foe more base and self-seeking. Both the system of republican government and the cause of civilization were bound up in the struggle.

Early efforts at unified defense proved futile because the masses, with cotton and the hopes it gave, could not muster the emotional response sufficient for action. They neither felt the inferiority suggested by economic dependence nor the compelling force-of-rights which gave no practical returns. They gladly accepted compromise in 1850 and were surprisingly unmoved throughout the next eight years. Leaders might support the fruitless Kansas-Nebraska Bill, as the Richmond *Enquirer* said, "solely for the reason that it would vindicate the equality and sovereignty of the states."[49] But the masses, to quote one individual, were "not a particle" excited. They knew, as this writer put it, that the struggle was over "a shadow."[50] Their outlook was as yet practical.

But the John Brown raid was another matter. It put reality into the much discussed program of Yankee "money-changers," "peasant farmers," and the "long haired men and short haired women" of the North. The sharpest resentments and deepest fears of which a people were capable broke loose. A race war was impending. And that was a poor man's problem. Albert G. Brown of Mississippi put it this way:[51]

> The rich will flee the country. . . . Then the non-slaveholder will begin to see what his real fate is. The Negro will intrude into his preserve . . . insist on being treated as an equal . . . that he shall go to the white man's bed, and the white man his . . . that his son shall marry the white man's daughter, and the white man's daughter his son. In short that they shall live on terms of perfect social equality. The non-slaveholder will, of course, reject the terms. Then will commence a war of races such as has marked the history of San Domingo.

49 Richmond *Enquirer,* March 10, 1854.

50 Josiah Evans to B. F. Perry, January 19, 1858, Perry Papers, Alabama Department of Archives and History; Jonathan Worth to John A. Gilmer, March 9, 1858, in J. G. de R. Hamilton (ed.), *The Correspondence of Jonathan Worth* (Raleigh, 1909), I, 55.

51 Quoted by Percy L. Rainwater, "The Presidential Canvass of 1860 in Mississippi," *Journal of the Mississippi State Bar,* V (1933), 279–80.

The triumph of the Republican party, sectional and containing, as it did, men as rabid as Sumner and as vague and shifting as Seward and Lincoln, drove the more inflamed Southerners to secession. Lincoln's refusal of compromise and his handling of Fort Sumter forced conservatives to follow. War had become inevitable. Fear and hate had taken charge.

By May, 1861, that staunch lover of the Union, Jonathan Worth, could write from peaceable old Randolph County in North Carolina: "The voice of reason is silenced. Furious passion and thirst for blood consume the air. . . . Nobody is allowed to retain and assert his reason. The cartridge box is preferred to the ballot box. The very women and children are for war."[52]

A little later the New York *Herald* solemnly reported from the battlefield of Bull Run that southern "fiends in human shape have taken the bayonets and knives of our wounded and dying soldiers and thrust them into their hearts and left them sticking there, and some of the Louisiana Zouaves have severed the heads of our dead from their bodies, and amused themselves by kicking them as footballs."[53]

The old Carolinian at Appomattox was right. It is a serious thing to love a country!

[52] Jonathan Worth to Gaius Winningham, May 20, 1861, in Hamilton (ed.), *The Correspondence of Jonathan Worth,* I, 149.

[53] New York *Herald,* July 24, 1861.

NOTE: It was never the intention of the author of this article to say that the Civil War was simply the product of emotions, as some have charged, but rather that the concrete problems might have been solved by the democratic process had they not been reduced to "right and wrong" and shot through with hatred and misunderstanding. The concrete issues, of course, were always real and dangerous, perhaps, uncompromisable, especially when reduced to emotionalized abstractions.

IV

THE REPRESSIBLE CONFLICT

The move for an independent South which came to a climax in 1861 did not arise from permanent physical and social conditions. It sprang rather from temporary emotional factors cultivated both without and within the section. Men fought because they had come to fear and hate—because they had at last accepted a distorted picture of both themselves and the people in other sections.

We have found little in the natural setup of the South to make a unity out of the varied states and regions stretching from Virginia to Texas. That had to be achieved through conflict. Nor have we found inherent differences great enough to make war "inevitable" or "irrepressible" between this section and other sections within the nation. That was to be an artificial creation of inflamed minds. Around the institution of slavery was engendered most of the bitterness which made war necessary. Yet slavery in itself, as we have seen, was not an all-inclusive institution. If it had not become a symbol first of sectional differences and then of southern depravity, or superiority, according to the point of view—it might have been faced as a national question and dealt with as successfully as the South American countries dealt with the same problem. Lincoln said he was fighting to save the Union and most certainly men of the South had been struggling for decades to save the Constitution on which that Union rested and was made possible. What we are slowly coming to realize is that war was the product, not so much of sectional differences as of emotions developed about differences, which by 1861 made it impossible to reason, to trust, or to compromise. Both sides believed the other to be composed of persons who could only be handled by force—fiends in human form whose lives need not be spared, whose homes could be pillaged and burned, and whose institutions must be destroyed. The North could say that it was fighting to save a Union which God had established as a great

Reprinted from *The Repressible Conflict* (Baton Rouge: Louisiana State University Press, 1939), pp. 63–97.

experiment in democracy and which Southerners would destroy and replace with chaos, aristocracy, and human bondage. That is the whole substance of Lincoln's Gettysburg Address. The South, on the other hand, could say that it was fighting to save the original Constitution and to defend rights granted under that Constitution; that Yankees would not respect either constitutions or rights—they would even, in John Brown fashion, stir racial wars.

Higher ideals and purposes have never actuated two belligerents. Worse qualities have never been attributed to enemies. Yet when the war had been over long enough for the historian to look back without passion or prejudice, he was to discover that in saving the Union the North had really achieved a nationalism, which in turn spelled centralization in the interests of industrialism and a new dominant section, which was to make colonial provinces of both South and West for the next generation or more, which was to crush the farmers of the nation and head them toward peasantry, and which was to create a new urban way of life which Spengler and his kind believe to be the last stage in the decline of Western civilization. Workers talking of "wage slavery"; capitalists piling fortunes high while poverty and starvation stalk the streets; culture, a bought and borrowed thing, stored in museums, with intellectual sterility everywhere save in a few provincial corners! To such ends did three decades of quarreling and four years of bitter warfare make substantial contributions.

To trace the steps by which the South was pounded into self-consciousness and moved to ultimate secession is not simple. We will ignore the early recognition of differences in Colonial days as the manifestation of a provincialism common to all the colonies. The old notion of Puritan in New England and Cavalier in Virginia does not hold water. The real distinction between the sections was one of commerce as against agriculture—a difference which manifested itself almost as soon as the colonists came together under a government of their own. In the Constitutional Convention, Charles Pinckney observed "a real distinction between the northern and southern interests arising from the character of their means of livelihood." Madison declared that "the great division of interest did not lie between the large and small states; it lay between the northern and southern."

In the debates over ratification of the Constitution, like opinions appear. Patrick Henry insisted that the proposed union was between units "naturally divided into carrying and productive states," and Governor Harrison of Virginia feared that under such a constitution, the southern states "would be little more than appendages to those northward" of the Potomac. Another citizen of the same state insisted that New England would soon be sending "revenue officers" to the South "instead of their onions and apples."

But real division did not appear until Hamilton began his program of centralization under funding, banking, and tariff schemes. It did not bring wide sectional response until that movement found its greater champion in John Marshall. When the struggle was fully developed, it revealed itself as a contest between those who farmed and those whose economic efforts were confined to the urban centers. Southern men assumed the leadership of the rural group only because their intellectual and social qualifications gave them the right to do so. They were the heirs to the economic-social philosophy of the early eighteenth century which French physiocrats had elaborated and English country gentlemen had practiced. They accepted as a matter of course the superiority of farming over all other forms of endeavor and assumed that, if economic affairs were left alone by government, the great mass of the people would be tillers of the soil and the great proportion of the nation's wealth would come from farming and remain in the hands of farmers. They believed that democratic government could succeed only when the people were largely engaged in agricultural pursuits and when their virtues were those developed and sustained by rural living.

When Hamilton's program was launched under the new government, men like Thomas Jefferson and John Taylor of Caroline drew back. Here was an attempt to create wealth by legislation and to raise a group of urban dwellers whose efforts were given to financial manipulation, to manufacturing, and to trade. Government was attempting to draw about itself a group of financial and industrial men through legislative favors. Money was to be taken in the form of taxes from the real producers and bestowed upon this "order of stockjobbers in loans, banks, manufactories, contracts." Money invested in government paper or in industries protected from competition would thus yield larger returns than if placed in agriculture. Capital would, under such conditions, soon flee the fields and be absorbed in "the legal monopolies of banking and manufacturing," leaving the farms in ruin and the farmers in despair. Population would shift from the country to the town, and political power would pass permanently into the hands of those whose interests and profits were created by legislation. Already, said John Taylor in 1803, Congress was "very visably against agriculturists." He believed that unless the farmers bestirred themselves, their fate was permanently sealed.

When John Marshall gave constitutional approbation to the centralizing trends which Hamilton had inaugurated and added his own contributions by decisions which subjected even the state courts to federal review, the agrarian spokesmen saw it all as a continuation of the scheme to exploit farmers in the interests of "legal factions." The passage of protective tariffs in the same period showed the aggressive interest of those in control of central government in the industrial parasites, and the efforts of the same group to lay restrictions on the state of Missouri as the price of admission to the Union had a like purpose when rightly understood. Agriculture was being crowded aside and plundered through the centralization of government in the interests of its own creatures—paper and industrial monopolies.

John Taylor described what had happened in this fashion:

> The great pecuniary favors granted by Congress to certificate holders begot banking; banking begot bounties to manufacturing capitalists; bounties to manufacturing capitalists begot an oppressive pension list; these partialities united to beget the Missouri project; that project begot the idea of using slavery as an instrument for effecting a balance of power; when it is put in operation, it will beget new usurpations of internal powers over persons and property, and these will beget a dissolution of the Union.

The checking of this evil was not wholly a southern problem. It was the farmer's problem wherever he might be. But since the South was the home of those who had most completely accepted the old physiocratic doctrines and since her planters had achieved the highest station reached by American agriculturists through the plantation system and staple crops, her leaders had long served as spokesmen for the rural group. As such they were thought of as the champions of these interests and had received all the hatred which the opposing element could muster. The defense, based on states' rights, which the farmers offered was destined to be considered her especial property even though it had wide and common use throughout the nation up to 1860. In this fight to defend agriculture through local democracy, the South came to be thought of as a section of peculiar unity and unusual self-consciousness.

This is a highly significant fact in the developments we are tracing and reveals so well the artificial process by which sectional consciousness was created that it needs added emphasis. The remedy which the "agrarians" offered to the consolidation program, and which was creating the new economic alignment, was one of strict construction of the Constitution in the interests of states' rights. The Virginia and Kentucky resolutions, framed by Madison and Jefferson and introduced in the case of the Virginia legislature by John Taylor, called attention to the fact of "delegated powers" and the necessity of adherence to the original grants. The campaign which brought Jefferson to the presidency in 1801 was conducted on like grounds. The same general political philosophy served through the next two decades while the Virginia dynasty ruled and broke forth with new force when the Missouri Compromise and Marshall's decisions showed again the rising power of the opposing economic group and their consolidation doctrines. The tariff controversy ending in nullification brought it to a climax.

It is not necessary to follow in detail this constitutional struggle. The significant point is that the states' rights doctrine had been brought forward in peculiar form to defend an agricultural group or "interest" against a commercial-urban-industrial group or "interest." The important fact is that this was not in reality a sectional struggle. The support for it was found among farmers and lesser elements throughout the nation. New England farmers and the agricultural and labor groups in the Middle States combined with southern men in what was a class struggle—an economic conflict. Their votes helped Jefferson to the presidency; Andrew Jackson found them behind him in the fight against the Bank. They resented the new-rich factory owner with a zeal quite comparable to that of the South Carolinian, and not until slavery entered the picture did they desert.

Nor was the support of consolidation by the opposing faction always sectional. There was a notable group of southern men who looked forward to a diversified economic life for their section and even favored protective tariffs. John Marshall was a Virginian and his Richmond group was as troublesome to the agrarians as were the traders and processors of the North. Yet the fact of southern leadership in the agrarian movement has fixed the false notion in American history of southern sectionalism as an early trait—of states' rights as its monopoly. The South Carolina nullification controversy, which would have been a minor incident of Hartford Convention proportions if South Carolina and Andrew Jackson had not given it picturesque flavor, has been singled out and distorted into a great prophetic event pointing inevitably toward civil war. The fact that the forces of moderation were nearly equal to those of aggression in South Carolina itself, and that not another southern state was ever in the slightest danger of joining in the movement, has been ignored, and the incident has been given sectional significance and related in direct fashion to the formation of the southern Confederacy.

Such an interpretation does violence to historical truth. By no stretch of imagination can we find sectional consciousness, or sectional unity in the South, save in the contest over Missouri, beyond that which a rural people, as such, were made to feel in the period from 1789 to 1830, when the urban-industrial interests were making their first great drive to establish themselves in American life. We may say that the South was forging weapons to be of use in later times. We may even say that leadership as well as logic was being evolved, but we cannot speak of unity in the face of so much division at home on all national questions. Furthermore, the entire back-country South at this time was finding new and different economic purposes and was chafing under the restraints imposed by its own state governments. More than half the southern people were quite uncertain as to what course, economic or political, they should follow. Even the men of the tidewater sections, under economic depression, were at loggerheads as to the best means for the promotion of their interests.

A survey of any southern state in the period of the 1820's and early 1830's will reveal internal conflict of the most intense kind. In legislatures and in conventions every question which was later to divide North and South was being fought out: the rights of minorities and majorities; the rights of property; the interpretation of constitutions; the merits of wide central government activity as against local action, including aid to economic endeavors; even the merits and the evils of slavery. In this contest appeared a group of leaders, perhaps representing a majority of the people of the South, who upheld the very positions which the North was to uphold on the eve of civil war. Every weapon of defense later used to combat the North was used to protect southern men from their fellow southern citizens! It is absurd to talk of a unique southern consciousness and common southern attitudes in this period!

If this analysis be correct, then the growth of southern consciousness and the final stroke for independent nationalism were the product of events and developments belonging in the main to the period after 1830. They had largely to do with the institution of slavery. Other issues, of course, entered into the picture, but in most cases slavery, sooner or later, managed to cast its distorting shadow over them and, ultimately, to make itself the symbol of sectional differences. The old idea of superiority and inferiority in social-economic life grew to new proportions as conflict became more bitter and the weapon of states' rights under the Constitution took on sharper edges as antagonisms developed. But the moral implications of the slavery controversy alone made hatred and distrust in degree great enough to require war.

Slavery as a reality and slavery as a symbol of southern life in its conflict with the North were, as we have seen, two quite different things. The one was left over from the eighteenth century and probably at this time rather near the end of its existence; the other was a creation of inflamed imaginations which endowed southern men and institutions with every quality desired and which extended its scope to cover all that was peculiar to the life of a section. The first was an economic fact, the other a psychological one. The first could be almost ignored in our study of sectional conflict had it not become the symbol of all sectional differences; the second leaves few pages of history from 1830 to 1860 untouched.

For our present purposes we need only notice that in the period before 1820 slavery had been sharply criticized as a social feature by farseeing men in all sections of the nation. Northern states, finding it unprofitable and in conflict with their ideals as emphasized by the Revolution, had abolished it. Southern leaders generally spoke of it as an institution which they confidently expected to pass in due season. The result was the localization of the institution, confining it to the South, and the creation of the idea that it was economically unprofitable and ethically unjustifiable. The colonization movement represented an effort to enable the work of manumission to proceed in those areas where the number of Negroes, if freed, was great enough to present a race question. It was to be a means of getting out of the frying pan without experiencing the unpleasantness of fire. Good men everywhere were expected to co-operate against a recognized evil. Only now and then did some stray voice dissent.

The debates over the Missouri Compromise brought the first indications that earlier attitudes were changing. They produced sharp condemnation of slavery and even the suggestion that Congress had the power to destroy it. Radicals, like Livermore of New Hampshire, asked: "How will the desire for wealth render us blind to the sin of holding both the bodies and souls of our fellow men in chains. . . . Do not, for the sake of cotton and tobacco, let it be told to future ages that, while pretending to love liberty, we have purchased an extensive country to disgrace it with the foulest reproach of nations!" Senator King of New York went so far as to insist that "no human law, compact, or compromise can establish or continue slavery. . . . There is no such thing as a slave."

Southern men, in turn, defended themselves, and a few began the partial defense of their institution. Most of them could have said with Reed of Georgia: "Believe me, sir, I am not a panegyrist of slavery. It is an unnatural state; a dark cloud which obscures half the lustre of our free institutions." All of them did agree with Barbour of Virginia who insisted that his opponent overstated its ills! "He has shaded it too deeply, with the coloring of his own imagination." But a few, like William Smith of South Carolina, "justified slavery on the broadest principles, without qualification or reserve." He pronounced it "right" and viewed it "as a benefit" which would be perpetuated.

The attack on slavery as a sectional institution had been launched; the proslavery argument as a sectional defense had been begun.

It is not necessary to follow the development of these two positions in the purely domestic conflicts in the several southern states. Nor need we do more than point out the widening national statements evolved in the contests over antislavery petitions in Congress and the sending of inflammatory materials through the mails. The effects were only to sharpen the opposing positions and to increase the sectional character of both attack and defense.

The rise of the professional spokesmen—called "abolitionists" on the one side and "fire-eaters" on the other—needs notice only because of the emotional flavor which they added to the contest. William Lloyd Garrison had the gift for making everyone mad—including himself. He had an unusual capacity for hating. If Southerners such as Dew and Harper and Ruffin were more dignified and logical, they were no less positive and one-sided. When the clergymen entered the field, and thousands of them did, they added righteous indignation to the conflict. The clan is notoriously efficient in uncomprising assertion of right and wrong. When one speaks for God, argument is useless; only combat is possible.

The significant thing about the antislavery men and movements and those who developed the abstract defense of the South is the picture of slavery and of society which they created. They were too extreme for any great following. Conservative men of the day dismissed them as fanatics and hastened to assure their friends in other sections that such voices did not represent the true opinions and feelings of their people. But these fanatics, unrestrained by fact, were creating clear-cut pictures of slavery, slaves, slaveholders, and southern and northern life positive enough to suit the needs of those engaged in conflict. When politicians became enraged in debate, when the sections became entangled in strife, these pictures were to serve wider purposes. The time would come when opponents needed just such distorted weapons—when false propaganda could take the place of truth. Then the conceptions of men and societies woven by these intense emotional voices of heaven would pass as sober truth. Enemies would become devils; friends, the incarnation of right and justice. Blood would have to be spilled.

The antislavery impulse as directed against that institution in the South began in the 1820's and lasted until emancipation and victory in battle brought it to an end. It passed through several distinct stages, the earlier ones being more or less pure social reform in character and the later ones so badly mixed with politics that it is difficult to tell what is political, what social, and what moral. It worked through every medium of individual and group contact known to the day and appealed to interest, conscience, emotion, and reason. Little children learned their A B C's from booklets which read:

> *A* is an Abolitionist,
> A man who wants to free
> The wretched slave—and give to all
> An equal liberty.

B is a Brother with a skin
Of somewhat darker hue,
But in our Heavenly Father's sight
He is as dear as you.

C is the Cotton field, to which
This injured brother's driven,
When, as the white man's *slave,* he toils
From early morn 'till even.

D is the Driver, cold and stern,
Who follows, whip in hand,
To punish those who dare to rest
Or disobey command.

And so on down through:

K is the Kidnapper, who stole
That little child and mother—
Shrieking, it clung around her, but
He tore them from each other.

L is the Lash, that brutally
He swung around its head,
Threatening that "if it cried again,
He'd whip it 'till 'twas dead."

And at the bitter end:

Z is a zealous man, sincere,
Truthful, and just and true;
An earnest pleader for the slave—
Will you not be so too?

With this as a beginning, the work of indoctrination was carried on by local and national organizations through means which ranged from songs and stories, pamphlets and books, conventions and lobbies, to the violent speeches of a Charles Sumner in the Senate or the more subtle statements of a Lincoln on the hustings in Illinois pointing out the moral wrong in human bondage and insisting that it be put on the road to ultimate extinction.

But regardless of time and place, type of antislavery men, or form of appeal, two great facts were being impressed upon the northern people: first, the Southerner was an aristocrat, an enemy of democracy in society and government; and second, he was a man of violent and generally uncontrolled passions which led him into intemperance, licentiousness, brutality, and disregard of others' rights. Most Southerners were supposed to be slaveholders and, as such, they constituted a single interest which could be designated as the slave power whose purpose was the rule or the ruin of the whole Union. As the *Philanthropist* said in 1840: "All the great changes of policy which have successfully involved in disaster each and every northern interest have been introduced by the dictation of the Slave Power."

In the widely read pamphlet entitled *American Slavery As It Is*, a writer spoke of the "savage ferocity" of southern men as "the natural result of their habit of daily plundering and oppressing the slave." He tells of perpetual idleness broken only by brutal cock-fights, gander pullings, and horse races so barbarous in character that "the blood of the tortured animal drips from the lash and flies at every leap from the stroke of the rowel." *Anti-Slavery Tract Number 7* declared that "a million and a half of slave women, some of them without even the tinge of African blood, are given up, a lawful prey to the unbridled lusts of their masters." Theodore Parker supplied the comment on this text by saying: "The South is full of mulattoes; its best 'blood flows in the veins of slaves.' . . . Girls, the children of mulattoes, are sold at great prices, as food for private licentiousness, or public furniture in houses of ill-fame." The *Liberator* referred to Southerners as "sagacious desperadoes and remorseless men-stealers"; and the section as "ferocious and despotic." Garrison insisted that it was as easy to "transform wolves and hyenas into lambs and doves" as to appeal to southern "understandings, consciences and hearts." He topped it all by saying: "We would sooner trust the honor of the country . . . in the hands of inmates of our penitentiaries and prisons than in their hands. . . . They are the meanest thieves and the worst of robbers. . . . We do not acknowledge them to be within the pale of Christianity, of republicanism, of humanity."

In such a picture, slavery was one round of cruelty. David L. Child honestly stated: "From all that I have read and heard upon the subject of whipping done by masters and overseers to slaves . . . I have come to the conclusion that some hundreds of *cart whip* and cowskin instruments, which I am told make the skin fly like feathers, and cut frequently to the bone, are in *perpetual daily motion* in the slave states." Charles Sumner's impressions, if we can judge by his speeches in Congress, were almost as harsh. Nor did he manifest the slightest interest in gaining better ones when the good Francis Lieber, himself an antislavery man, informed him that "my wife read [your speech] . . . and exclaimed at the picture you give of slavery, 'How untrue.' It seems to me slavery may be attacked without fiction such as you state. . . ."

The final logical conclusion of all this discussion was stated by Theodore Parker in 1851 when he declared:

> The South, in the main, had a very different origin from the North. I think few if any persons settled there for religion's sake; or for the sake of the freedom of the State. It was not a moral idea which sent men to Virginia, Georgia, or Carolina. "Men do not gather grapes of thorns." The difference in the seed will appear in the difference of the crop. In the character of the people of the North, and South, it appears at this day. . . . Here, now, is the great cause of the difference in the material results, represented in towns and villages, by farms and factories, ships and shops. Here is the cause of differences in the schools and colleges, churches, and in the literature; the cause of difference in men. The South with its despotic idea, dishonors labor, but wishes to compromise between its idleness and its appetite, and so kidnaps men to do its work.

"Two opposing civilizations are in conflict here, and have been from the infancy of our Union," said Professor Austin Phelps of Andover Theological Seminary.

The full effect of such distortion was not apparent at once. The historian can judge its real force only on that bitter July day in 1861 when the *New York Herald* carried to a receptive nation the story of southern atrocities committed on the battlefield at Bull Run.

> A private of the First Connecticut Regiment found a wounded rebel lying in the sun, and lifted him up and carried him to a shade, where he gently layed him and gave him to drink from his canteen. Revived by the drink, the ingrate drew his pistol and shot his benefactor through the heart. Another instance is related of a troop of rebel cavalry deliberately firing upon a number of wounded men, who had been placed together in the shade. . . . It is said by Virginians who have come from the battlefield that these fiends in human shape have taken the bayonets and knives of our wounded and dying soldiers and thrust them into their hearts and left them sticking there, and that some of the Louisiana Zouaves have severed the heads of our dead from their bodies, and amused themselves by kicking them about as footballs.

All of which, as the *Cincinnati Enquirer* added, was "attributable to the barbarism of slavery, in which and to which the southern soldiers have been educated. . . ."

For a generation southern men and women lived under such an attack. It began, as we have said, as a simple questioning of the justice of human slavery by a few earnest, if fanatical, humanitarians. It ended on the level of a high moral crusade, the justice of which few northern men questioned, and tended to include in its sweep of purpose the overthrow of the whole southern way of life. Garrison and Phillips and Parker became as well known in the South as in the North. In fact, one writer has recently evaluated Garrison in the antislavery impulse as more important for the hatred he stirred below Mason and Dixon's line than for the influence he wielded above it. Gradually the South became conscious and bitter. It turned in self-defense. A "refutation of the calumnies circulated against" the section appeared almost as soon as the attack was begun. It showed that emotions had been stirred and revealed the possibility of a sectional response. Edwin Holland asked his neighbors to present facts in refutation of charges made and referred to the "abundant testimony of the hostile and unfriendly spirit with which the most vital interests" of the South were discussed. He declared that "the North and East" were "or affected to be, totally ignorant of the actual state and character of our Negro population; they represent the condition of their bondage as a perpetual revolution of labor and severity, rendered still more deplorable by an utter destitution of all the comforts of life. . . ." He charged "malignity of design" and "utter contempt of truth in such statements" and declared them uttered without "the most ordinary regard for our feelings."

By 1854 the Macon *Georgia Telegraph* could say that "the grand question . . . is what shall be done to protect the South from this everlasting enmity and turmoil, which tears the country to pieces . . . when any question arises which . . . affects the question of slavery." It felt the Union could stand anything but

> the insolent and insidious rust of a progressing, perverted, and corrupt public opinion, which we know has been manufactured with more than Jesuitical zeal and perseverance for a quarter of a century in a portion of this Confederacy. The pseudo ministry . . . of our country . . . take the child's young mind and preoccupy it by many species of lying and blasphemous outcry . . . and follow the child into manhood with this sort of teaching as regards Southern people, until lies and sophistry and false information about us have become ingrained into the very intellect and hearts of Northern people.

A more positive reply was offered in the ingenious "proslavery argument" which was evolved in the South from 1820 to 1860. From a half-apologetic defense of slavery as a necessary evil, it grew to an aggressive glorification of a way of life. The Bible, the Past, Nature, and Civilization were all appealed to, and when the task was completed the Southerner stood before the world a superior man in a superior society. An early group attempted to point out the benefits of slavery to the Negro himself. The Reverend J. C. Stiles showed that slavery had turned twice as many heathens into Christians as all other missionary efforts combined, and Reverend Stringfellow was certain that God had confined the institution to the South because of the superior qualities in its people for lifting ignorant Negroes to culture! Others pointed out the inability of the Negro to be of economic benefit to himself and society without the supervision and direction which slavery afforded. A few with a scientific bent, such as Van Everie and Nott, insisted on the unique origins of the Negro and his peculiar physical and mental traits which predestined him to servitude. The clergy, even then a bit skeptical of science, accepted the differences but explained them by the curse of God on Ham.

From such beginnings, the defense went on to ingenious refinements as men discovered that slaves were better off than factory workers; that all labor, regardless of the system, was exploited; that republican government could exist only where all white men were free from drudgery; and that without slavery in agriculture all farmers were destined to a degrading peasantry. It reached its fullness in the staunch belief that under slavery, the South had achieved a vastly superior civilization toward which the rest of the world must move. Here was a society without a labor conflict, without race conflict, and without social agitation. There was no unemployment and no old-age worries for its toilers. Culture and refinement prevailed, and the ruin which urban life produced in "depravity of morals . . . increase of want, and of crime," as Edward Fisher charged, was lacking. Slavery had marked the beginning of man's upward climb, as Professor Dew had early declared, and it now marked its highest peak. When war broke, the Reverend J. H. Thornwell could say:

The parties in this conflict are not merely abolitionists and slaveholders; they are atheists, socialists, communists, red republicans, jacobins on the one side, and the friends of order and regulated freedom on the other. In one word, the world is the battle ground, Christianity and atheism the combatants, and the progress of humanity the stake.

What stands out in all this is the belief in the peculiar quality and character of the South; the growing emotion involved in attack and defense; the assumption of differences inherent and persistent. There was a North, and there was a South. They represented entirely different values and qualities. They were by nature enemies. And, what is most significant, *moral* values were involved—things affecting humanity, civilization, God's purposes in this world. Those are things for which men give their lives, for which holy wars are fought. National consciousness is woven from fear and resentment as well as from conviction and faith. Material realities shrink into insignificance when brought into comparison.

Meanwhile the "average American" went about his busy way. The nation had entered a new period of expansion which carried it across the plains and mountains to the Pacific. The Indian and Mexican learned anew the meaning of Manifest Destiny. Behind frontiers, old Wests found their lands and crops in competition with those ahead and readjustments forced upon them which ran back in waves even to the eastern seaboard. The old western demands for lands and better ways to improved markets thus gained new strength, especially in the region above the Ohio, and the banner of democracy was hoisted over every demand. Americans had a right to prosperity as well as to freedom and equality. In the deep South, cotton erected its kingdom to strengthen the hold of agriculture below Mason and Dixon's line, and in the Northeast the Industrial Revolution reached maturity great enough to produce a depression. The nation grew "fearfully"; inequality increased at an even greater rate.

Such expansion inevitably exaggerated the already great sectional division and conflict, and soon the sectional spokesmen, in the struggle for place and advantage, were making telling use of emotions generated in the slavery controversy. James McDowell, in 1832, had told the slaveholders of Virginia that "a Crusade, in the name of liberty, *but with the purpose of plunder*, will be preached against the States that protect it [slavery]—that they will be held up as the common enemies of man whom it will be a duty to overthrow and justice to despoil. . . ." Events now proved the soundness of his warning, but they also showed that he had seen only half of the truth. Southern leaders too would make use of slavery sentiments to forward their ends and to produce unity among their followers.

After 1840 few issues were allowed to stand on their own merits. Individuals and groups, consciously and unconsciously, used slavery to aid their interests. John C. Calhoun and John Quincy Adams, seeking political advantage, tangled slavery hopelessly with the western demand for the annexation of Texas. David Wilmot introduced his trouble-making Proviso as part of a political game which he and his friends were playing. The repeal clause in the Kansas-Nebraska Act was the afterthought of a mere handful of politicians and not a move in response to southern demands. The Appeal to Independent Democrats which Chase and his group used to stir the Northwest was false in its assertions and unfair in its purposes, but it was politically effective. The damaging section in the Dred Scott Decision was an *obiter dictum*, forced, according to the late Professor Hodder, by the political ambitions of dissenting judges. John Brown, who reduced rabid talk to action, is frankly considered insane by his most able biographer.

Yet these uncalled-for moves and this irresponsible leadership were the very things which lifted the crusade of a band of "crackpot reformers" in the North and an extravagant group of "fire-eaters" in the South to the proportions of a national conflict adjustable only by civil war. Texas and slavery combined begot the Wilmot Proviso, which, in turn, forced the crisis of 1850. The repeal of the Missouri Compromise begot the Republican party and ultimately the combination of a political party and a moral crusade. The Dred Scott *obiter dictum* justified the continuation of that party as a perpetual guard against the aggressions of the South. John Brown brought the race question to the fore and added the final emotional appeal needed to pound the divergent classes of the South into a working unity.

The politician thus gave an air of reality to the abstractions of those who had evolved the slavery question into a struggle of civilizations. In his hands the conflict between freedom and slavery became a sectional contest for lands, internal improvements, tariffs, and new areas for expansion. The continuation of material well-being and the existence of fundamental rights were linked with the spread or the restriction of the "peculiar institution." An emotional fervor and moral force, which only slavery could create, was thus thrown about a whole set of very practical and concrete problems. Two ways of life and two opposing sets of constitutional principles were thus forced into an irrepressible contest for supremacy. Yet, as a matter of fact, few actual gains or losses were involved. Texas would have progressed about as it did if slavery had never been mentioned. There were only two slaves in Kansas in 1860, and there never was the slightest chance of slavery's entering Kansas or Nebraska. All well-informed men knew that by 1857, and many were saying so at the very time Lincoln was making political capital out of proslavery danger. A dozen *obiter dicta* would not have spread slavery over the North, and a hundred John Browns could not have produced a general revolution among the slaves.

The combined efforts of reformer and politician gradually created the notion of the "slave power" and of "Black Republicanism." Each of these creations was supposed to consist of a well-organized force and program. The one was determined to spread slavery throughout the land. The other was determined to wipe out the institution of slavery even at the cost of a race war. Both were fictions. Yet partisans were able to bring all the fears and apprehensions, all the noble purposes and sentiments aroused by the antislavery and the proslavery crusades, to their side and to pour all the bitter distortions of that conflict upon their opponents. They made a conscious North and a conscious South. Each could fight for God against the Devil and his human allies. One would struggle for Union and democracy, the other for self-rule and the Constitution untarnished. Sane men on both sides, and they constituted a majority even in 1861, were helpless before fanatics armed with such holy weapons.

Today, as we look back, we discover that the net results of a war which blackened the years from 1861 to 1865 must be couched in terms of the triumph of industry over agriculture; of centralization over local democracy; of one section over another; of the Republican party, representing bourgeois acquisitiveness, over its Democratic rival, representing an older agrarian ideal. Hundreds of thousands lost their lives, and property damage ran into billions of dollars. The victors abandoned the Negro in 1876 and permitted him to escape little of the hard fate destined for his race in 1850. Inferior social and economic status and segregation in poor neighborhoods are his lot North and South alike. The race question still awaits solution. The balance in American economic development kept by natural sectional and class differences was completely upset. Industrial capitalism, with the banners of righteousness, patriotism, and progress over its head and with all critics hushed in disgrace and defeat, went on to its fullness and perhaps its ruin. Men today are looking back regretfully toward a Constitution which might have protected rights, an agrarian way of life which might have fostered a rich American culture and a sane economic order, a decentralized government wherein individuals and localities might have realized a more satisfactory democracy. We are back where we started. We have begun to realize what it costs a people to permit emotion to rule and to allow pious men to lead them into "irrepressible conflicts."

V

THE CIVIL WAR AND THE DEMOCRATIC PROCESS

The Civil War is the most significant event in the domestic history of the United States. It marks the dividing line between an old order and Modern America. It eliminated the South as an important factor in shaping national policies and ended the domination of rural groups in American life. It opened the way for modern industrial and finance capitalism. It put the major control of national affairs into the keeping of the urban dwellers of the Northeast. It was, indeed, what Charles A. Beard has called it, "The Second American Revolution."

And the significant thing about the American Civil War is that it represents a complete breakdown of the democratic process in the handling of national problems. Men ceased to reason together. Discussion of issues turned to incrimination; compromise or delay in action became impossible. Men firm in the conviction that the totality of right and justice was on their side faced each other with a willingness and a determination to use violence for the achievement of their ends. In the end, opponents were beaten into submission in bloody combat in complete contradiction of the basic assumption on which the whole American political structure had been erected, namely, that men are endowed with reason enough to rule themselves and that they have consciences which impel them to deal justly with their fellows; that rational discussion of issues, compromise of differences, and delay in action where adjustment is not reached constitute a procedure by which groups that vary as much as did the colonies of Massachusetts and South Carolina could live and work in unity forever.

For these reasons the Civil War continues to be a matter of vital

Reprinted from the *Abraham Lincoln Quarterly,* IV, No. 6 (June, 1947), 269–92. An address given at the annual meeting of the Abraham Lincoln Association, Springfield, Illinois, February 12, 1947.

interest to all historians of the United States and one about which there has been less agreement than about any other event in the history of the nation. Historians are far apart in their interpretations and, strangely enough, in a field so complicated that any honest effort to throw light into darkness should be welcomed, there has been little of co-operation and much of name-calling, distortion of positions, and open charges of bias. The passions of 1860–65 seem still to exist, especially among those who have done little research in the vast materials on both sides, and the hope for a better understanding of America's greatest tragedy is yet a long way off.

It is not my purpose to attempt any full discussion of events and factors that entered into the making of a civil war in the United States. I only wish to suggest to you certain approaches to the matter of the breakdown of the democratic process in 1860, which may have some permanent value to those who still retain their faith in that process as the best way for humble men to govern themselves.

I would begin with two great American documents and their differences in emphasis—the Declaration of Independence and the Constitution of the United States. I would like to suggest a dilemma inherent in their implications and in their significance in American life.

When the Continental Congress, on July 2, 1776, had passed the Virginia Resolutions officially declaring our independence of Great Britain, they thought it necessary to justify the step they had taken. So they appointed a committee, of which Thomas Jefferson was a member, to make such a statement. It presented, on July 4, 1776, a document that has ever since been known as The Declaration of Independence.

That document contained two things: a political philosophy justifying rebellion and a statement of the grievances of the colonies against the British king.

The statement of grievances was a rather labored affair not always exactly sound from an historical point of view and, strangely enough, completely ignoring the British parliament against whose acts and encroachments they had for years been complaining. It served their purposes, however, and has since been largely ignored even by scholars who are seeking the facts as to the causes of the American Revolution.

The ringing phrases of the political philosophy, on the other hand, quickly became a part of the American heritage, a weapon to be used against tyranny of every kind, a constant prod toward making American practices coincide with American ideals:

> We hold these truths to be self-evident, That all men are created equal, that they are endowed by their Creator with certain unalienable rights; that among these are life, liberty, and the pursuit of happiness; that to secure these rights, governments are instituted among men, deriving their just powers from the consent of the governed; that whenever any form of government becomes destructive of these ends, it is the right of the people to alter or to abolish it, and to institute new government, laying its foundation on such principles, and organizing its powers in such form, as to them shall seem most likely to effect their safety and happiness.

The ideas here expressed were not new. They were a part of the Natural Rights philosophy, used first to justify rebellion against the English king in 1688 and widely current in the eighteenth century when the works of Isaac Newton became generally known. With Newton, God had withdrawn from the immediate and direct manipulation of the universe and had left it to be run by laws which gave order and security. By his intelligence, man could know these laws; by conformity he could avoid disaster and turn them to his benefit. And God as the creator of man had also created a moral law for man's government and had endowed man with reason by which to comprehend it and a conscience that created the obligation to obedience. "Underneath and supporting human society, as the basic rock supports the hills, was a moral order which was the abiding place of the eternal principles of truth and righteousness."

That meant that there was a right and a wrong in social things, that there was a good society and a bad society, that the laws and institutions of man should approximate the moral law and the moral order. If they fell short, then there was the "higher law," and "civil disobedience" became a virtue. Social conduct was thus a matter of conscience rather than obedience to existing law. Social justice was an obligation, and the existence of conditions which reason and conscience condemned was a matter for concern and action. The fight for social justice became a part of "the eternal struggle between right and wrong." Politics and Christianity had common ends. To secure the equality of all men, to guarantee to them life, liberty, and the pursuit of happiness was a moral obligation. And all just men, through reason and conscience, knew exactly what each of these things meant.

Out of Revolutionary thinking and the trends of the age came a second document, the Constitution of the United States. In resisting England and the acts of the British parliament, the colonists assumed that they had certain rights which belonged to them as Englishmen. They believed that there was a great body of English precedent, a set of British documents, which guaranteed to Englishmen everywhere and at all times, certain rights and the protection of certain interests. Some spoke as though these formed a British constitution, and as though this constitution was a bulwark against oppression and injustice—that it permanently fixed relations within the empire.

So when they had declared their independence, they followed a growing practice of the age and put down in written form a description of their common government and its rights and limitations. When this proved inadequate, they formed "a more perfect Union" and established "this Constitution for the United States of America." Here they described the machinery and functioning of government and the distribution of powers between its agents and listed the powers of the central and the state governments. As completed, it revealed a government of checks and balances that was to be altered only by prescribed methods. It too, when amended with a Bill of Rights, was to be a bulwark against aggression, a shelter behind which both men and states and their rights would be secure.

And since the Fathers who framed the Constitution were just men, men who gave full play to reason and conscience, it could be assumed that the grants and restrictions placed in the Constitution aimed at a good society and at the approximation of the moral order that all Americans accepted.

Now here were two fundamental American documents—the one framed to *establish* a government, the other framed to *justify revolution* against a government. The one intended to set up a more perfect Union and protect the fixed rights of men against the whims and passions of those who might destroy, the other intended to stress those abstract rights of mankind which grow and expand and change almost constantly—rights of human beings ultimately resting on the "higher law" that knows no fixed bounds save those of a just and moral universe.

As a pure abstraction such differences were of no consequence, but what if some fine day one group of Americans should appeal to one of these documents to prove and protect *its* rights and interests and another group of Americans should appeal to the other document to prove and protect a conflicting set of rights and interests? What if the law of the land as embodied in the Constitution should not remain in accord with some men's reason and conscience and they should appeal to the Declaration of Independence and the higher law it justifies? Then, perhaps, the Constitution would be burned and the phrases of the Declaration would be dismissed as mere "glittering generalities"—as doctrine, both "false and foolish."

That, I judge, would constitute a conflict of basic values, of moral standards, of the most fundamental things in the national makeup and create a situation where discussion would be utterly useless and compromise impossible.

The second situation was the heavy strain placed on the American political structure by the rapid growth and expansion of the period from 1830 to 1860. These years, the life span of a single generation, saw population increase nearly two and a half times and spread, with gaps on the plains and in the mountain regions, to the Pacific coast. A great Southwestern kingdom was added by the annexation of Texas and by conquest from Mexico. The industrial revolution reached maturity in the Northeast, and New York City, Boston, and Philadelphia became centers of commerce and finance, national and international in scope. Agriculture more than kept pace. In the northwest the kingdom of wheat, and, in the Southwest, the kingdom of cotton, poured out surpluses capable of caring for the needs of both Europe and America. Steam applied to transportation on land and on water shrank space by halves and thirds and altered all the concepts of distance held by the generation that framed the Constitution.

Growth and expansion produced two conflicting results which bear directly on the problem we are considering. Developments of different kinds in different parts of the nation tended to exaggerate sectional interests and attitudes. Regions already distinct in character and needs became more so under augmenting forces. Sectional consciousness increased and sectional rivalry became more intense. Westward expansion increased the demand for more liberal land legislation and for government aid in building internal improvements along which western produce could move to market. Opposition by South and East to such measures stirred deep resentment and bitter words. The growth of industry brought quick demands for protective tariffs from men of the Northeast, and the spread of cotton across the South brought equally strong demands for free trade. Banking and commercial interests in the North found need for a stronger central government; the planting interests with slave labor turned more and more toward the state for security and approval. Men began to talk about civilizations based on "peculiar" interests and values that were rising in different corners of the nation.

But that was only one side of developments. The *facts* of *increased interdependence* and growing *national interest* were even more important. Vastly more significant than sectionalism was the fact that the United States was becoming a great nation among the nations of the earth. By 1860 its population had passed that of the United Kingdom and was rapidly closing the gap on France and Germany. Foreign immigrants, who knew nothing of sections, were pouring into the country. Floods of native Americans swept westward across state line after state line in answer to the call of gold or fertile soils. Where in earlier days foreign commerce dominated, now internal trade came to the fore to signify "the transition from colonial to national economy." That meant sectional interdependence. The South, with its heavy concentration on staple crops, formed a splendid market for the horses, mules, tobacco, bagging, and surplus slaves of the border states, for the foodstuffs of the Northwest, and for the manufactures of the Northeast. It provided opportunities to ships and shippers of the North and to bankers of eastern cities who often financed both the production and the marketing of southern crops. Its cotton, in turn, kept northeastern factories busy, and its rice and sugar added to the nation's food supply. The Northwest, as an expanding frontier, needed manufactured goods as well as financial assistance in the purchase of lands and the building of internal improvements which could be secured only from the Northeast and from Europe. The Northeast needed raw materials for its factories and food for its dependent urban workers which could come only from the South and West. And thus the packet, the steamship and the railroad shuttled back and forth between supply and demand to weave the pattern of a national economy and to demonstrate the interdependence of life in the modern world.

Nor had Americans been unconscious of the significance of these developments or lacking in national pride because of them. This consciousness showed itself in the swaggering demands for territorial expansion that passed under the guise of "Manifest Destiny," in the sharp reaction against foreign immigrants who might ruin the great experiment in democracy, in the strident efforts of "Young America" to intervene in behalf of battling European liberals, in the quick emergence of a native literature that began its statement by insisting: "Our day of dependence, our long apprenticeship to other lands, draws to a close. . . . We will walk on our own feet; we will work with our own hands; we will speak our own minds."[1]

Other peoples also felt the force of the new national consciousness. Our dealings with Mexico were brusque enough to produce war and the open charge of aggression from half the nation itself. Great Britain bristled at Polk's bumptious diplomacy and then good-naturedly yielded to compromise. Spain, less graciously, accepted disavowal of swashbuckling efforts to force her to yield Cuba, and the sullen Indians retreated step by step in front of settlers bearing letters of marque from God.

The strain on the political structure produced by sectional growth and rivalry was, indeed, great. The question of national policy in regard to lands, internal improvements, tariffs, the bank, and expansion all brought bitter strife in Congress and, on one occasion, a move by South Carolina for nullification. Every man who aspired to national leadership had to voice the demands of his own section in regard to each of these issues and, at the same time, shape his appeal in such a way as to win support in other sections or at least to soften opposition. Most programs offered had a double purpose or appeal. Calhoun's land cession bills were framed both to win western support, by land and internal improvement aid, and to prevent an increase of tariff rates. Clay's American system offered tariffs to industrial areas and internal improvements to the needy agricultural belts. His bills for the distribution of the proceeds from public land sales were intended not only to settle the land question but also to deplete the public treasury and thereby justify tariff increases. Benton linked pre-emption and graduation together in order to please both the older and newer public land areas, and Webster frankly stressed the national appeal in order to weaken opposing combinations that threatened New England tariffs.

Yet, in spite of all differences and all individual maneuvering, one agent stood out above all others to weaken local loyalties and to bind divergent geographic elements into national unity. That was the na-

[1] Ralph Waldo Emerson, *Works* (Riverside edition, 1883), I, 113–14.

tional political party. Whether Whig or Democrat, Americans manifested the most ardent devotion to party and the most intense feelings against party rivals. For party's sake, men were willing to sacrifice sectional interest and to yield even personal principles. The very fact of membership in a party and allegiance to its platform was a personal compromise, and the party, as such, could yield where individuals could not. Men with consciences could belong to parties that had none. And party loyalty, reaching beyond all local borders, worked steadily for sectional agreement and for national compromise.

Political parties, nevertheless, felt the strain of sectional strife and alternated control of the national government from 1836 to 1856. No party could succeed itself and no president could secure a second term. No important party leader reached the presidency, and dark horses and figurehead candidates were put forward in every election.

The strain was heavy; yet the strong national undercurrent held the parties together and prevented either Democrats or Whigs from assuming a strictly sectional character. The level of debate in Congress was high, and workable compromises or adjustments were reached on lands, tariffs, internal improvements, and even finances. A successful foreign war was fought, with considerable opposition it is true, but with all the bipartisan support necessary. The democratic process was functioning well. Policies were being established and issues adjusted. The nation was moving steadily forward to maturity and strength. The experiment in democratic government, at least up to 1848, seemed to be succeeding. It was, however, a purely political success—one which accepted the claims of sectionalism and established ways as equal to those of a crowding, driving, modern nationalism with its new technologies and social interdependence.

Historians generally agree that the complete breakdown and ultimate abandonment of that process in the next thirteen years was due to the institution of slavery. To read some of their writings one would think that "the dark cloud of slavery" appeared suddenly out of nowhere in the years around 1850, that, for the first time men had become conscious of its evils and launched a great moral crusade against an institution that had no place in the modern world. As a matter of fact the whole situation had existed for over two hundred years. Slavery in the United States just before the Civil War was most certainly a more humane affair than it had been in earlier times. Nor had it lacked critics. All through the years some men had complained of its injustice, its evil effects on both master and slave, and its violation of every ideal held by both democrats and Christians. As late as 1832 members of the Virginia House of Delegates had denounced the holding "of any part of the human race in bondage" as an act "of injustice, tyranny, and oppression." They had pointed out its baneful effects on both blacks and whites; they had called it a "transcendent evil . . . a mildew which has blighted in its course every region it has touched, from the creation of the world . . ."; they had ascribed the backward condition of agriculture and industry in Virginia to its presence, and had insisted that the day when men would listen to its defense with patience or forbearance had gone forever.

The historian's problem is, therefore, *not* whether slavery was a great evil or whether there was just at this time a sharp moral reaction against it which had a major part in producing the Civil War. Both those things can be taken for granted, and let me say once and for all that I know of no historian who has ever questioned either of them. The real problem is how did the slavery issue happen to take the form it did take in these years, and why did it produce the effects it did produce.

In the first place the opposition to slavery which brought the final break was not opposition to slavery per se or even opposition to slavery in the states where it existed. It was simply opposition to *the extension of slavery*. It was being carried on, not by anti-slavery societies, but by politicians and political parties. The abolitionist was still at work, even though his organizations had split and weakened, but the men who led the new and fatal drive against slavery had almost as little use for the abolitionist as did the slaveholder himself. And it was the election of a president who gave ample assurance to the people of the South that he would not directly or indirectly interfere with the slaves or with them about their slaves[2] and who had publicly declared his belief in white supremacy that produced secession.

This is not to say that these men did not think slavery wrong. They most certainly did, and they said so! It was a moral issue, but their determination not to see it spread to the territories had back of it something more in their firm belief in the capacity of a free democratic society to produce an ideal economic and social order.

[2] See Roy P. Basler (ed.), *Abraham Lincoln: His Speeches and Writings*, p. 580.

Slavery was a blight. Southern life was backward. Slaves were wasteful; southern fields were tumble-down; the South was out of step with progress. Freedom alone would give the greatest prosperity and alone permit advancement toward that social-economic millennium which was being realized in these free United States. They linked the growth of industry and commerce and agriculture with a free democratic order. They believed that they were achieving something of the perfect society made possible by the laws of nature and nature's God. The very growth of northern and western population, the rise of northern cities, northern commerce, and northern industry all demonstrated the value of freedom and the fact that these people were in step with the nation's true destiny.

That what was evolving was finance and industrial capitalism did not matter just then. The problem was one of checking slavery as the great enemy of democratic progress. That was as much a moral job as was the destruction of slavery itself.

In addition to this, there had grown up, since Polk's election in 1844, a strong belief that the Democratic party was becoming the party of slavery. Texas was annexed, but the Oregon boundary was not pushed to 54° 40′. The Walker tariff moved sharply toward free trade, and a river and harbor bill met the president's veto on constitutional grounds. Homestead legislation seemed further off than ever. For the first time northern men talked of "the slave power" and linked the policies of government with its influence. The Wilmot Proviso, which they devised to check slavery's advantage in lands acquired from Mexico, was their answer. Back of it was not only a determination to check the spread of slavery but also an equal determination to check the "slave power." And that, more and more, meant checking the Democratic party. As Wyndham Robertson complainingly put it: "The possession of the power of the Federal Government by the Democratic party . . . furnished the pretext . . . to confound the whole slaveholding interest as absolutely identical with Democracy, and thus to turn and direct opposition, for whatever cause, to the policy and acts of the Democratic party, into apparent opposition to the slaveholding interests." "This ruse," he charged, "fused . . . and united into a common line of policy, some who merely opposed the administration on political grounds, with its opponents on the slavery issue."[3]

This belief in the Democratic party as the agent of "the slave

[3] "Speech of Wyndham Robertson, Esq. . . . on the State of the Country," March 5 and 6, 1860 (reprint).

power" reached a climax, when Stephen A. Douglas introduced his Kansas-Nebraska Bill. The "Appeal of the Independent Democrats" which Chase and his fellows issued was a call to revolt. The formation of the Republican party which followed was the political answer to a political situation in which, as they believed, slavery dominated the Democratic party. The combination of opposition to the extension of slavery and such material things as tariffs, railways to the Pacific, river and harbor improvements, homesteads, and encouragement of immigration in the Republican program was natural and necessary. The purpose and end of both was one and the same, freedom and progress!

But there was more in the way than the Democratic party. Increasingly it was apparent that the Constitution of the United States was being used to check northern demands and to protect slave interests. First it had been the tariff which South Carolina had attempted to check on grounds of unconstitutionality. Then Polk had rejected the much-needed river and harbor bill on constitutional grounds, and Pierce had followed the precedent. In the territorial struggle Southerners had insisted both on the constitutional obligation of Congress to protect slavery in the territories and on the unconstitutionality of congressional interference with slavery in the territories. The courts had aided by declaring the Missouri Compromise unconstitutional and had repeatedly upheld the rights of masters to recover their fugitive slaves.

Through southern statements of the period ran the world "Constitution" like the repeated call of a whippoorwill. "We invoke the spirit of the Constitution, and claim its guarantees," said the resolutions of the Nashville Convention.[4] "We will stand by the right; we will take the Constitution; we will defend it by the sword with the halter around our necks," avowed Robert Toombs in the Senate.[5] ". . . The South should never yield one atom of her full, just, and *equal* rights under the Constitution," wrote H. L. Berguin.[6] If it be true . . . that there is a large majority of the people of the North who are unwilling to stand by the constitutional guarantees," spoke Alexander H. Stephens, "I, for one, am for tearing asunder every bond that binds us together. . . . Any people capable of defending themselves, who would continue their allegiance to a government which should deny them a clear, un-

[4] M. W. Cluskey (ed.), *Political Text Book,* p. 597.

[5] *Congressional Globe,* 36 Cong., 2 sess., p. 270.

[6] *Considerations Relative to a Southern Confederacy,* pp. 28–29.

questionable, constitutional right of the magnitude and importance of this to the people of the South, would deserve to be stigmatized as poltroons."[7] And when steps to disunion were already under way it was Stephens again who pleaded with the people, saying: ". . . We are pledged to maintain the Constitution. . . . If all our hopes are to be blasted, if the Republic is to go down, let us be found to the last moment standing on the deck with the Constitution of the United States waving over our heads. Let the fanatics of the North break the Constitution, if such is their fell purpose. Let the responsibility be upon them. . . ."[8]

To meet such appeal to rights under the Constitution there were only two methods. First, the Constitution could be burned. That Garrison and his friends adopted. The second method was to turn to that other equally good American document, The Declaration of Independence. That the Republicans did. Here was a document which Southerners had already declared to be both "false and foolish," but one which had deep meaning for those who would ponder its phrases.

Seward early declared: ". . . I know that there are laws of various sorts which regulate the conduct of men. There are constitutions and statutes, codes mercantile and codes civil; but when we are legislating for states, especially when we are founding states, all these laws must be brought to the standard of the laws of God, and must be tried by that standard, and must stand or fall by it."[9] Later he declared that ". . . The abstractions of human rights are the only permanent foundations of society. It is by referring to them that men determine what is established because it is RIGHT, in order to uphold it forever; and what is right only because it is established, in order that they may lawfully change it, in accordance with the increase of knowledge and the progress of reason."[10]

To Seward slavery was clearly one of the things that "the increase of knowledge and the progress of reason" had left back in the "Dark Ages." He was certain that "we cannot, in our judgment, be either true Christians or real freemen, if we impose on another a chain that we defy all human power to fasten on ourselves."[11] And if some defended it because it was "established" by the Constitution,

[7] *Cong. Globe,* 32 Cong., 1 sess., Appendix, p. 460.

[8] Alexander H. Stephens, *A Constitutional View of the Late War between the States,* II, 281.

[9] George E. Baker (ed.), *The Works of William H. Seward,* I, 66.

[10] *Ibid.,* p. 102.

[11] *Ibid.,* p. 67.

then there was "a higher law than the Constitution," which, in the case of slavery in the territories, devoted them "to union, to justice, to defence, to welfare, and to liberty," as a part "of the common heritage of mankind, bestowed upon them by the Creator of the universe."[12] And to sustain his position he quoted Algernon Sidney:

> If it be said that every nation ought in this to follow their own constitutions, we are at an end of our controversies; for they ought not to be followed, unless they are rightly made; they cannot be rightly made if they are contrary to the universal law of God and nature.[13]

For these reasons Seward felt assured "that slavery must give way, and will give away, to the salutary instructions of economy, and to the ripening influences of humanity; that emancipation is inevitable, and is near; that it may be hastened or hindered; and that whether it shall be peaceful or violent, depends upon the question whether it be hastened or hindered; that all measures which fortify slavery or extend it, tend to the consummation of violence; all that check its extension and abate its strength, tend to its peaceful extirpation."[14] It was all "part of the eternal conflict between truth and error."[15]

Here was the supreme confidence, or the extreme arrogance, according to the point of view, of a man in step with progress, a man who knew the right as based on the universal law of God and nature and expressed in the Declaration of Independence.

Abraham Lincoln's own final judgment regarding the sectional conflict was that it was part of "the eternal conflict between right and wrong." On his way to assume the presidency he declared that the great principle or idea that had kept this confederacy together was "not the mere matter of the separation of the Colonies from the mother land; but that sentiment in the Declaration of Independence which gave liberty, not alone to the people of this country, but, I hope, to the world for all future time. It was that which gave promise that in due time the weight would be lifted from the shoulders of all men. This is a sentiment embodied in the Declaration of Independence. . . ."[16] And in his first message to Congress he insisted that the whole struggle was "for maintaining in the

[12] *Ibid.*, pp. 74–75.
[13] *Ibid.*, p. 108.
[14] *Ibid.*, p. 87.
[15] *Ibid.*, p. 88.
[16] *New York Tribune*, February 23, 1861. (Speech at Independence Hall, February 22, 1861.)

world that form and substance of government whose leading object is to elevate the condition of men; to lift artificial weights from all shoulders; to clear the paths of laudable pursuit for all; to afford all an unfettered start and a fair chance in the race of life."[17]

No wonder he hailed Thomas Jefferson as the man "who, in the concrete pressure of a struggle for national independence by a single people, had the coolness, forecast, and capacity to introduce into a merely revolutionary document, an abstract truth, applicable to all men and all times, and so to embalm it there, that to-day, and in all coming days, it shall be a rebuke and a stumbling-block to the very harbingers of re-appearing tyranny and oppression."[18]

The full implication of a genuine acceptance of the doctrines of the Declaration of Independence and the moral law which it carried was not fully understood even by those who professed it. Seward did say bluntly that "slavery and freedom are conflicting systems, brought together by the union of the states, not neutralized, nor even harmonized," and that though "you may slay the Wilmot Proviso in the Senate chamber, and bury it beneath the capitol to-day; the dead corse, in complete steel, will haunt your legislative halls to-morrow,"[19] yet he did not believe the Union in danger. Lincoln, in turn, talked of "a house divided against itself," that could not stand, yet he did not believe that it would fall. Both attempted while they preached the revolutionary doctrines of the Declaration, to retain respect for the Constitution *as they interpreted it.* They, of course, had to reject the Supreme Court's interpretation of the Constitution and good Republicans even talked of reconstructing the Court so as to secure the kind of decisions they wanted. Yet some men more logically and boldly said: "The fact that a law is constitutional amounts to nothing, unless it is also pure; it must harmonize with the law of God, or be set at mought by all upright men."[20]

The *Chicago Tribune* put it bluntly this way: "The Republican victory would be incomplete if it did not promise sooner or later to reform the United States Supreme Court. That bench full of southern lawyers, which gentlemen of a political temperament call an

[17] Basler, *op. cit.*, p. 607.

[18] *Ibid.*, p. 489. Letter to H. L. Pierce and others, April 6, 1859.

[19] *The Works of William H. Seward,* I, 108–9.

[20] William Hosmer, *The Higher Law,* pp. 176–77. Quoted in Jesse T. Carpenter, *The South as a Conscious Minority,* p. 159.

'august tribunal,' is the last entrenchment behind which despotism is sheltered; and until a national convention amends the Constitution so as to defeat the usurpations of that body, or until the Court itself is reconstructed by the dropping off of a few of its members and the appointment of better men in their places, we have little hope for congressional action in the way of restricting slavery."[21]

The development of southern attitudes paralleled that of the North. Slavery gradually became a "positive good" and southern society, under slavery, an ideal society. God had created the Negro an inferior. His natural status was that of servitude; ". . . the division of mankind into grades, and the mutual dependence and relations which result from them," said Edward Brown, "constitute the very soul of civilization."[22] It was "as much the order of nature," said Chancellor Harper, "that men should enslave each other, as that other animals should prey upon each other."[23]

So because southern society was based on nature's laws, it was a stable society. It was exempt, as one editor said, "from all those distresses which periodically affect the northern and English communities,—labor riots, . . . strikes of vast bodies of operators, . . . bad seasons or hard times . . . when the community seems disorganized [and] its equilibrium destroyed. . . ."[24] Best of all it was free of all those *isms* which kept free society in constant turmoil and change. Southern prosperity, in 1857, when the North suffered panic and depression, proved the point to their satisfaction.

The constant effort of free society to get around the Constitution in order to secure tariffs, internal improvements, and homesteads only showed their lack of respect for that document. Their appeal to "a higher law" than the Constitution marked the end of orderly government. Speaking in New York in October, 1858, Jefferson Davis declared: "You have among you politicians of a philosophic turn, who preach a high morality; a system of which they are the discoverers, . . . They say, it is true the Constitution dictates this, the Bible inculcates that; but there is a higher law than those, and they call upon you to obey that higher law of which they are the inspired givers. Men who are *traitors* to the compact of their fathers—*men who have perjured the oaths they have themselves*

21 *Chicago Tribune*, March 4, 1861.
22 *Notes on the Origin and Necessity of Slavery*, p. 38.
23 "Memoir on Slavery" in *The Pro-Slavery Argument*, p. 14. See also Avery Craven, *The Coming of the Civil War*, pp. 151–74.
24 *New Orleans Daily Crescent*, May 26, 1859.

taken . . . these are the moral law-givers who proclaim a higher law than the Bible, the Constitution, and the laws of the land . . . *These higher law preachers should be tarred and feathered, and whipped by those they have thus instigated* . . . The man who . . . preaches treason to the Constitution and the dictates of all human society, is a fit object for a Lynch law that would be higher than any he could urge."[25]

And as to the Declaration of Independence, it was nothing more than a bundle of "self-evident lies." Its assertions, said the Reverend Fred A. Ross, "were denied and upset by the Bible, by the natural history of man and by Providence in every age of the world."[26] The Constitution alone was sound and enduring. The Democratic party provided the only defense remaining. Even that had to be purged and split in order to be safe.

The final effect of such developments was to reduce the whole sectional struggle to a conflict of civilizations. The South would yield, said Seward, because this was "the conflict of man against the obstacles which oppose his way to an ultimate and glorious destiny." It would yield because "nations which were prudent and humane, and wise . . . have done so already."[27] And the good Reverend J. H. Thornwell, of South Carolina could answer:

> The parties in this conflict are not merely abolitionists and slave holders; they are atheists, socialists, communists, red republicans, jacobins on the one side, and the friends of order and regulated freedom on the other. In a word, the world is the battle ground, Christianity and atheism the combatants, and the progress of humanity the stake.[28]

Such attitudes, if confined to idealistic reformers, would not have wrecked a nation. When held by politicians and made a part of party politics, they meant the end of national parties and the building up of sectional parties pledged to action. What that meant, Alexander H. Stephens made perfectly clear to Abraham Lincoln in December, 1860, when he assured him that the South did "not entertain any fears that a Republican Administration . . . would attempt to interfere *directly* and *immediately* with Slavery in the

25 Dunbar Rowland (ed.), *Jefferson Davis, Constitutionalist,* III, 337–38.
26 Fred A. Ross, *Slavery Ordained of God,* p. 104 (Letters to Rev. Albert Barnes).
27 *Works of William H. Seward,* I, 88.
28 J. H. Thornwell, *The Rights and Duties of Masters,* p. 12.

States."[29] What the South objected to was the entrance of Anti-slavery "as an element into Party organizations."[30] When that happened there was "no telling where . . . impulses or passions may drive."[31] Stephens knew that honest men would not long accept evil, even though that evil be legal, that forward-looking men would not long tolerate outgrown systems that impeded progress. He also knew that though slavery was to the North only an evil, an outworn system, it represented in the South millions of dollars in property and the solution of a race question that, even yet, seems unsolvable. It was also a right supposedly protected by the Constitution of the United States.

If the destruction of slavery was inevitable, as Seward said, the bitter resistance of Southerners to the destruction of their property rights and their social order was also inevitable. The rational discussion of such issues and the compromising of differences, was not possible. Resort to violence was at hand.

What stands out in this story is the simply fact that issues dealing with right and wrong and issues that have to do with the fundamental structure of society do not lend themselves to the democratic process. Discussion proves efficient, as Carl Becker says, only "when there is nothing of profound importance to discuss and when there is plenty of time to discuss it."[32] Perhaps it is as T. V. Smith has said: ". . . that when groups fall in love with perfection they grow intent upon power with which to implement their perfection; and when conscience-driven men get together freedom is always at stake."[33] And, he might have added, property is even more in danger. Yet society cannot stand still. An inherited conception that insists that good has already been delivered and cannot be altered is even worse than the fanatic's constant push for perfection. Growth seems necessary even for remaining alive. If the politician and the political party dare not sometimes reach beyond the mere realm of policies, by what means can democratic society progress? Perhaps that is the great weakness in our system of government. Perhaps that is why the major parties always tend to become more or less alike; why there is so much of drifting, so much

[29] Stephens, *A Constitutional View of the Late War between the States,* II, 267.
[30] *Ibid.*
[31] *Ibid.*
[32] Carl Becker, *New Liberties for Old,* p. 106.
[33] T. V. Smith, *Atomic Power and Moral Faith,* p. 15.

blundering along trusting to fortune. Seward was probably right when he insisted that "the fierce conflict of parties" in the 1850's was only "the agony of distracted parties—a convulsion resulting from the too narrow foundations of both the great parties, and of all parties—foundations laid in compromises of natural justice and of human liberty." Because ". . . a moral question, transcending the too narrow creeds of parties" had arisen and "the public conscience" had expanded with it, "the green withes of party associations" were giving way, breaking, and falling off.[34] What he did not understand was that parties based on "natural justice" and "human liberty" might threaten vested interests and create conditions in which calm and rational discussion, tolerance of differences, and compromise, would be impossible.

[34] *Works of William H. Seward,* I, 81.

VI

THE 1840's AND THE DEMOCRATIC PROCESS

The most significant thing about the American Civil War is that it represents a complete breakdown of the democratic process.[1] After years of strain, men ceased to discuss their problems, dropped the effort to compromise their differences, refused to abide by the results of a national election, and resorted to the use of force. After four years of bloody civil strife, one side was beaten into submission and the other had its way in national affairs. The emergence of modern America was largely the product of that outcome.

If the breakdown of the democratic process is the significant thing about the coming of the Civil War, then the important question is not *what* the North and South were quarreling about half so much as it is *how* their differences got into such shape that they could not be handled by the process of rational discussion, compromise, or the tolerant acceptance of majority decision. The question is not "What caused the Civil War?" but rather "How did it come about?" The two questions are quite different, yet hopelessly tangled. The effort to distinguish between them, however, is important and needs to be stressed.

If one were to discuss the causes of the Civil War, he might begin with geography, move on to historical developments in time and place, trace the growth of economic and social rivalries, outline differences in moral values, and then show the way in which personalities and psychological factors operated. The part which slavery played would loom large. It might even become the symbol of all differences and of all conflicts. State rights, territorial expansion, tariffs, lands, internal improvements, and a host of other things, real and imagined, would enter the picture. There would be economic causes, constitutional causes, social causes, moral causes, political causes involving the breaking of old parties and

Reprinted from the *Journal of Southern History,* XVI, No. 2 (May, 1950), 137–47.

[1] This paper was read at the annual meeting of the Southern Historical Association, November 12, 1949.

the rise of sectional ones, and psychological causes which ultimately permitted emotion to take the place of reason. There would be remote or background causes, and immediate causes, and causes resting on other causes, until the most eager pedagogue would be thoroughly satisfied.

The matter of how issues got beyond the abilities of the democratic process is, on the other hand, a bit less complex and extended. It has to do with the way in which concrete issues were reduced to abstract principles and the conflicts between interests simplified to basic levels where men feel more than they reason and where compromise or yielding is impossible because issues appear in the form of right and wrong and involve the fundamental structure of society. This is not saying, as some have charged, that great moral issues were not involved. They certainly were, and it is a matter of choice with historians as to whether or not they take sides, praise or condemn, become partisans in this departed quarrel, or use past events for present-day purposes.

As an approach to this second, more modest problem, a correspondence which took place between Abraham Lincoln and Alexander H. Stephens between November 30 and December 22, 1860, is highly revealing.[2] On November 14, Stephens had delivered one of the great speeches of his life before the legislature of Georgia. It was a Union speech. He had begged his fellow Southerners not to give up the ship, to wait for some violation of the Constitution before they attempted secession. Equality might yet be possible inside the Union. At least, the will of the whole people should be obtained before any action was taken.[3]

Abraham Lincoln, still unconvinced that there was real danger, wrote Stephens, as an old friend, for a revised copy of his speech. Stephens complied, and he ended his letter with a warning about the great peril which threatened the country and a reminder of the heavy responsibility now resting on the president-elect's shoulders. Lincoln answered with assurance that he would not "*directly*, or *indirectly*, interfere with the slaves" or with the southern people about their slaves, and then closed with this significant statement: "I suppose, however, this does not meet the case. You think slavery is right and ought to be extended, while we think it is *wrong* and ought to be restricted. That I

[2] Alexander H. Stephens, *A Constitutional View of the Late War between the States: Its Causes, Character, Conduct and Results* (2 vols.; Philadelphia, 1868–70), II, 266–67, insert.

[3] *Ibid.*, pp. 279–300.

suppose is the rub. It certainly is the only substantial difference between us."[4]

The reduction of "the only substantial difference" between North and South to a simple question of *right and wrong* is the important thing about Lincoln's statement. It revealed the extent to which the sectional controversy had, by 1860, been simplified and reduced to a conflict of principles in the minds of the northern people.

Stephens' answer to Lincoln's letter is equally revealing. He expressed "an earnest desire to preserve and maintain the Union of the States, if it can be done upon the principles and in furtherance of the objects for which it was formed." He insisted, however, that private opinion on the question of "African Slavery" was not a matter over which "the Government under the Constitution" had any control. "But now," he said, "this subject, which is confessedly on all sides outside of the Constitutional action of the Government so far as the States are concerned, is made the 'central idea' in the Platform of principles announced by the triumphant Party." It was this total disregard of the Constitution and the rights guaranteed under it that lay back of southern fears. It was the introduction into party politics of issues which projected action by Congress outside its constitutional powers that had made all the trouble. Stephens used the word "Constitution" seven times in his letter.[5]

The significant thing here is Stephens' reduction of sectional differences to the simple matter of southern rights under the Constitution. He too showed how completely the sectional controversy had been simplified into a conflict of principles. And he with Lincoln, speaking for North and South, emphasized the fact that after years of strife the complex issues between the sections had assumed the form of a conflict between *right* and *rights*.

To the scholar it must be perfectly clear that this drastic simplification of sectional differences did not mean that either Lincoln or Stephens thought that all the bitter economic, social, and political questions could be ignored. It simply meant that *right* and *rights* had become the symbols or carriers of all those interests and values. Yet it is equally clear that as symbols they carried an emotional force and moral power in themselves that was

[4] *Ibid.*, pp. 266–67, insert.
[5] *Ibid.*, pp. 267–70.

far greater than the sum total of all the material issues involved. They suggested things which cannot be compromised—things for which men willingly fight and die. Their use, in 1860, showed that an irrepressible conflict existed.

The question as to whether the Civil War was "a needless war" has, therefore, little to do with the bungling statesmanship of 1860–61. It has much to do with the matter of how problems got beyond the ability of the democratic process. And as to that, we do know that the author of the Declaration of Independence, on which the Lincoln position rested, was a slaveholder. So was Madison and many other important leaders of the first great democratic drive in national life. The three men whom Arthur M. Schlesinger, Jr., names as the ones who carried the democratic torch on down to the age of Jackson[6]—John Randolph, Nathaniel Macon, and John Taylor of Caroline—were also slaveholders, as were Jackson himself and Thomas Hart Benton and Francis Preston Blair, his chief lieutenants. Even the father of Martin Van Buren held slaves.[7] Evidently, in these years only a generation away from Civil War, the belief that slavery was morally wrong did not constitute "the only substantial difference" between those who sought to forward government "of the people, by the people, for the people" and their reactionary opponents.

Nor, by the same token, was everyone in the early South agreed on the value of slavery or its constitutional right to immunity from public criticism and political action. In the Virginia constitutional convention of 1829–30 and in the legislature of 1832, men questioned the economic benefits of slavery, pointed out its social dangers, and shamed its violation both of Christian and democratic values. Bills were introduced and voted upon. True, it was a case of a state discussing and acting upon its own domestic affairs, but these men were talking about slavery as an institution, not as just a Virginia practice, and they were thoroughly conscious of the larger national implications of what was going on. Robert Stanard spoke of the impulse begun in Virginia passing "with the rapidity of lightning across the whole extent of this Union." James Monroe frankly admitted that he looked "to the Union to aid in effecting" emancipation, and James M'Dowell, Jr.,

[6] Arthur M. Schlesinger, Jr., *The Age of Jackson* (Boston, 1945), pp. 18–29.

[7] William E. Smith, "Martin Van Buren," in Allen Johnson and Dumas Malone (eds.), *Dictionary of American Biography* (21 vols. and index; New York, 1928–45), XIX, 152.

bitterly denounced slavery because it created "a political interest in this Union" and produced conflicts in Congress and dissension in the nation. He saw the day when a national crusade against slavery would unite all rival interests against the South.[8]

Slavery took its blows in other states as well, and there was anything but general agreement on how to protect constitutional rights when South Carolina tried nullification. However much they might dislike the tariff, the other southern states had not as yet returned to the old anticonsolidation states'-rights position of their elder statesmen. The issue outside of South Carolina was generally one of the merits of the tariff rather than the constitutional rights of a state. The younger Southwest, moreover, had its own attitudes toward lands and internal improvements which kept these issues on the level of interest rather than on that of constitutionality.[9]

The next few years, however, brought important changes. The growing realization of failure to share equally in national expansion, the new demand for slaves with the spread of cotton, and the increasing agitation against slavery all contributed to a feeling of resentment and insecurity on the part of the South. Where the coming of the Industrial Revolution to the Northeast upset life to its very roots and forced a reconsideration of every old value and every relationship, Southerners, who had experienced only the extension of old agricultural patterns into new agricultural areas, knew no sharp break with their pasts and found no reason to question the soundness of old social and political institutions and relationships. Conditions under the Constitution, as the fathers had made it, were quite satisfactory.

Yet the matchless material growth that had come to the nation in these years, the deep ferment of ideas, and the rapid increase in the means of communication denied the South the chance to live alone. The nation was, in fact, in a state of transition, politically, economically, and socially. The attempt to apply old forms to constantly changing conditions put heavy strain on institutions

[8] *Proceedings and Debates of the Virginia State Convention of 1829–30* (Richmond, 1830), pp. 149, 306; *Speech of James M'Dowell, Jr. in the House of Delegates of Virginia on the Slave Question, delivered Saturday, January 21, 1832* (2d ed.; Richmond, 1832).

[9] Richmond *Enquirer,* April 24, December 13 and 15, 1832; Charles S. Sydnor, *The Development of Southern Sectionalism, 1819–1848* (Baton Rouge, 1948), pp. 208–9, 218–19.

and agencies created in more simple times and tended to thrust forward for decision the questions of just what kind of a government we had set up in the United States, what provisions it made for the protection of minorities, and just what the relations were between government and business. Nor could southern institutions escape the scrutiny that was being given to all institutions and relationships in this age of transition. The whole Northeast, under the pressure of forces that would ultimately produce modern America, was rapidly becoming the center of social unrest and of efforts at reform. The new age was revealing too many contradictions between profession and practice. Where before in a simple rural order the true and the good were not beyond the comprehension of every man through a direct moral approach, and a good society was simply one composed of good men, they now found environment a force of major importance. The living of the many was passing into the hands of the few. Everywhere men were losing their independence, and forces quite beyond individual control were shaping the lives of the masses. Neither Christianity nor democracy seemed to be working. Something was wrong and it should be righted. The Declaration of Independence with its emphasis on freedom and equality ought again to become a force in American life.

Out of the welter of reform movements that resulted from such convictions came the antislavery impulse and the resulting struggle over antislavery petitions in Congress. Joining hands with the great religious revivals that were burning their way through the lives of men and women in a region spreading east and west from upper New York, a group of earnest souls had lighted the fires of moral indignation against the sin of slavery and was pouring a flood of petitions into Congress demanding various steps against the evil. The South thus found itself faced by danger on a new front. It was thrown on the defensive. The Constitution and its clear statement of rights also needed to be brought back into American consciousness.

Already, in the tariff controversy, Robert J. Turnbull had argued that under changing conditions it was in the interest of the North and West to make the government "more national," while the interest of the South was to continue it "Federal."[10] In

[10] Robert J. Turnbull (Brutus), *The Crisis; or, Essays on the Usurpations of the Federal Government* (Charleston, 1827), p. 11.

opposing Jackson's Force Bill, John C. Calhoun had insisted that the real issue was whether this was a federal union of states or a union of the American people in the aggregate. He made it perfectly clear that he thought it was the former and that "To maintain the ascendency of the constitution over the law-making majority" was the great and essential thing for the preservation of the Union.[11] When the petition struggle developed, he quickly picked up the charge that slavery was "sinful and odious, in the sight of God and man," and pronounced it "a general crusade against us and our institutions." "The most unquestionable right may be rendered doubtful," he insisted, if slavery were "once admitted to be a subject of controversy." The subject was beyond the jurisdiction of Congress—"they have no right to touch it in any shape or form," he said, "or to make it the subject of deliberation or discussion." And then, ignoring his own words, he bluntly pronounced "the relation now existing in the slaveholding States" between the two races to be "a positive good." Even though opposition to the very popular right of petition might weaken friends in Congress and strengthen the abolitionists, the enemy must be met "on the frontier"; this was the southern "Thermopylae."[12]

Later, on December 27, 1837, Calhoun introduced a series of resolutions which carefully defined the character, purposes, and powers of the government under the Constitution. It had been adopted by the "free, independent and sovereign States" as security against all dangers, "*domestic*, as well as foreign." The states retained the sole right over their domestic institutions, and any intermeddling with those institutions by other states or combinations of their citizens was unwarranted and "subversive of the objects for which the constitution was formed." And it was the duty of the government to resist all such meddling.

Negro slavery, he declared, was an important domestic institution in southern and western states and was such when the Constitution was formed. "No change of opinion or feeling, on the part of other States of the Union in relation to it, can justify them or their citizens in open and systematic attacks thereon." To do so was a "breach of faith, and a violation of the most solemn obligations,

[11] Richard K. Crallé (ed.), *The Works of John C. Calhoun* (6 vols.; New York, 1853–56), II, 197–262.

[12] *Ibid.*, II, 481–90, 625–33.

moral and religious." Furthermore, to attempt to abolish slavery in the District of Columbia, or in any of the territories, on grounds that it was immoral or sinful "would be a direct and dangerous attack on the institutions of all the slaveholding States"; and to refuse to increase the limits or population of these states by the annexation of new territory or states on the pretext that slavery was "immoral or sinful, or otherwise obnoxious" would destroy the equal "rights and advantages which the Constitution was intended to secure."[13]

To resist the moral attacks of what was then a comparatively small group of Americans, who were none too popular in their own neighborhoods, Calhoun had asked Congress and the American people to accept his interpretation of the character of our government and his evaluation of the institution of slavery—accept them at a time when the whole course of developments in the Northeast, and to an increasing degree in the Northwest, was toward a more interdependent nationalism and a more humane and democratic social order. Calhoun had reduced the struggle to the level of abstract principles at the very moment when every principle for which he stood was being abandoned by the whole Western world and invalidated by the onward rush of the incoming modern age.

It was a serious mistake. Or was it clear insight into realities which discerned the inevitable course of events and dictated a bold stroke at the very threshold in an effort to ward off consequences? Most leaders at the time thought it a serious blunder. Garret Dorset Wall of New Jersey thought the resolutions were just "political abstractions" of which the Senate ought not to take cognizance. John Jordan Crittenden of Kentucky declared, "More vague and general abstractions could hardly have been brought forward," and agreed with James Buchanan of Pennsylvania that they would serve only to stir more agitation. Robert Strange of North Carolina added, "Agitating this question in any shape was ruinous to the South." Thomas Hart Benton, at a later time commenting on results, said that it gave to the antislavery forces "the point to stand upon from which they could reach every part of the Union. . . . Mr. Calhoun was a fortunate customer" for the abolitionists.[14]

[13] *Ibid.*, III, 140–42.

[14] Thomas H. Benton, *Thirty Years View* (2 vols.; New York, 1854–56), II, 134–43.

The roaring decade of the 1840's quickly demonstrated the soundness of Benton's opinion. They were spacious days. They brought the great developments in national life to a point where final patterns were quite discernible. The era of transition was coming to an end. Economic groups and geographic sections were becoming increasingly conscious of their unique interests, and the nation of its manifest destiny.

In these years the Cotton Kingdom rounded out its borders and demonstrated its right to speak for the section. The old South began to find its way through the difficulties that had beset them, some states to draw closer to the Cotton Kingdom, others to drift away into border-state position.

Meanwhile, the rapid expansion of New England and New York peoples along the Great Lakes and the rise of a Kingdom of Wheat where they and large bodies of foreign immigrants settled sharply altered the balance in the Old Northwest where, until now, close alliance with the South had been taken for granted. A hungry home market for wheat and a Canadian demand for any surplus gave early prosperity but produced a harsh depression when they failed. That turned attention to the English Corn Laws and produced a close alliance between the free-trade, antislavery elements in the two countries. That gave strange new support to the low Walker tariff, the passage of which, in turn, smoothed the way for Britain's acceptance of a compromise Oregon boundary. Thus while the antislavery men of the upper Northwest talked free trade and joined in the drive for a homestead law, they were, in spite of surface appearances, drawing closer to the older portion of the Northwest along the Ohio River, whose leaders were bitterly denouncing their fellow southern Democrats for betrayal of the Oregon-Texas bargain. The Old Northwest, too, was becoming self-conscious and independent in attitude. Henceforth it would seek its own interests and determine its own values.[15]

In this same period, industry entered a new phase in the northeastern corner of the nation. Hard times and bitter competition wrecked weaker concerns and left the field to the large, well-financed

[15] See Thomas P. Martin, "Free Trade and the Oregon Question, 1842–1846," in Arthur H. Cole, A. L. Dunham, and N. S. B. Gras (eds.), *Facts and Factors in Economic History* (Cambridge, Mass., 1932), p. 480; Dwight L. Dumond (ed.), *Letters of James Gillespie Birney, 1831–1837* (2 vols.; New York [1938]), I, 574, 581, II, 604; Thomas P. Martin, "Cotton and Wheat in Anglo-American Trade and Politics, 1846–1852," *Journal of Southern History,* I, 293–319.

corporations. Work was speeded up, and wages remained low. Strikes became frequent. Gradually the native girls gave way before the Irish and French-Canadians, and the factory and the factory town reached maturity. Industry sent its spokesmen into legislative halls, and the ardent complaint against local ills gave way steadily to the attack on southern slavery. A general acceptance of the new age of interdependent nationalism, already a business reality, marked the section. The questioning and criticism represented in Fruitlands, Brook Farm, and the Fourier associations gradually lost force. A new feeling of being in step with progress took its place. The development of a complex industrial order was a part of the nation's manifest destiny. Men, therefore, fell into line on domestic issues, but they did not yield their tough Puritan estimates of the ways of other Americans. Meanwhile the growth of internal commerce, now far more important than foreign trade, fostered the growing cities along the Atlantic coast, and the canal and the railroad, as the great new agents of transportation, more and more linked the interests of the Northwest to those of the commercial-industrial Northeast.

By these quick and drastic developments, the problems of lands, internal improvements, tariffs, and expansion were thrust forward in aggravated forms. They took on the character of sectional struggles. They became part of the right and the effort to achieve a manifest destiny. Sooner or later every one of them became tangled with slavery and from it took new strength with which to wage their battles. Both Calhoun and the abolitionists connected slavery with the annexation of Texas. Benjamin Lundy declared the Texas revolution a scheme to wrest that territory from Mexico in order to establish a slave market, and John Quincy Adams and twelve associates denounced annexation as a proslavery scheme. Calhoun gave substance to their charge by insisting on annexation as necessary for the protection of southern slaveholders.[16] Others connected it with the tariff and internal improvements. Joshua Giddings of Ohio in May, 1844, called attention to the balance and rivalry between North and South which produced a deadlock in legislation. "So equally balanced has been the political power," he said, "that for five years past our lake commerce has been utterly abandoned; and such are the defects of the tariff, that for years our revenues are unequal to the support of government." The annexation of Texas,

[16] Avery Craven, *The Coming of the Civil War* (New York, 1942), pp. 189–96.

secured "obviously to enhance the price of human flesh in our slave-breeding states," would now place "the policy and the destiny" of this nation in southern hands.

"Are the liberty-loving democrats of Pennsylvania ready to give up our tariff?" he asked. "Are the farmers of the West, of Ohio, Indiana, and Illinois, prepared to give up the sale of their beef, pork, and flour, in order to increase the profits of those who raise children for sale, and deal in the bodies of women? Are the free states prepared to suspend their harbor and river improvements for the purpose of establishing their slave-trade with Texas, and to perpetuate slavery therein?" "Our tariff," he added at a later time, "is as much an anti-slavery measure as the rejection of Texas. So is the subject of internal improvements and the distribution of the proceeds of the public lands. The advocates of perpetual slavery oppose all of them, they regard them as opposed to slavery."[17]

Giddings represented an extreme position, but the proposed tax on tea and coffee brought from more moderate western men the charge that it was "a sectional tax." It was "wrong, unequal, and unjust," because while all free western laborers used these articles, the three million slave laborers scarcely touched them at all. President James K. Polk was asking for a war tax on tea and coffee "to make southern conquests, while northern territory [meaning Oregon] is given away by empires."[18]

Slavery was also blamed for Polk's veto of a river and harbor bill intended largely to benefit shipping on the Great Lake. Is it not strange that enlightened men of the South cannot be persuaded that our lakes are something more than goose ponds?" asked the Chicago *Democrat*. "If we were blessed with the glorious institution of slavery this comprehension would not be so difficult."[19] The Chicago *Daily Journal* was more blunt. It charged Southerners' opposition to western internal improvements to the fact that they were "slaveholders" but "not Americans." "If no measures for the protection and improvement of anything North or West are to be suffered by our Southern masters," it said, "if we are to be downtrodden, and all our cherished interests crushed by them, a signal revolution will eventually ensue."[20]

[17] Joshua R. Giddings, *Speeches in Congress* (Boston, 1853), pp. 98–105, 151–56; Giddings to Oran Follett, November 18, 1844, in Historical and Philosophical Society of Ohio, *Quarterly Publication,* X (1916), 20.

[18] Jacob Brinkerhoff of Ohio. *Congressional Globe,* 29 Cong., 1 sess., Appendix, pp. 784–85 (June 30, 1846).

[19] Chicago *Democrat,* September 15, 1846.

[20] Chicago *Daily Journal,* August 19, November 19, 1846.

By the close of the Mexican War, which brought proslavery charges to a climax, some men were frankly saying that the whole business had become a struggle for power. The extension or non-extension of slavery in the territories acquired from Mexico was a matter of increasing or decreasing the strength of parties in Congress. Robert Barnwell Rhett of South Carolina was convinced that "Political power, the power of the different sections of the Union, seeking the mastery, is undoubtedly a strong element in the proposed exclusion of slavery from our territory."[21] George Oscar Rathbun of New York was more explicit. He had figured out that by its three-fifths representation of slaves the South gained some twenty-three members in Congress. With this vote the section had "turned the scale upon every important question that had divided this country for the last forty years." The South had by this advantage elected presidents, filled the speakership, ruled the army and navy, and placed southern men in the office of Secretary of State during most of those years. Rathbun was, therefore, opposed to slavery in the territories because it gave "representation and political power." If the South would yield the three-fifths rule, he was willing for Southerners to go into any territory and freely to take their slaves with them.[22] Southerners made it just as clear that the exclusion of slavery from the territories meant the reduction of their section to the position of a permanent minority and the ultimate destruction of their institutions. They were contending for equality in the nation.

The Wilmot Proviso was unquestionably, in part, a move to check southern strength in Congress and to end the restraints placed on northern and western development. It was, however, considerably more than that. It was an assertion of the fact that North and West had now definitely caught step with the modern world and had reached the point where they knew both their minds and their strength. They knew that the future belonged to urban industrial and financial capitalism, to democracy, and to a more social Christianity. They understood that slavery, as an impediment to each of these things, had no place in a nation whose manifest destiny was to round out its boundaries on this continent and, perhaps, to right the social and political balances in the whole Western world.

That understanding gave a positiveness to northern opposition to the extension of slavery that knew no yielding. It easily took on

21 *Cong. Globe,* 29 Cong., 2 sess., Appendix, p. 246 (January 15, 1847).
22 *Ibid.,* pp. 364–65 (February 9, 1847).

the flavor of a moral crusade. Politicians and "sober, deliberate, and substantial men," who had "the good of the country at heart," as Charles Hudson of Massachusetts described them, let it be known that slavery could not advance a foot farther.[23] Anyone who has read the debates in Congress on this issue knows that the question of whether slavery had reached its limits in the United States is a thoroughly academic one. And the answer has nothing to do with geography or profits. It could go no farther for the simple reason that the North had made up its mind and had the strength to enforce its will.

And, regardless of how complex were the forces operating to produce this situation, the argument that carried the day was that slavery was a moral wrong and an impediment to progress. In the great debates on compromise which followed, Horace Mann and William H. Seward, not Daniel Webster, made the important northern statements. Mann insisted that to spread slavery was to "cast aside, with scorn, not only the teachings of Christianity, but the clearest principles of natural religion and of natural law." It was to sink back to the Dark Ages. To insist that men and women could rightly be called property was a trick for which any "juggler or mountebank" would be hissed off the stage in any respectable village. "I deliberately say, better disunion, better a civil or servile war—better anything that God in his providence shall send, than an extension of the boundaries of slavery."[24] Seward declared that we could be neither Christians nor real freemen if we imposed on another the chains we defied all human power to fasten on ourselves. He insisted that the Constitution had created a consolidated political state in which the states had "submitted themselves to the sway of the numerical majority." The same Constitution had devoted the territories to freedom. And what was just as important, slavery itself in the long run would have to give way "to the salutary instructions of economy and to the ripening influences of humanity." It was only a question of whether it be done peacefully or by force. And to those who offered the Constitution as an impediment to the forward sweep of material and moral progress, he offered the "higher law."[25]

Some day the historian will understand that there is no break between Henry David Thoreau's "Civil Disobedience," William

[23] *Ibid.*, pp. 51–52 (December 16, 1846).
[24] *Ibid.*, 31 Cong., 1 sess., Appendix, pp. 219–24 (February 15, 1850).
[25] *Ibid.*, Appendix, pp. 260–69 (March 11, 1850).

Lloyd Garrison's burning of the Constitution, and Seward's higher law. He will also understand the obligation which northern men felt to bring profession and practice into harmony in a nation whose manifest destiny was to uphold Christianity and democracy throughout the Western world.

The South, on its part, met the Wilmot Proviso with an uncompromising insistence on the right to an equal share in the territories won by the common blood of the nation. Calhoun, as usual, brought forward a series of resolutions, declaring the territories to be the property of "the several States composing this Union" and denying the right of Congress to discriminate between the states or to deny to their citizens the full and equal opportunity to migrate to the territories with their property. Others took up the cry of "indefeasible right," and through their statements rang the word "Constitution" like the repeated call of the whippoorwill. "We invoke the spirit of the Constitution, and claim its guarantees," said the resolutions of the Nashville Convention. "I, for one, am for tearing asunder every bond that binds us together," said Alexander H. Stephens. "Any people capable of defending themselves, who would continue their allegiance to a Government which should deny to them a clear, unquestionable, constitutional right of the magnitude and importance of this to the people of the South, would deserve to be stigmatized as poltroons."[26] Jefferson Davis summed up the situation as one in which the North was determined to deny to slavery its constitutional rights for "the sole purpose of gaining political power."

Some day the historian will also understand that there is no break between southern abhorrence of the strife and ferment in northern and European society and its deep reliance on the Scriptures and the Constitution for defense of a stable order. He may even come to understand that few peoples on this earth have ever extended freedom of speech to the point of permitting agitation that would destroy a goodly percentage of their material wealth and completely upset the existing structure of society. Southerners too felt an obligation to manifest destiny.

The struggles of the 1840's had thus gone a long way toward becoming a matter of *right* and *rights*. Issues had been caught up

[26] *Ibid.*, 32 Cong., 1 sess., p. 460 (April 27, 1852); M. W. Cluskey (ed.), *Political Text-Book, or Encyclopedia* (Washington, 1857), p. 597; Crallé (ed.), *Works of John C. Calhoun,* IV, 348.

in the great fundamental developments of the age. "Right" had become a part of what men were calling progress, a part of a nation's manifest destiny—its obligation to the democratic dogma and experiment. "Rights" too had become a part of something fundamental in terms of a superior way of life, a sound form of government, and a sane treatment of property.

It seemed for a time that the final crisis had been reached, that the Union would go to pieces. Some expressed the hope that it would. That it did not do so was due largely to the strength of political party ties. Whigs and Democrats, North and South, still felt the tug of party loyalty and still retained confidence in the integrity of their fellows. By a supreme effort they forced the conflict back to the concrete issues involved in the immediate difficulty and were able to secure a compromise. It was a slender thread, but it held. It promised, however, little for the future, for third parties had already appeared and the rift in each of the dominant parties had perilously widened. They might not survive another crisis. And what was equally alarming was the growing tendency of issues, however material, to fall into the pattern of *right* and *rights* and to be linked to the matter of progress and national destiny. It might not be possible next time to throw aside this covering and to return to concrete issues.

The 1840's had certainly shown the weakness of the democratic process in dealing with issues cast as moral conflicts or having to do with the fundamental structure of society. It seemed to show, as Carl Becker has said, that "government by discussion works best when there is nothing of profound importance to discuss, and when there is plenty of time to discuss it. The party system works best when the rival programs involve the superficial aspects rather than the fundamental structure of the social system, and majority rule works best when the minority can meet defeat at the polls in good temper because they need not regard the decision as either a permanent or a fatal surrender of their vital interests."[27]

That, however, was only half of the difficulty. The 1840's had also shown that a democratic society cannot stand still. The conservative urge to hold fast to that which has been established may prove as fatal as the fanatic's prod to constant change. Those who profess a belief in democracy must ever remember that alongside the Constitution of the United States stands that other trouble-

[27] Carl Becker, *New Liberties for Old* (New Haven, 1941), pp. 106–7.

some document, the Declaration of Independence, with its promise of greater freedom and equality. If politicians and parties do not sometimes give it heed, they may learn to their sorrow that the great document was written to justify revolt. That too may be a fatal weakness in the democratic process.

VII

BACKGROUND FORCES AND THE CIVIL WAR

It is usually possible, when two nations have gone to war, to find plausible reasons for their action. Disputes over boundaries; the aggressive acts of one people against another; the lust for power on the part of rulers; these and other matters of the same general kind can, as a rule, be pointed out as having provoked the quarrel which eventuated in open warfare.

Even when motives are clouded and confused, there is always the treaty of peace at the end of the struggle which reveals something of the purposes which inspired the victor and which led the vanquished to risk defeat. Historians may shy a bit at listing exact causes, but most of them have been willing to designate what they call "background causes" and "immediate causes" for international struggles.

In the case of a civil war, however, the matter is entirely different. Here the usual reasons for force on the part of nations are not present. The parties to the quarrel dwell within the same geographic limits and are heirs to the same national, social, and political traditions. Their past is a common possession. The lines which divide one group from the other are often so blurred and indistinct that great numbers have difficulty in choosing sides and getting themselves into a fighting mood. The final break is usually the product of a long accumulation, and the immediate occasion may seem comparatively trivial and unconvincing. Through long association, personalities have become tangled with concrete issues, and close, intimate connection may have become a larger reason for strife than the lack of understanding between two foreign peoples. And for the same reason, emotions may have been raised to a more intense pitch and an unforgiving bitterness developed. Civil wars have, therefore, been marked by unusual ruthlessness, dogged de-

Lecture delivered at Hampden-Sydney College, April, 1959, and printed in *The American Tragedy: The Civil War in Retrospect,* by A. O. Craven and Frank E. Vandiver (Hampden-Sydney, Va., 1959), pp. 5–18.

termination, and an aftermath of guerrilla fighting. Family feuds have left ugly scars.

Then, to add to the difficulties, there is no negotiated peace at the end of a civil war. They are struggles between whole peoples and are waged for total victory. They come to an end only when one party is crushed in complete exhaustion, its armies scattered and disbanded, its political institutions dissolved, its values discredited, and its flag and all the agencies by which civil life has been carried on discarded and robbed of all authority and meaning. The victor alone is left to carry out his will to any extent that vindictiveness or generosity may inspire.

The American Civil War followed these patterns with only such variations as local circumstances dictated. The geographic line that supposedly separated the North and the South was never a fixed and certain one. Even if slavery be accepted as forming a physical distinction, we must remember that four slaveholding states remained loyal to the Union, that three-fourths of those who lived south of the Mason and Dixon's line held no slaves, and that until the mid-1830's, the attack on slavery centered in the South.

And so deeply ran the devotion to common practices and values, that the Confederacy adopted the Federal Constitution for its own with only minor changes. Its military leaders were so heavily West Point trained and the knowledge of what to expect from an opponent so general that the military character of the struggle was quickly reduced to pattern. Meanwhile, citizens on both sides continued to behave like Americans whose individual rights had at all times to be respected.

As a result, neither North nor South achieved a unity at any time comparable to that of a nation at war. Lincoln found it necessary to suppress newspapers, to suspend the right of *habeas corpus*, and to ship protesting citizens across the border into the Confederacy. The term "Copperhead" came into wide use, and the soldier vote had to be relied upon to insure victory. Jefferson Davis, in turn, had his troubles. They sometimes ran on a higher level where Alexander H. Stephens, his vice-president, seemed to think that his job was primarily that of obstructing and criticizing the administration, and Zeb Vance of North Carolina and Joe Brown, of Georgia, on occasion, all but took their states out of the Confederacy by open defiance and independent state action.

Then to make the problems more difficult, the President whose election in 1860 precipitated secession had only recently said: "I am not, nor never have been in favor of bringing about in any way the social and political equality of the black and white races . . . and I will say in addition to this that there is a physical difference between the white and black races which I believe will forever forbid the two races from living together on terms of social and political equality. . . ." And, who on assuming office, gave assurance that he had "no purpose, directly or indirectly, to interfere with the institution of slavery in the states where it exists."

And it was the greatest soldier which the Confederacy produced who, at the very same time, was saying that "in this enlightened age" there were few who would not acknowledge "that slavery as an institution" was "a moral and political evil" and who sadly wrote: ". . . I am unable to realize that our people will destroy a government inaugurated by the blood & wisdom of our patriot fathers. . . . I wish to live under no other government & there is no sacrifice I am not ready to make for the preservation of the Union save that of honour. . . ."

Evidently Lincoln and Lee, as individuals, had little to quarrel about.

The historian is thus left to puzzle over a quarrel that has no definite beginning and no definite ending—a quarrel between two parties which could not agree among themselves and which had much in common with their opponents. It is easy, of course, to go back after the break occurred, and to point out cases where sharp differences existed; it would be just as easy to run over the record and to find agreement. So all the historian can safely say is that national consolidation and states' rights, Negro slavery and anti-slavery, agriculture and industry, fears and anger, and a lot of other things played some part in producing conflicting views which, in turn, resulted in a quarrel.

In approaching the problems involved in understanding the American Civil War, it is necessary first to look at the setting in which events developed, at the Age itself, and at the unique conditions existing in the United States.

In the year 1815, a new era opened for the whole Western world of which the United States had, from earliest settlement, been a part. The almost continuous state of war, which had involved the nations of western Europe for centuries and which had embroiled the American people throughout colonial and early national days, came to a sudden end. For the next hundred years there would be peace. True, there would be local struggles, but no worldwide wars. Three generations of fortunate men who lived around the Atlantic Basin could center their thoughts and efforts on peaceful endeavors.

The matchless age that now had a chance to reach maturity was characterized by an intensification of national feelings and a corresponding increase in central government activity; by the coming of the Industrial Revolution to full growth through the perfecting of the steam engine; and by the spread of a deep democratic-humanitarian impulse. These forces, which had been slowly emerging in the past decades and which had been held back by warfare, now gained their freedom.

With sullen determination, the peoples on both sides of the Atlantic Ocean quickly pushed aside the heavy restraining hand of Metternich, and nationalism began its heady advances. The factory system and the city as an industrial center came into their own. Men, regions, and even nations altered their ways of living and became interdependent to new degrees as both industrial and raw producing areas specialized according to their peculiar abilities. *Where* men lived; *how* they lived; *what their environments* were like; *who* controlled their very existence; and even *what they thought was right or wrong* was determined to a large degree by the new machines of the new age.

The gap between industry and raw producer widened with industrial maturity and, in the end, brought about a new kind of colonialism in which those who fed the machines and consumed their goods lost much of their former independence. Cities grew at astonishing rates and ceased to depend on their immediate neighborhoods for supplies and markets. The steam engine, applied to transportation, cut space, opened the great land masses, and shrank continents to convenient size. Wealth and plenty reached new levels, while growth and expansion took on new meanings.

As wealth centered in fewer hands and poverty pressed on greater numbers; as the ways of doing business became more complex and labor became dependent on the capital for even the right to work; as men struggled to learn how to live in cities; and as the moral code that had served the past became obsolete, a strange mixture of democracy and humanitarianism became a permanent part of the new day. New ways of thinking were needed where new ways of living and working already existed. Thus western Europe and the United States entered a new era. Water on wheels and steam in engines were proving to be even more revolutionary forces than wind in sails had been four centuries earlier. The Modern World was emerging.

It is not necessary, for our purposes, to follow in detail the course of developments in the United States as the Modern World crossed the Atlantic. It is only important to stress the fact that each and every one of the forces which entered into the making of the new era operated in quite a different way on what ultimately became spoken of as "the North" and "the South."

Of first importance is the fact that the Industrial Revolution brought its benefits and its problems primarily to the northeastern corner of the nation. On foundations that were laid well before the War of 1812, the textiles now moved rapidly into the factory stage. After a few uncertain days in which the least efficient were crowded out, Lowells and Lawrences and Chicopees were scattered about wherever favorable locations could be found. A new capitalist group and a new kind of American worker made their appearance. A sag in commerce made capital available to younger men who entered the industrial field and by the application of Yankee genius saw their profits mount and their investments reach out into banking, insurance, lands, and railroads, and their dominance in legislative halls made secure. Women and children, meanwhile, came down from the countryside to toil long hours in lint-filled rooms and to find their efforts to increase wages, shorten hours, and improve working conditions rejected as interference with American freedom. Nor did their menfolk who came down to find jobs in the growing cities fare any better. They too met with the same resistance and were soon speaking of themselves as "despised and trampled upon by the drones and minions of fortune."

The farmers in the region, too lost their old self-sufficiency based on agriculture and household industry combined. A few adjusted their efforts toward supplying the specialized crops needed for the support of the spreading urban centers, but the many turned cityward or toward the West where old methods and crops could still exist. Their surpluses would soon rebuild the import and export trade on which the merchants in the seaport cities would thrive.

In this fashion a new industrial belt, stretching from New Hampshire to Pennsylvania, was created to take the place of the old rural-mercantile order that had formerly existed. It was a region which expected the central government to protect and forward its interests; whose leaders looked to all parts of the nation for raw materials and markets; whose bankers and investors would finance the staple crops of distant farmers and build the railroads or provide the ships to carry them to market. It was a region where the Modern World had had its way.

The coming of the Modern Age touched and affected the American South quite differently. The South had long been a region where staple-crop agriculture had dominated and where a certain rural way of life had shaped the social order. Its economy had suffered much in late colonial, Revolutionary, and early national days. Markets had failed, and efforts at recovery had not been successful. Slavery, as a labor system, had weakened and, in some cases, had become both an economic burden and a matter of moral concern. Migration to the West was becoming heavy, and demands for reform were plaguing those in political control.

The great forces of the Modern World reached the South only indirectly. Since the Industrial Revolution found its most spectacular expression in the textiles, the major task assigned to agriculture was the production of an adequate supply of cotton. That demand fitted magnificently into the southern situation where a start at cotton production had already been made, some of its technical problems solved, and where a great belt superbly fitted to cotton growing could be opened along the Gulf. The plantation system with an adequate supply of slaves, now becoming a burden to their masters, provided the large scale unit needed to meet the almost unlimited demands for raw material, and the restless southern small farmer, crowding the Indian ahead, had already begun the westward push and shown his eagerness and his ability to raise a share of the valued crop. Flush times were on their way to Alabama and Mississippi.

The result was the rise of the Cotton Kingdom—a new plantation-farming world where slaves would again become profitable, and a new crop of Southerners could at least dream of reproducing old social patterns. It did not, it must be noted, involve the revolutionary changes in ways and values that had been required in the northern industrial belt. The southern response to the demands of the new day represented only the expansion of established patterns. The effect would still remain the production of an agricultural staple. The agencies of production would remain the same. Some adjustments would be necessary because of frontier conditions and because cotton was not tobacco or rice, but nothing revolutionary would occur.

Nor would old social, moral, political values be invalidated by what was being done. It did not in any way undermine the Southerner's reliance on local and state government. It did not weaken men's confidence in the superiority of a rural way of life or their belief that slavery in southern hands was beneficial to the Negro, to the white man, and to society as a whole. Southern values were still those which the Fathers had accepted and approved.

The South's mission in the days ahead would thus be one of defending the old—in holding fast to those things in society and government which had already proved themselves. New "isms" would not attract. Yet such a course would subject the South to that fate which the Modern Age had prepared for those who merely supplied the raw materials and the markets. Its people would not share, to any great extent, in the rich rewards of industry. It would not have its share of prosperous cities with their merchants, bankers, and capitalists. It would be dependent on others for most of the good things of the new day, and its influence in government would, of necessity, at some point have to give way. In other words, its course would lead towards a colonial status. It would be guilty, in terms of the Modern World, of being backward.

But cotton was not the whole southern story. The old seaboard states had not shared in its benefits and had lost heavily both in white and Negro slaves by its spread. Tobacco had not recovered from its long drawn out depression, and rice had long since reached its limits of production. Efforts at readjustment had not made much headway and internal strife had not improved matters. The Old South had not found a place in the modern world.

It is thus clear that some men in both North and South had profited, at least temporarily, from the revolutionary changes that had been wrought in their lives and regions. Some men had caught step with the forces that were molding a new age all about the Atlantic Basin. Others in both North and South had suffered from its coming and were ready to raise the grave question as to its benefits and its soundness. Whole groups had lost status and were ready to argue whether the new order was in keeping with the old American values and purposes. The great debate which followed forms a watershed in American history.

Never before or since have the American people looked so intensely at themselves. Never have they so carefully and so thoroughly examined their institutions, their social ways, and their values. Never have they reached such positive conclusions. Never have they been willing to die for so many things.

Throughout the 1820's and 1830's the debate went on. Economic values, social values, political values, and even those which had to do with things of the spirit, lost their sacredness and moved into the field of questioning and decision. Every problem ranging from the kind of government we had established to the merits of human slavery was discussed, argued, and firmly settled in the minds of the contestants. By the 1840's most Americans knew exactly what they thought about most things.

These Americans had come out of the Revolutionary struggle with rather well-fixed opinions about the national purposes and the course to be run. They had incorporated them into the Declaration of Independence and later into the Constitution. There was considerable question as to exactly what each of these great documents implied, but something of balance had been reached in the years before the War of 1812. Nor was men's understanding of what was honest in business and moral in conduct less fixed. They had very definite notions as to cheating and stealing and even as to sound financial undertakings. Their laws had been framed to take care of such matters. They were just as certain as to what was good and what was bad in the social order. Now, however, everything had again been thrown into confusion and uncertainty by the great forces that were creating a new America and invalidating much that men had thought fixed and certain.

It is possible to speak only of a few basic subjects which the Americans of this period thoroughly discussed and on which they came to differing, but firm, conclusions. Each represents the American reaction to some phase of the oncoming Modern Age. The first of these had to do with the character and powers of the United States government. It arose with the spread of nationalism.

In the first flush of national pride in 1815, the men of North and South had united in establishing a new National Bank, passing tariff measures for the protection of manufacturies, building a National Road to unite East and West, and announcing to the world in the Monroe Doctrine that we had reached national maturity. John

Marshall, of Virginia, followed with his centralizing Court decisions, and Daniel Webster of Massachusetts, with his flaming national oratory. Most Americans had seemingly caught step with the rest of the Atlantic Basin.

United action, however, had already begun to weaken as men in the depressed Old South saw the danger to their agriculture and their labor system in an all too active central government. John Taylor, in Virginia, and Robert Turnbull, in South Carolina, insisted that "there are many states in America, but no state of America or any people of an American state." Ours, they said, was a league of sovereignties—a federal union, not a consolidated nation of peoples. Congress was exercising "powers never contemplated by the framers of the Constitution." "The more National, and the less Federal the government becomes," said Turnbull, "the more certainly will the interests of the great majority of the States be promoted, but with the same certainty will the interests of the South be depressed and destroyed."

The argument reached a climax in nullification and in the passage of the Force Bill, which Calhoun declared "proceeded on the ground that the entire sovereignty of this country belongs to the American people as forming one great community, and regards the States as mere factions or counties." "I know," he went on to say, "that it is not only the opinion of a large majority of our country, but it may be said to be the opinion of the age, that the very *beau ideal* of a perfect government is the government of a majority . . . without check or limitation on its power; yet, if we may test this theory by experience and reason, we shall find that . . . the necessary tendency of [such] . . . governments . . . is to faction, corruption, anarchy, and despotism. . . ."

In these words, the man whom John Quincy Adams had pronounced the most national and the least provincial of Americans took his stand for the federal character of our government against the majority and the age itself. He did not, however, carry the South as a united section with him. That would not come until after the debate had ended.

Nor did the doctrine of consolidated nationalism receive solid sectional support at the North. New Englanders would hold their Hartford Convention, and northern men and states would feel perfectly free to indulge in open resistance to the nation at war with Mexico. Consolidated nationalism would become good northern doctrine only when William H. Seward announced, in 1850, that "the States . . . as States had (in forming the Constitution) surrendered their equality as States, and had submitted themselves to the sway of the numerical majority without qualifications or checks."

A second basic issue discussed and reduced to positive opinion in this period had to do with the relative importance of persons and property. It arose, as a rule, over the growing demand for universal suffrage as a part of the great democratic impulse of the new day. It involved the legal or constitutional rights of minority interests as against population majorities.

In the New York Constitutional Convention of 1821, the wealthy land owners opposed the popular move to grant voting rights to all adult white males who had paid taxes either in money or services. Advocates saw this as mere justice under the Declaration of Independence. Opponents saw it as revolution. Said Abraham Van Vechten: ". . . Life and liberty are common to all, but the possession of property is not. Hence the owners of property have rights which, in relation to those who are destitute, are separate and exclusive." From this he concluded that "the right of suffrage should be so arranged as to give due weight to property as well as to personal rights."

Chancellor Kent was even more emphatic. He noted the tendency of universal suffrage to "jeopardize the rights of property . . . of majorities to tyrannize over the minority and to trample them down." He feared what he called "the extremes of the democratic doctrines" and viewed with alarm the rise of the cities with their docile factory workers who would soon outnumber the sturdy and dependable rural peoples.

In the Virginia Constitutional Convention of 1829–30, the problems were much the same and the arguments offered strikingly similar. The only major difference was that the property involved consisted of Negro slaves; the threat to security, however, was still from "King Numbers." Men from the western part of the state were demanding a broader franchise and a more just representation; the planters of the east were struggling to retain the right to count three-fifths of their slaves as population and thus to be able to protect themselves from heavier taxation.

Judge Upshur spoke for the planters, saying there were two kinds of majority. "There is a majority in interest, as well as a majority in numbers" and "those who have the greatest stake in the government [should] have the greatest share in the administration of it." He spoke of the slave as "a peculiar kind of property," which, because of its nature, required "that kind of protection which flows from the possession of power."

What he meant was made clear by another speaker who explained that "The property we seek to protect . . . consists of intelligent, sentient, responsible beings that have passions to be inflamed, hearts to feel, understandings to be enlightened, and who are capable of catching the flame of enthusiasm from the eloquent effusions of agitators. . . ." Another insisted that all minorities should have the legal right to protect themselves from unwise majorities.

Their opponents questioned the value of slaves even to their owners and ascribed the backward conditions in affairs to their presence. They talked of the rights of majorities to dominate, and bluntly suggested that "if no such thing as slavery existed," the men of the East would grant suffrage on a free-white basis. One even hinted that this fact "offered the greatest of all temptations to make constant war on it." All of which caused John Randolph to speak of "the fanatical spirit existing in the West on the slavery issue." He too demanded control in government by the slaveholders, for, as he said: "Sir, I would as soon trust the Quakers of Pennsylvania as the Quakers of any county of Virginia. I would as lief trust the Fanatics of Free-Masons Hall, London, as any other Fanatics, for Fanatics, like madmen, are on a par."

There were many other problems given a thorough airing in this period which I have called "the great debate"—issues on which positive convictions on both sides were ultimately formed. Time permits only a brief mention of two that developed in the economic field as the nation hurried out of the simple, personal handicraft stage into the impersonal complexities of modern industrial society. The first of these had to do with finances.

The coming of the Industrial Revolution to the United States created a new kind of businessman. He was both ignorant and contemptuous of the traditional practices and moral codes that had characterized business in the more sober eighteenth century, and he was bent on getting rich quick in an America that seemed to be especially designed for that purpose. Men of the old business cult called him "vulgar" and his ways "contemptible." Yet the Modern

World was in his keeping. Armed with the matchless energy supplied by steam, confident that it was the nation's business to see that every man prospered, and overjoyed by the discovery that "promises to pay" could be used in place of gold and silver, he denounced the Second National Bank as "a Monster" for its efforts at restraint and threw caution to the wind. In the process he not only produced an economic panic but a moral one as well. For, as Bray Hammond says in speaking of the fraudulent banking practices of the day: "The simpler forms of cheating and stealing were well enough known but the more complicated dishonesty of distinguished looking persons who sat at their desks month after month in plain view while appropriating other people's funds to their own use through bookkeeping entries, false reports or no reports, substitutions, and euphemisms—all this was beyond the simplicities of the common law and was something with which the legislators had still to cope." Embezzlement was something new that belonged to a new day. "The great debate" in this field thus had to be both economic and moral.

The second economic problem to be discussed had to do with capital and labor. As we have said, the coming of finance-industrialism produced in the North a new and powerful group of business leaders and a new and uniquely dependent body of workers. It had given slavery a new hold on the South and had spread the plantation system widely over a new geographic region. It had thus greatly altered the old relationship between employer and employee in the North but had not greatly changed the character of Negro slavery at the South. The sharpest debate on issues would, therefore, of necessity take place in the northern industrial belt.

Here the right of labor to organize and to strike was bitterly contested between employers, who had the courts on their side, and the workers, who had only numbers. Judges ruled that organization and strikes were "acts injurious to trade" and declared: "It is important to the best interests of society that the price of labor be left to regulate itself." "Competition," they added, "is the life of trade." Strikers were, therefore, fined and thrown into prison.

Labor answered by saying: "If this is not Slavery, we have forgotten its definition. Strike the right of associating for the sale of labour from the privileges of freemen, and you may as well at once bind them to a master. If it be not in the color of his skin, and in the poor franchise of naming his own terms in contract for work, what advantage has the labourer of the North over the bondsman of the South?" They spoke of the Judges and Aristocrats "hung over our heads as a grim skeleton to frighten us into a still deeper vortex of degradation, that we may become mere tools to build up princely fortunes for men who grasp at all and produce nothing."

Conservatives, on the other hand, saw it all as a prelude to revolution—a repetition of what had occurred in France, where, as Phillip Hone observed, it had destroyed "everything good and lovely and of good report." "Virtuous men," he wrote in his diary, "have begun to fear the worst. Now is the critical moment of our country's fate." William Leggett, however, saw deeper. "The times have changed," he said, "though the courts remain the same. . . . Has [labor] not the right to act in concert, when their opponents act in concert? . . . The rich perceive, acknowledge, and act upon a common interest, and why not the poor?" Capital, he thought, was again using the language of the feudal barons—the language which despots had used towards their serfs.

Others, as respectable as Orestes Brownson and Theodore Parker, turned savagely on the new capitalists. They talked of them as men who lived by the toil of others but contributed nothing themselves. Parker accused them of never being on the right side of any question, of never asking what could be done for labor but always what could be done with it. They too spoke of northern slavery, and Brownson added: "Wages is a cunning device of the devil for the benefit of the tender conscience, who would retain all the advantages of the slave system, without the expense, trouble, and odium of being slaveholders." He was of the opinion that the southern slave had all the advantages in the bargain. Parker warned that if powerful men will not write justice with black ink on white paper, ignorant and violent men would write it on the soil in blood.

Southern slavery, which had been in the United States for two hundred years without bothering the consciences of many, other than the Quakers, now became an object, along with other social ills, to be quickly removed. The new movement was primiarily, at first, part and parcel of a reform effort centering in the evangelical revival belt of the Northeast. Slavery was viewed as one of the flagrant evidences of sin which should be removed before the impending millennium. It bore little evidence of a sectional crusade.

Nor was the drive confined to the North as a section. Most of the early antislavery societies and most of the first antislavery publications were to be found in the southern states. While not confined to Virginia, by any means, the most spectacular attack, or shall we call it a debate, occurred in the Virginia House of Delegates in the session of 1831–32. There everything any later abolitionist would say against the institution was said by Virginians talking to their fellow Virginians. And there, strangely enough, few of the things which men would later say in its defense were said. It was called a blight that cursed every region it touched. It was denounced for the division of Negro families, for the damage it did to both morals and the economy, and for the danger of insurrection which it held perpetually over the community. It was defended as a necessary evil but in not a single instance as a positive good. What could be said in its defense was soon said by Professor Dew of William and Mary, who had only recently been sharpening his wits at an Old World university. It was a native Virginian, however, by the name of Jesse B. Harrison who answered him with an equally thorough denunciation of the institution.

Now the significant thing to be noticed is that the thorough discussion of American institutions, American society, and American values, stirred by the impact of a new age on a growing, expanding nation, had been carried on largely at a local level. The problems men saw were those in their immediate neighborhoods. The evils to be eliminated or the good to be preserved were local ones. The discussion of values, pro and con, had been carried on by local men representing local interests. Yet, the final, fixed opinions and the deep convictions reached, had to do with basic issues that were becoming more and more a permanent part of national life in the new age. All the forces it brought were bringing men closer together, making them more interdependent, weaving them into an indestructible whole. The era of debate had reached the point of affirmation at a critical period in American history. Issues raised at the local level would become sectional issues.

We now realize that finance-industrial capitalism reached maturity in the United States somewhere around 1845 and began its drive for national domination. We also know that at about the same time it became perfectly clear that the South had been forced into an inferior colonial position. It had become dependent for its finances, its insurance, its marketing, and its supplies on the North. Southern men were soon saying that "from the rattle with which the nurse tickles the ear of the child born in the South . . . to the shroud which covers the cold form of the dead, everything comes from the North." They must look to local government for protection.

There was, however, more to it than being dependent. The southern planter and farmer, in spite of certain concessions in ways and values to the new age, had retained a degree of respect for the old moral and human values of the rural eighteenth century. Tobacco, rice, sugar, and cotton had never quite destroyed the obligations that went with being a gentleman, however much diluted. The Southerner had kept the ideal, at least, and the pushing, hard drives of business had not ended paternalism or completely destroyed his notions of honor. He had not become a typical businessman of the new age. He and his section were a bit backward, and he had made a virtue out of it. He kept his slaves and his old ideas of honor in business.

Then to bring all that had happened into the open, the nation, in the 1840's, entered a period of rapid expansion which pushed differences in values into conflict. All issues would now be at the national level and, as such, would reveal the extent to which the consolidation of convictions on fundamental issues had drawn a line between North and South. It was not long until men were talking about two civilizations in conflict—of peoples that were as separate as England and France, Carthage and Rome. Then it became clear that consolidated nationalism and states' rights, majority rule, and minority rights under the Constitution where a peculiar property was involved—all tangled together with differing moral and social standards, had drawn a line between the sections and that the issues between them had to do with *right* and *rights*. The whole struggle would henceforward be waged between abstract values and not between adjustable concrete interests.

The annexation of Texas and the settlement of the Oregon boundary line were normal events in the life of a young and growing nation. Even the Mexican War was not so much out-of-line. Yet each of these quickly became tangled with slavery as a sectional interest and the nation started drifting toward a serious crisis. Political parties began to divide within themselves over issues that, until now, had made no difference. Democrats who had no fault with such slaveholders as Andrew Jackson, Thomas Hart Benton, Francis Preston Blair, and James K. Polk began to draw away for conscience' sake. Ardent Whigs, such as Abraham Lincoln and Alexander H. Stephens, who had stood solidly together on all party issues in the early 1840's, now found their ways in opposite directions. Talk of a slave power brought new parties into existence, and the Wilmot Proviso became sound doctrine for both wavering Whigs and Democrats at the North, and a reason for breaking up the Union by equally wavering Whigs and Democrats at the South. Compromise was achieved in 1850 when principles were pushed aside and men discovered that they could deal rationally with concrete issues.

After that, facts made little difference. Reactions in both North and South were stereotyped. Ends began to justify means, and men as unfitted to shape the course of a nation's life as Charles Sumner, John Brown, Robert Barnwell Rhett, William L. Yancey, and their fellow travelers, began to wield unwarranted influence. Conservatives and moderate men, who probably constituted a majority in both sections, lost ground and numbers as irritations accumulated and at last tumbled a whole people into a war few wanted and no one could prevent. What the situation had become is nowhere better illustrated than by the fact that secession followed the perfectly legal election of a moderate middle-of-the-road man who was steadily insisting that he would do nothing that would provoke trouble.

And then, to turn tragedy into irony, after four years of bitter warfare, the North, and then the South belatedly, hurried as rapidly as possible into the Modern Age.

VIII

LEE'S DILEMMA

In his sketch of Robert E. Lee in the *Dictionary of American Biography,* the late Douglas Southall Freeman states that Lee made his decision to follow Virginia into secession "without mental debate." The only question with Lee was "simply whether his first allegiance was due to his state or the Union." So when Virginia acted, Lee "instinctively . . . cast his lot with her." It was "the answer he was born to make."

Freeman also notes that Lee followed this course in spite of the fact that he was "warmly devoted to the Union," did not believe in the right of secession, and was no defender of slavery in the abstract. He deliberately chose the path of revolution.[1]

For this, Freeman offers no apology, no defense, and apparently thinks it requires no explanation. He accepts Lee's action as the natural one for a Virginia gentleman with Lee's background to have taken.

Allan Nevins, on the other hand, speaks rather contemptuously of the ease with which Lee made his decision. With more cynicism than truth, he implies that Lee's only reason for hesitancy, and the only struggle it cost, was over separation from the Army, not from the Union. Then, in order to make Lee's action more clearly "the product of instinct, not deep reflection," he lays heavy emphasis on Lee's expressed "contempt for the business of secession" and on his frank statement that "the framers of the Constitution would not have exhausted so much labor, wisdom and forbearance in its formation and surrounded it with so many guards and securities, if it was intended to be broken up by every member of the Confederacy at will. It was intended for 'perpetual union.' . . . It is idle to talk of secession."

Reprinted from the *Virginia Magazine of History and Biography,* LXIX, No. 2 (April, 1961), 131–48; Paper delivered as the annual address to the Virginia Historical Society, January 19, 1961.

[1] *Dictionary of American Biography,* XI (New York, 1933), 122.

After admitting that "nobody today dreams of questioning Lee's sincerity," Nevins concludes by saying: "But we may well question whether the man who thus preferred State to nation did not lack a certain largeness of view, did not respond to a parochial type of patriotism, and did not reveal an inadequate comprehension of the American destiny."[2]

It is not my purpose to defend Robert E. Lee against the charges of provincialism and narrowness of view. If Douglas Freeman, speaking to the future, saw no reason for explaining Lee's action, I most certainly can find no excuse for doing so here. I need only to say, in passing, that to me the real significance, and the true value in Lee's action, lie in the very things to which Nevins objects. Lee, in reality, took the hard road. He chose to yield deeply held convictions regarding immediate concrete issues in order to stand by those intangible, yet more profound values which had to do with honor, with self-respect, and with duty. The important truth, on which all else turns, is that Lee did genuinely and deeply love the nation. He had long grieved over its troubles and had sincerely declared that "there is no sacrifice I am not ready to make for the preservation of the Union save that of honour." "My own troubles, anxieties & sorrows," he added, "sink into insignificance when I contemplate the sufferings present & prospective of the nation." He had denounced secession, declared himself unable to realize "that our people will destroy a government . . . that has given us peace & prosperity at home, power and security abroad, & under which we have acquired a colossal strength unequalled in the history of mankind." He had as frankly said: "There are few in this enlightened age who would not acknowledge that slavery as an institution is a moral and political evil."

The cruel fact is that Lee, like the majority of Southerners in 1861, had no choice that could be made by a mental process. He and they had been driven into a corner and caught between conflicting values. On charge of being sinners, they were being forced either to yield their convictions in regard to slavery and secession or to subject the land of their birth to an impending social-economic revolution which would wipe out millions of dollars of invested capital and plunge their section into racial chaos.

Developments at the North, which had climaxed in the birth of

[2] Allan Nevins, *The War for the Union: The Improvised War, 1861–1862* (New York, 1959), pp. 109–11.

the Republican party, had produced a holy crusade armed with a law higher than the Constitution which had been framed supposedly to protect local and minority rights. Slavery had become the symbol of all sectional differences, and slavery, as a sin, must at once be put on the road to ultimate extinction. Christianity, democracy, and progress all required it. Southern men saw it as a case of submission or secession.[3]

Now the tragedy in the situation was the fact that three-fourths of those who lived south of Mason and Dixon's line held no slaves. The majority of them, like Lee, were unquestionably opposed to secession. Yet, in the end, these men were forced to fight under Lee, as few humans have ever fought, to preserve the Confederacy born of secession and anchored to Negro slavery. *That is one of the great tragedies of history.*

Then, to turn tragedy into irony, present-day historians are more and more inclined to view the war in which Lee and his men fought so bravely as "a needless war." They see it as the product of "the demagogy, selfishness, and blindness" of a "blundering generation." With equal assurance, they insist that, in that war, "the South stood face to face with a socio-economic revolution from which not even victory could extricate it." The Industrial Revolution, enlisted on the northern side, had made the southern cause a lost cause even before the fighting began.[4]

And it must also be remembered that Robert E. Lee, more than any other single individual, was responsible for prolonging that "needless, hopeless war" which cost half a million lives and more than nine billion dollars and which made possible the bitterness of Reconstruction and the extravagance and brutality of the Age of Big Business. To Lee and his gallant men, it brought only failure and defeat. Yet failure and defeat for which both North and South are endlessly grateful. To the North, it brought victory, but at the cost of decades of political corruption, wasteful and unbalanced economic development, and social problems which the next two generations would spend most of their efforts trying to solve.

It is thus only in terms of tragedy and irony that Robert E. Lee's

[3] Avery O. Craven, *Civil War in the Making, 1815–1860* (Baton Rouge, 1959), pp. 3–32.

[4] Nevins, *The War for the Union: The Improvised War,* Preface, p. v; J. G. Randall, "The Blundering Generation," *Mississippi Valley Historical Review,* XXVII (1940), 3–28; Allan Nevins, *The War for the Union: War Becomes Revolution* (New York, 1960), p. 483.

story has meaning. It is only in such terms that the War between the States has lessons to teach a nation that still stumbles and blunders. It is, therefore, without apology, that I ask you to admire the man who, as a soldier, did so much with so little and who turned failure into greatness to take a new look at the events which led a whole people into this ironic tragedy.

A wise English historian has divided the historiography of civil struggles into two stages. The first he calls the "Heroic" stage, in which the victors write their own chronicles, gloat over the defeated, count their trophies, commemorate their achievements, and boast of how righteousness triumphed over evil.

The second and more mature stage comes much later when the defeated side has had a hearing and all passion has been spent. Then the historian can see that it was a conflict between one half-right that was perhaps too willful and another half-right that was perhaps too proud and that even back of *this* lay "a terrible predicament," which had the effect of putting men at cross purposes with one another, causing situations to harden, events to tie themselves into knots, and one party or another to be driven into a corner.

When this stage is reached, the historian can feel sorrow for each side and give due weight to the "fundamental human predicament—one which we can see would have led to a serious conflict of wills even if all men had been fairly intelligent and reasonably well-intentioned."[5]

I would like to approach the bitter struggle which, one hundred years ago, divided North and South into warring factions from this point of view. I would like to select just one single event which had a vital part in tying things into knots and hardening situations and which so brutally reveals the sad predicament that lay behind it. I have chosen the John Brown raid on Harper's Ferry.

On the sixteenth of October, 1859, a little band of silent, determined men left an old farmhouse on the Maryland side of the Potomac River and headed towards Harper's Ferry. They carried rifles under their long gray shawls, and a farm wagon, creaking down the dark road behind them, was heavily loaded with sledges

[5] Herbert Butterfield, *History of Human Relations* (New York, 1952), pp. 10–14.

and pikes recently fashioned in New England shops. Their rifles were of a kind widely known as "Beecher's Bibles."

At their head strode a grim and gaunt old man, Kansas battle-scarred, who, according to Wendell Phillips, carried "letters of marque from God." He and his men had come South for the purpose of turning slaves into freemen and to arouse a nation to the necessity of getting on with business long overdue.[6]

What happened that night and the next days at Harper's Ferry was, from any *legal* point of view, simply a raid on public property by an irresponsible band of armed outlaws. What happened from any *common sense* point of view was pathetic tragedy. The John Brown raid on Harper's Ferry was *from any point of view* childlike both in conception and in execution. It was, as Robert E. Lee said, "the attempt of a fanatic or madman which could only end in failure." What temporary success it had was due entirely to the mistaken belief that large numbers were involved and to the general notion that nothing so absurd could possibly be undertaken.[7]

What John Brown had in mind if we can believe his own statement was nothing less than the stirring up of "a servile war on the borders of Virginia, which he expected to extend . . . through the State and throughout the entire South." By seizing the government arsenal at Harper's Ferry, he expected to establish a base to which the slaves and the non-slaveholding whites would flock in great numbers. "When I strike," he said, "the bees will swarm." At this base, his forces would be armed with the pikes and guns which he had brought from the North and with those captured at the arsenal.

With an army thus formed, he would move southward along the mountain ridges which extend from Virginia far down into the heart of Alabama. He would conquer and gather forces as he moved along. Then he would create a new and greater state out of this conquered territory, powerful enough to defend itself against the old slaveholding states and against the United States government itself if necessary.

For the administration of this vast conquered region, a plan of government had already been drawn. At a Constitutional Convention held at Chatham, Canada, on May 8, 1858, a "Provisional Con-

[6] Avery Craven, *Edmund Ruffin, Southerner: A Study in Secession* (New York and London, 1932), pp. 169–70.

[7] The material on the raid is from the *Report [of] the Select Committee of the Senate Appointed to Inquire into the Late Invasion and Seizure of the Public Property at Harper's Ferry . . .*, 36th Cong., 1st sess., Senate Report No. 278.

stitution and Ordinances for the people of the United States" had been framed and adopted. In its preamble it declared slavery to be "none other than a most barbarous, unprovoked, and unjustifiable war of one portion of its citizens upon another portion . . . in utter disregard and violation of those eternal and self-evident truths set forth in our Declaration of Independence." Since the present government did not protect all men in their rights, it had become necessary to form a new one.

With the purpose stated and justified, the forty-eight articles which followed projected a government of three departments—legislative, executive, and judicial—with the duties and responsibilities of each carefully described. Then followed provisions for an army under a "Commander-in-chief" who was to exercise unusual powers throughout the entire government. In fact, the whole organization seems to have been planned with the conquest and control of "conquered territory" in mind. Even the procedure for making "treaties of peace" was included, together with regulations dealing with captured or confiscated property, neutrals, prisoners, and persons placed on parole.

Social life, under the new government, was to be carefully regulated. Needless waste, profane swearing, filthy conversation, indecent behavior or indecent exposure of the person, intoxication, and quarreling were not to be tolerated. Schools and churches were to be established and high morals and personal cleanliness encouraged. Individuals in "conquered territory" were not to be allowed to carry *concealed* weapons, but those of good character and sound mind who were members of the organization were to be encouraged to carry arms *openly*. This state would face its moral obligations.

To inaugurate this vast scheme for the ending of slavery in the United States by the use of force, John Brown brought along only twenty-two men. Some of these were boys in their teens, and only one of the group had ever had any professional experience either in things military or in things political. Nor did they possess, other than in animal courage, the qualities necessary for such a bold venture. In spite of the fact that secrecy was absolutely necessary, even for establishing a base at the Ferry, Brown permitted a night train bound for Baltimore to proceed on its way after it had been delayed at the Ferry bridge long enough for its crew and passengers to understand clearly what was taking place.

Equally fatal was the seizure next morning of a nearby schoolhouse for the storage of pikes and guns to be used by revolting slaves. School was in session and some thirty frightened children, ranging in age from eight years to fifteen, were permitted to scatter to their homes and to spread the alarm.

Nor did Brown's men inspire the terror necessary for quick success. Important slaveholders who were seized in order to serve as hostages did not react to the name of John Brown as had settlers in Kansas. When his men demanded from Colonel Lewis W. Washington his watch and money, the dignified and courageous refusal in the face of their guns brought only the remark, "Take care, Sir!" And when pressure was offered by mention of Ossawatomie Brown, Washington declared that he had never heard of him, and that whenever he saw the word "Kansas" in a paper, he turned the page and refused to read it.

Nor were Terence Byrne and his brother any more impressed. They refused to surrender their slaves voluntarily or to help Brown's men to find them. "Hunt for them [as I do] when I want them," was the answer.

Somehow the advantage in men and guns did not meet a situation where gentlemen retained their dignity and composure. Brown's men could only waive their demands.

Nor did the slaves respond to Brown's call. A few frightened groups were rounded up and pikes placed in their hands. None, however, resorted to violence and all, at the first opportunity, dropped their pikes and returned to their homes. Regardless of what they thought of slavery, they showed no signs of being ready to revolt or to injure their masters. The name of John Brown held no meaning for them. Not a single recruit was found in all Virginia.

Under these circumstances, the whole movement collapsed as suddenly as it had begun. In taking possession of the arsenal, it was necessary to seize only one man, and the shooting of a Negro, who approached the railroad station, was both foolish and unnecessary. So quickly and easily was the work done that it was possible almost immediately to send out men for the purpose of collecting hostages and slaves. Not until morning and the arrival of armed men from the surrounding area did resistance develop.

During the course of that one day of unorganized snipe shooting, all of Brown's party, except those who had remained behind on the Maryland side, were either killed or captured or were driven within the engine house. The final blows were struck early next morning when a small detachment of United States Marines under Colonel Robert E. Lee broke down the engine-house doors and brought the raid to an abrupt end. As Colonel Lee said in his official report: "The whole [affair] was over in a few minutes." Brown and all but one of his men were seriously wounded and taken captive. The raid on Harper's Ferry had come to nothing.

The trials and conviction of John Brown and the other survivors from his band were more or less matters of observing legal forms rather than of determining guilt. The facts were too clear and the admissions too frank and open. The question of insanity might have been given more consideration, but Brown's own firm demands and the ultimate realization by friends that Brown dead was more valuable to their cause than Brown merely insane made that impossible. Perhaps the most significant development between the capture and the execution was the pious indulgence in falsehoods both by Brown and by those who had provided him with money and arms. Both were trying to transform a criminal into a martyr. Their effort, as Robert Penn Warren says, was "all so thin that it should not have deceived a child, but it deceived a generation."[8]

From this brief statement of facts, it would seem that, under ordinary circumstances, the whole incident, which in itself was little more than a tragic fiasco, would soon have been forgotten. Brown's efforts would have been judged for what they were, and his name would have had little place in American history. The raid in itself was too absurd in character and too local in its physical effects to have become a matter of national importance.

That Brown's efforts were not forgotten and that they assumed historical significance had nothing to do with the man John Brown or his raid on Harper's Ferry. The significant thing about this insignificant affair, like much else that occurred in this period, is the light it throws on American thinking and on the desperate and tangled situation into which the nation had fallen. It was a situation in which violence, that reached the status of private warfare, had not only been permitted but openly encouraged in Kansas. Pious men, on their own responsibility, had enlisted soldiers and provided arms and money for leaders as irresponsible as John Brown. Wil-

[8] Robert Penn Warren, *John Brown; The Making of a Martyr* (New York, 1929), p. 414. Warren is speaking of Brown's statement of his intentions made to the Court on November 2. "Unhappily, every reference to fact in that oration was a lie." Emerson said it ranked with Lincoln's Gettysburg Address.

liam H. Seward in Congress had shouted: "Come on then gentlemen of the slave states, since there is no escaping your challenge, I accept it in behalf of the cause of freedom. We will engage in competition for the virgin soil of Kansas, and God give victory to the side that is stronger in numbers as it is in right."[9]

With this understanding of personal responsibility outside the law, well-armed individuals from Missouri had poured across the border to face the challenge of the equally well-armed men from New England and New York. Civil war and every kind of violence that could be covered by a supposedly holy cause soon produced what came to be known as "Bleeding Kansas." The United States Army and civil officials, though present, played little part. Under the guise of accomplishing pious ends, the individual had come to believe that the law and the government had failed, and that he alone had become the agent of truth and right and God's will. It was, indeed, a sad predicament.[10]

To understand the relationship of this to Harper's Ferry, we must go back to the simple fact that John Brown's entire effort was based on "expectations" and "assumptions," not on cold fact. When Governor Henry A. Wise asked him after the raid what and how much support he counted on in men, he replied "from three to five thousand, if we wanted them." At which one of his wounded companions interrupted to say that "he was not sure of any aid, but he only *expected* it." He assumed that thousands like himself were anxious to shed southern blood. Furthermore, he assumed that every slave in the South was ready to rush into rebellion at the slightest opportunity and even to slay his master. He assumed that rich and powerful men in New York and New England, who had already provided him with money and arms, would back his efforts as they had done in Kansas; that they believed in a moral law higher than the laws passed by legislative bodies; that ends justified means; and that guns provided the only means for checking and destroying an aggressive slaveocracy.

These "expectations" and "assumptions" proved to be rather weak weapons in an emergency, but, were they not based on fairly reasonable grounds? Had not men been poured into Kansas by the thousands to fight slavery and to create free territory? And had

[9] *Congressional Globe,* 33 Cong., 1 sess., Appendix, pp. 768–71.

[10] James C. Malin, *John Brown and the Legend of Fifty-six* (Philadelphia, 1942), pp. 16–210.

they not been provided with "Beecher's Bibles" with which to fight? Had not the abolitionists pictured slavery as a state of constant war and rebellion and had not the "underground railway" been functioning on that assumption? And was it not William H. Seward, Mr. Republican, who had originated the "higher law doctrine" which Joshua Giddings told the congressional committee he had been expounding in public lectures? And had not two of the North's greatest preachers, Theodore Parker and Thomas Wentworth Higginson; two of its most prominent teachers, Dr. Samuel Gridley Howe and Franklin B. Sanborn; and two of its men of wealth, Gerrit Smith and George L. Stearns, secretly permitted guns and money contributed for Kansas to fall into Brown's personal possession?[11]

No, it was not John Brown who was confused. He knew exactly what he wanted to do. It was the people of the nation, both North and South, who were confused. Northerners were trying to live under both the moral law and the law of the land. They were saying that slavery was *wrong*—was a *sin* that must be done away with but which had a perfectly *legal* right to exist in the United States. No wonder they had begun to talk about a "higher law." Southerners, for their part, saw only property rights involved and refused to see that the whole Western world viewed slavery as a moral blight. They saw the "higher law" as only an excuse for selfish gain—for denying rights guaranteed by the Constitution! The historian can only conclude that each was half-right and each half-wrong.

The reactions to the John Brown raid showed this plainly.[12] An affair that never reached beyond the borders of a sleepy little village and involved a handful of unimportant men stirred a nation to its depths. Southerners magnified it into positive proof of all that had been charged against the abolitionists, the Republicans, and the North as a whole. A wave of anger, insecurity, and fear swept the section. No other single occurrence played so decisive a part in convincing the masses of their own danger and of the depravity of their enemies.

Northern reactions varied. Republicans were generally quick to disavow any connection or approval of Brown's deeds. The political

[11] J. C. Furnas, *The Road to Harper's Ferry* (New York, 1959), pp. 326–82.

[12] For a more extensive discussion of reactions to the raid, see Avery Craven, *The Coming of the Civil War* (New York, 1942), pp. 407–12.

stakes were too high. A few even condemned Seward and the "higher law." Democrats, of course, were quick to see the connection between Brown's deeds and the words of Seward, Hale, and Sumner. "They, not the crazy, fanatic Brown, are the real culprits," said one editor. They matched him in all but courage. They were as deserving of the gallows as was Brown himself.

The little group of prominent men who had backed Brown with money and arms suddenly saw this as a possibility. Stearns, Sanborn, and Howe fled to Canada. Smith found shelter in insanity and was confined to an asylum. His secretary hurried off to England. Parker, already safely in Italy, expressed regret that he was not at home to use his remaining strength "in defense of Truth and Right." Only Higginson stood his ground and turned on his colleagues with the scornful remark: "Is there no such thing as *honor* among confederates?"[13]

Most Northerners, however, still thought, as did Abraham Lincoln, that "even though he [Brown] agreed with us in thinking slavery wrong," that did not "excuse violence, bloodshed, and treason." They and he were still trying to keep their moral convictions and their legal obligations in separate compartments.

Unconsciously the contradiction implied in such a situation led gradually to a realization that, though most Northerners could not accept Brown's *means*, they did approve of the *ends* which he sought. That realization completed the transformation of a man whose career had been marked by business failure, sprinkled with "flagrant dishonesty," and by violence, climaxed by open theft and brutal murder, tangled with a passionate hatred of slavery, into a martyr and an American saint.

Intellectuals and clergymen began it. The Reverend Charles Gordon Ames found fault with Brown's head but honored his heart. "I regret his blundering haste and his rash, foolish violence, but I love and glory in the cause for which he died." The Reverend J. M. Manning of Old South Church, Boston, saw Harper's Ferry as "an unlawful, foolhardy, suicidal act" but added that he stood "before it wondering and admiring." "That he violated statute enactments is true," said the Reverend Stephen H. Taft, "and so did the Prophets; so did the Apostles; so did the Savior of men. . . . If

[13] Mary Thacker Higginson, *Thomas Wentworth Higginson: The Story of His Life* (Boston and New York, 1914), pp. 190–214; Ralph Volney Harlow, "Gerrit Smith and the John Brown Raid," *American Historical Review,* XXXVIII (1932–33), 32–60.

John Brown was a law-breaker . . . , so were Moses and Daniel; so were Peter and John; so were all the martyrs of all ages. If John Brown deserved death, then much more did Warren, Adams, Hancock, and Washington." His final conclusion was that John Brown had "reproduced before the world that grand sublime type of heroism which dignifies humanity, and inspires anew in the heart of man his faith in God and truth. He has done more to lift humanity towards God than any other man of this age."[14]

No wonder the Boston *Post* remarked that if John Brown were insane, "then one-fourth of the people of Massachusetts are madmen," and perhaps three-fourths of the ministers of religion. To which the Reverend Freeman Clarke replied that Brown's madness was "the madness of Curtius leaping into the gulf which yawned in the Forum; the insanity of a Roman Consul, who, dedicating himself to the infernal gods, plunged alone and in full armor into the ranks of the enemy as a sacrifice for his nation. . . . It is the kind of insanity of which a few specimens are scattered along the course of the human race—and wherever they are found . . . make the glory of human nature, and give us faith in God and man."

Parker, Thoreau, and Emerson rounded out the picture. Parker pronounced Brown "not only a martyr, . . . but also a saint." Thoreau praised him as one who "did not recognize unjust human laws, but resisted them as he was bid. No man in America has stood up so persistently and effectively for the dignity of human nature, knowing himself for a man and the equal of any and all governments. . . . I rejoice that I live in this age, and that I was his contemporary." In a plea for Brown's life, he added: "A man such as the sun may not rise upon again in this benighted land. Into whose making went the costliest material . . . , sent to be the redeemer of those in captivity. . . . You who pretend to care for Christ crucified, consider what you are about to do to him who offered himself the savior of four million men." Emerson brought it all to a climax when he described Brown as "The saint, whose fate

[14] Charles Gordon Ames, *The Death of John Brown: A Discourse Preached on the Occasion of His Public Execution, Delivered in the Free Congregational Church, Bloomington, Ill., Dec. 4, 1859* (Bloomington? 1909?); S. H. Taft, *A Discourse on the Character and Death of John Brown, Delivered in Martinsburg, N.Y., Dec. 12, 1859* (Des Moines, 1872); the Reverend J. M. Manning is quoted in C. Vann Woodward, "John Brown's Private War," *America in Crisis*, ed. Daniel Aaron (New York, 1952), p. 115; James Freeman Clarke, *Causes and Consequences of the Affair at Harper's Ferry, A Sermon Preached in the Indiana Place Chapel, on Sunday Morning, Nov. 6, 1859* (Boston, 1859).

yet hangs in suspense, but whose martyrdom, if it shall be perfected, will make the gallows as glorious as the cross."[15]

It is perfectly clear that these intelligent, high-minded men were not talking about the real John Brown or the real raid on Harper's Ferry. They had forgotten the man and the means; they were thinking only of the fact that a blow had been struck at slavery; and *that* was an end much to be desired. They were thinking of themselves as Americans who were responsible for a democratic dream, a moral principle. They literally radiated self-righteousness. They were convinced that they faced an unprincipled foe bent on destroying all the things which God had entrusted to their keeping. If the government did not act, it was time, as the Reverend Thomas Wentworth Higginson said, to give up what he called "that spirit of blind, superstitious loyalty to the U.S. government" and to fight "any opponent, state or federal." He was ready, with Gerrit Smith, not only to have slavery "repulsed with violence, but pursued even unto death, with violence." Ends justified means.[16]

Nor were southern reactions to the raid any more in line with actualities. The deeds of a mere handful of extremists and the approval of a few idealists were taken as positive proof of the fanatical intentions of the whole Republican party—perhaps, of the entire North. A reign of terror brought every stranger under suspicion, led to a liberal application of tar and feathers, and silenced moderate voices. After the John Brown raid, even "fervid Union" men declared themselves willing to risk the evils of secession "sooner than submit longer" to what they called "*Northern* insolence and outrage."[17]

Now what needs to be better understood is that this same situation had existed for a decade or more. Something deeper than immediate events had been producing reactions all out of proportion to the events themselves. Southern reaction to the Wilmot Proviso shows this clearly. That document *did* reveal a growing northern opposition to the expansion of slavery, and it did constitute a sharp protest against the course of the Democratic administration, but it

[15] For this and other reactions of a like kind, see James Redpath, *Echoes of Harper's Ferry* (Boston, 1860); Ralph L. Rusk, *The Life of Ralph Waldo Emerson* (New York, 1949), p. 402.

[16] Harlow, "Gerrit Smith and the John Brown Raid," *American Historical Review*, XXXVIII, 34–37.

[17] Avery O. Craven, *The Growth of Southern Nationalism, 1848–1861* (Baton Rouge, 1953), pp. 306–11.

never seems to have had the slightest chance of enactment into federal law, and it did not in any way determine the fate of slavery in California. The people of California themselves, of their own free will, did that, and no section, no national political party, or no administration can be blamed for the decision reached. It represented neither aggression nor injustice. Yet southern men fumed and raged and threatened secession. They rejected a free California as *northern* denial of southern rights. They precipitated a national crisis over what was at that time purely an abstract question—the right to share equally in territory acquired from Mexico, for which they had no immediate use. Yet, in the debates which followed, they harked back to the Northwest Ordinance, to the Missouri Compromise, to Oregon, to fugitive slaves, and to slavery and the slave trade in the District of Columbia. They made it perfectly clear that back of their reactions to the Wilmot Proviso and California lay the haunting fear that something more dangerous was threatening them with permanent inequality, perhaps even with inferiority.

As a matter of cold fact, harsh words and threats aside, the only cases of open northern aggression on clear-cut southern rights, prior to the John Brown raid, had to do with fugitive slaves. Even here the United States Census Bureau in 1860 estimated that only one thousand out of the three million slaves held in 1850 were fugitives. They constituted only three one-hundredths of one percent. And as Professor Edward Channing says, there is absolutely no way of knowing how many of these crossed Mason and Dixon's line. It might even be a safe guess that the majority who did were from the border states, which showed little enthusiasm for secession in 1860.[18]

Nor were reactions to Douglas' Kansas-Nebraska Bill any more in line with actualities. That act never produced one foot of slave territory and neither its author nor intelligent Southerners expected it to do so. The feeble southern effort to carry slaves to Kansas and the quick acceptance of defeat when the people of Kansas themselves chose freedom confirms the oft expressed statement that a recognition of abstract equal rights, not slave territory, was the real southern objective.

Yet that bill set the North on fire. Sane and pious men accepted as fact the absurd charges made in the Appeal of the Independent

[18] Edward Channing, *A History of the United States* (New York, 1905–25), VI, 94.

Democrats (written, incidentally, by men who were not Democrats), supported private warfare in Kansas, and openly declared: "The worthlessness of the Union to all who love liberty and hate oppression ought to be shown up" and "idolatry" of it "be rebuked and ridiculed."

Kansas made possible the absurd reactions to the John Brown raid and both suggest the tragic predicament into which the nation had fallen. A situation had developed in which events had meaning only in terms of civilizations in conflict. That was why a novel which had no great literary merit, and which quickly degenerated into a neglected Civil War relic, became a best seller surpassed only by the Bible. That is why Charles Sumner and Preston Brooks each became a sectional hero for conduct equally absurd.

Now it seems perfectly clear that back of the absurd gap between events and the reactions they produced, lay the ever widening gap between northern and southern economic and social values. The emerging Modern World in its uneven course was pushing them steadily apart and deepening their apprehensions of disasters yet ahead. Under its impact, nothing had remained static. Few things had retained their original form or meaning, and those who traveled at an uneven pace were destined to misunderstanding, fear, and hatred. It was this which, to use our English historian's words, was setting them at cross purposes and rendering them "embittered by the heat of moral indignation . . . just because each was so conscious of its own rectitude, so enraged with the other for leaving it without any alternative to war."[19]

The fashion of the age, as Calhoun put it, lay in the direction of the consolidated nation and its more active central government, of finance-industrial capitalism, and of a more democratic social order. The Northeast and gradually the Northwest had caught stride with the emerging Modern World, while the South, with cotton and slavery, had lagged behind. Neither section had deliberately chosen its course. The North had only gradually and reluctantly accepted its new capitalists, its factories, its cities, and its new communications based on steam. Some had questioned whether its wage workers were any better off than the Negro slave. Some had thought the machine was a curse, not a blessing. They had only slowly discovered that the good outweighed the bad and had come to hail it

[19] Butterfield, *History of Human Relations*, p. 21.

all as progress. Only gradually had they brought their old social and moral values into line and to the support of the new day. The crusade against slavery both as an impediment to progress and as a moral blight belonged largely to the last two decades. Even then it was against the so-called Slave Power as a political rival that a working unity was achieved.

The South had more readily accepted the task of supplying the new age with cotton, but it did not deliberately choose between free-white labor and Negro slavery for its cotton fields. It simply took what was at hand in the mad hurry to reap profits. Virgin soils and high cotton prices only gradually silenced the harsh criticism of slavery which, up until the mid-1830's, had found wide and open expression in the Old South. Not until then was slavery called "a positive good" and the idea evolved that it constituted the foundations of a superior society.

Under such conditions, the average Southerner really never had a fair chance to compare the merits of the old order with those of an urban-industrial society. They met the Modern World only as profits in cotton produced by slave labor and as a hostile force to be resisted, not evaluated. Yet, throughout the 1850's, they had shown enough interest in scientific agriculture, the building of factories, and what they called "the mechanic arts," to suggest that under normal conditions, they, too, might in time have known its transforming power.

But the spread of cotton as the South's share in the Modern World meant only the continued dominance of a rural-agricultural interest and a new field for the spread of slavery. It did not require a change of opinion regarding institutions and values. The federal character of our government and the powers granted under the Constitution remained the same. Southerners knew little of the growing interdependence which goes with an urban-industrial society, and which, at the North, was making disunion not only unthinkable but impossible. Southerners were not indifferent to the nation's growth nor were they lacking in loyalty to it. They had simply been driven into a corner where, as a permanent minority, they were forced to defend institutions and values which were no longer valid by appealing to constitutional principles already outgrown.

The futility of it all and the growing certainty of defeat bred a feeling of helplessness, bitterness, and anger. Southerners were right when they said that their institutions and their values were no longer safe in the Union. It was just another way of saying that they were no longer safe in the Modern World.

Northerners, on the other hand, were conscious of their growing superiority in numbers and in material strength. They were impatient of the restraints imposed by southern opposition to tariffs, internal improvements, and homesteads. Their course into the Modern World and the realization of their potentialities were being impeded by a backward South whose notions of government and whose labor system belonged, as Seward said, to the Dark Ages. Progress, Christianity, and democracy all demanded that something be done about it. In the Republican party, they created a means to that end. They had, in fact, created the political agent through which the nation would make its way into the Modern World. It was the vague realization of this fact which permitted the southern states to believe that they faced submission or secession on the perfectly legal election of a Republican President pledged to do them no immediate harm. It was this which reduced all issues to those of *nationalism versus states' rights* and *freedom versus slavery*. Both had to be settled as the price for entering the Modern World. In fact, the most important positive result of the Civil War was to permit the United States, freed of restraints and taught the importance of "plan and control in war days, to enter the age of consolidated nationalism and enlarged freedom."

Now these two issues may have been unsolvable as abstractions this side of war or they may not. No one can say with certainty. But in the light which the John Brown raid throws on the mental distortions of the period, does it not seem intelligent to suggest that when John C. Calhoun asserted that each state was still sovereign, he was dealing in abstractions regarding an issue which the necessities of his own day under steam were already dissolving? When William H. Seward so boldly announced that in forming the Constitution, the "States . . . as States . . . had submitted themselves to the sway of the numerical majority without qualifications or checks," was he too dealing in abstractions, only recently discovered, which unnecessarily added to the fears and apprehensions of the day and which bore little resemblance to statesmanship?

And is it not sound to ask, when the historian assumes that slavery created two social-economic orders so incompatible that one whole section of the nation had to be destroyed in order that the other might live, whether he is not forgetting that three-fourths of those who lived in the slave states held no slaves; that four slave-holding states did not join the Confederacy; and that the real battle against slavery up to the middle of the 1830's was waged in the southern states themselves? It does, indeed, take quite a stretch of imagination to take seriously Lincoln's assertion that the nation was in danger of becoming all slaveholding. And it takes even more imagination to believe the southern assertion that the whole world would again accept slavery as a positive good.

So now that we are a hundred years away from the passions of that day, is there not some sense in asking what might have happened had slavery been dealt with, not just as a *sin* to be immediately given up, but as a national economic problem involving millions of dollars in invested capital, as a social problem carrying with it a race question not yet solved, as a political interest where three-fifths of the slaves were counted as population in determining representation?

We do not know. It was never tried. Instead men faced each other with a growing feeling of self-righteousness, with hurt pride and growing fears and distrust. Each accused the other of aggression. Each believed that the central government had become the tool of an unprincipled foe. Congress became a place where men met to air their grievances and to make speeches intended largely for home consumption. Reformers occupied the seats intended for politicians, if not for statesmen, and the democratic process ceased to apply. In the end, each accepted war as a kind of romantic adventure without the slightest realization of the destructive character of modern warfare. Such men deserve our sympathies, not our apologies.

It was into such an atmosphere that John Brown came to perform his acts of violence with complete confidence of success and wide approval. Since reason had been abandoned, force was the only logical answer. Wise and good men had already proclaimed the higher law which set aside the restraints imposed by courts and legislatures. They had announced an irrepressible conflict which, of course, had to be settled sooner or later. The struggle was now one clearly between good men and bad men, between justice and injustice, between progress and backwardness, between civilizations.

John Brown was, therefore, simply a normal product of an abnormal situation. He may or may not have been insane. That made no difference. He did kill innocent people, and he did attempt to stir up the worst of social disasters—a servile insurrection. He did lead a body of outlaws in the seizure of government property, but none of these things made any difference. The point is that he represented in himself the tragic predicament into which men's minds and relationships had fallen—that narrow line that separates social sanity from surrender to the mad forces of destruction. His raid came only a year before South Carolina, in much the same mood, would take matters into her hands and secede from the Union—only a short span before the legal call for troops to put down insurrection and to plunge the nation into civil war.

It was, therefore, not surprising that the soldier boys who soon marched off to accomplish, in the end, what John Brown attempted, should have found him walking in front of the armies. They sang his song and kept step with his soul as it marched along, gun on shoulder, headed for the front line. Rumor had it that dead men and madmen had seen him standing over many a battlefield, bullets whistling through his shadowy figure, as he wielded a sword whetted sharp on a Bible.

And so I come back to Robert E. Lee and to Douglas Southall Freeman. In concluding his magnificent biography of Lee, three-fourths of which deals with battles and campaigns, Freeman refuses to have "this study of a man who loved peace interpreted as glorification of war." "Each new inquiry," he writes, "has made the monstrous horror of war more unintelligible to me. It has seemed incredible that human beings endowed, with any power of reason, should hypnotize themselves with doctrines of 'national honor' or 'sacred right' and pursue mass murder to exhaustion or ruin. I subscribe with my whole heart to the view of General Lee that 'had forbearance and wisdom been practiced by both sides' the great national tragedy of 1861 might have been prevented."

IX

THE FIRST COLD WAR

Each nation is important to its own people. Some nations, however, occupy a peculiar place in the history of mankind because of the contribution they have made to civilization as a whole. The United States, "conceived in liberty and dedicated to the proposition that all men are created equal," has always thought of itself as earth's great experiment in democracy, and others have generally accepted that estimate.

Back in the 1830's young Alexis de Tocqueville confessed that "in America he saw more than America." As he put it: "I sought the image of democracy itself, with its inclinations, its character, its prejudices, and its passions, in order to learn what we have to fear or to hope from its progress." Sixty years later, Lord Bryce still viewed the United States as "an experiment in the rule of the multitude tried on a scale unprecedently vast, the results of which everyone is concerned to watch." Yet, he added, "they are something more than an experiment, for they are believed to disclose and display the type of institutions towards which, as by a law of fate, the rest of mankind are forced to move, some with swifter, others with slower, but all with unresting feet."

Consciousness of its democratic mission has been a part of the American story from the day when Thomas Jefferson penned the Declaration of Independence to that in the twentieth century when the United States threw its "moral and physical force into the scales of European republicanism," once to help make the world "safe for democracy," and once to advance the "four freedoms."

Yet in less than three generations after Jefferson had written his immortal document, the democratic process in the United States hopelessly failed. Men ceased to discuss their problems in a rational manner, refused to tolerate differences, rejected compromise, and

Reprinted from *Civil War in the Making, 1815–1860* (Baton Rouge: Louisiana State University Press, 1959), pp. 89–115.

defied the will of the majority. Then for four long, bitter, bloody years the armies of one group of Americans battled against the forces of the other, until one was victor and the other lay in ruin and helpless defeat.

There had been physical and social differences in various corners of the United States from the beginning, but these had not prevented the realization of the need for union. There had been issues before the Congress on which there had been sharp disagreement and sometimes harsh words. Yet, in spite of considerable grumbling, compromise or yielding had always been possible. When, however, issues began to involve the matter of right or wrong, of honor and self respect, of equality and rights, then compromise or yielding, or even rational discussion of issues, was no longer possible. To hold to one's position was a matter of principle—something to fight for or even to die for.

The historian's problem is, therefore, as has been said, largely one of trying to find out *how* and *why* issues increasingly tended to get into such abstract shapes that they could not yield to the democratic process; why *right* and *rights* crowded everything else aside. If he accepts Lincoln's statement that the government resorted to the use of force only to save the Union, and the southern insistence that resort to secession was necessary for the protection of their domestic institutions (primarily slavery), then the historian must conclude that the elevation of nationalism to a supreme value on the part of the North and of slavery to an equal value on the part of the South was the work of a single generation. An intense love of the Union and a willingness to accept its acts had not characterized all of the North in the days of the embargo and the War of 1812. The Hartford Convention of 1815 was not exactly an expression of good will toward sister states or the rule of the majority. As an English writer has said: "The mind of New England in this critical period . . . baffles inquiry." Nor, on the other hand, could one charge a section with knowing loyalty only to the state which gave a Washington, a Jefferson, a Madison, a Monroe, a John Marshall, an Andrew Jackson, and a James K. Polk to the cause of nation-building.

The historian must also remember that the harshest attacks on slavery in the 1820's and early 1830's were launched by Virginians, North and South Carolinians, the men of Tennessee and Kentucky.

Everything the most rabid northern abolitionist would later charge against the institution was charged in the legislative halls of these states and backed by antislavery societies, most of which at that time existed in these same states. Slavery, it should be remembered, had existed in the southern states for over two hundred years without becoming a heavy burden on many northern consciences. That too was a recent development.

Something indeed must have happened between 1830 and 1860 which strangely altered the patterns of American thought, pulled North and South apart and instituted a cold war between them. The period is highly complex, and one can hardly hope to explain all that happened or played a part in producing a nation's tragedy. Yet a brief look at some of the forces at work in that period may give a few clues and may serve, as the late Charles A. Beard once said, as "a damn dim candle over a damn dark abyss."

In the decades preceding the Civil War, two great forces were fundamentally altering the lives of men everywhere around the Atlantic Basin. The first of these, the Industrial Revolution, had already brought the factory, mass production, world markets, and the concentration of capital for economic effort to much of western Europe. It had spread to the northeastern corner of the United States and had turned the South into a great cotton field. What we think of as the Modern World was rapidly being created.

The material changes wrought everywhere by the Industrial Revolution require no comment. The term itself is enough to suggest them. But, for our purposes, one profound social change needs emphasis: *The total effect of the Industrial Revolution was vastly to increase the interlocking of human interests and the dependence of man on man.*

With the factory, labor became dependent on capital even for the right to work; capital, in turn, became dependent on machines and the labor to man them. Both became dependent on the producers of the raw materials that went into their product and on the markets which consumed their mass production. Cities grew with industry, but no city could feed itself or consume the goods which its industries produced. They became increasingly dependent on the rural areas for food and most of the other necessities of life. Without widespread markets, they would have perished. Nations which became thoroughly industrialized, as did England by 1845, abandoned their tariffs on foodstuffs and reached out all over the world for markets and raw materials. Mankind was being bound together and made interdependent as never before in all the history of the world. The call for centralized political efficiency in the form of nationalism had never been so loud. No other force had ever worked so insistently to link the interest of individuals in different nations and within nations themselves so closely together.

In the United States the growth of interdependence was as marked as elsewhere. New England textile mills each year took a larger percentage of the southern cotton crop. In return, the South increasingly depended on the North for its plantation supplies. By the 1850's, speakers often referred to New York City as "the prolongation of the South," and in late June and early July her hotels were filled with southern merchants and planters and her newspapers with advertisements addressed to Southerners. They had come for their annual supply of dry goods, hardware, boots and shoes, and other merchandise. J. P. Marshall and Company, Rogers and Company, and Phelps-Dodge and Company had branch houses in New Orleans; some, like Trenholm Brothers, had branches in Charleston, while others, like Daniel Parish and Company, had branches in five different Southern cities.

The planting of the cotton crop was financed by advances made by northern firms and paid for at harvest with drafts on New York banks. It was shipped in northern vessels, insured by northern companies, and handled by northern factors. In fact, as Professor Foner says, "Down to the outbreak of the Civil War, New York dominated every single phase of the cotton trade from plantation to market."

Meanwhile the farmers of the Northwest sent enormous quantities of corn, salt pork, flour, and whiskey down the rivers to southern plantations, and the market gardeners of Virginia, each night, loaded their ships with potatoes, cabbages, fresh vegetables, and berries, according to the season, for the morning markets in Philadelphia, New York, and Boston.

In spite of surface differences and all that historians have said, the most glaring reality of the day was interdependence—the uncomfortable fact that, in an economic sense, this was a single nation—"One World."

The second force, working toward the same end as the first, was the application of steam and electricity to communication. The first gave the railway, the steamship, and the power press. The second gave the telegraph. The effect of both was to cut space and to bring men closer together. Where up until now, the vast spaces of the earth had been conquered by following waterways—the oceans between continents, and the lakes and rivers through continents—the railroad could penetrate great land masses and go wherever human needs dictated. Where before space was covered by the force of wind or animal and human exertion, now the tireless machine took over and began the task of shrinking the nations into convenient size.

The telegraph brought men separated by great distances within a few seconds of each other, and the power press made possible the creation and spread of common ideas from continent to continent and from one end of a given nation to the other. Dr. Channing has even argued: "Modern life in all its branches from day to day, in peace and war, depends on the mobility of men and of things."

The United States, with greater spaces to be covered than any nation save Russia, made the most of these forces in the decade before the Civil War. Railroad-building became a veritable passion as states vied with each other in the piling up of debts. Most of the mileage ran from east to west, but North and South were also joined along the eastern seaboard and from the Gulf to the Great Lakes. Other lines were projected or under construction by 1860 that would have cut diagonally from Charleston to Cincinnati and from Pensacola to New York. The telegraph followed the railway lines, and publishing for national consumption was a reality well before the outbreak of war.

How dependent the sections had become upon each other as producers and markets was strikingly expressed by a speaker at a southern commercial convention in 1855. In a plea for greater home production, he declared: "From the rattle with which the nurse tickles the ear of the child born in the South to the shroud which covers the cold form of the dead, everything comes from the North. We rise from between sheets made in Northern looms, and pillows of Northern feathers, to wash in basins made in the North, dry our beards on Northern towels, and dress ourselves in garments woven in Northern looms; we eat from Northern plates and dishes; our rooms are swept with Northern brooms, our gardens dug with Northern spades and our bread kneaded in trays or dishes of Northern wood or tin; and the very wood which feeds our fires is cut from Northern axes, helved with hickory brought from Connecticut and New York." The picture was balanced by the confident assertion that if the cotton supply were cut off from northern factories or the Mississippi River closed, the economy of the North would fall in ruin.

Again we must insist that the most patent social-economic fact of the period from 1815 to 1860 was the bringing of men closer together and the increase of *interdependence* to the point where the peace and security of all depended on an equal increase of that humility and intelligence and patience which make the democratic process work. Tolerance of differences, rational discussion of problems, and compromise where possible, would be the price men would have to pay for continued piece. No people could insist that their pattern was the one which all must accept. No people, with any grasp on the basic physical-social facts of the age, could have accepted disunion as a rational step. The United States had become an indivisible unit.

Yet the irony in the situation was that, in these very years, two distinct and differing social-economic systems were evolving side by side in the United States. One was predominantly agricultural; in the other, commerce, industry, and finance were increasingly important. The one depended on free-white labor; in the other, by 1860, there were nearly four million Negro slaves.

The Industrial Revolution had played a mean trick on the United States. It had set one part of the nation to producing cotton to feed the hungry machines of Europe and given it a swaggering prosperity such as few Americans had ever known. Yet the spread of cotton and the creation of a new Lower South had not upset old institutions or old values. It only meant the spread of an agriculture based on the continued employment of the plantation system and Negro slave labor. It had not undermined men's reliance on local and state government as Thomas Jefferson and John Taylor of Caroline had said should be the case. It had not weakened the belief in a rural-agricultural way of life as the only sound foundation for democracy and as the producer of those qualities in men designated as "gentle." It had justified in their minds the continued holding of slaves as beneficial to the Negro, to the white man, and to society as a whole.

This, however, was not the whole story. The rapid expansion of an agricultural area for the production of the raw materials needed in industry meant an unbalanced interdependence in which the raw producer moved steadily towards a colonial status. The advantages in the Modern World were all with those who owned the factories and those who controlled finances and marketing. Old World developments had already shown that, and the American South would soon find it out.

And, while the Industrial Revolution was spreading cotton and slavery over the Lower South, it was, as we have seen, also altering another part of the nation—the Northeast—by building factories and factory towns where young girls came from the neighboring countryside to toil, creating great cities with their prosperous merchants and their restless working classes, and spurring on a westward-moving farm population whose families provided the laboring force.

It was a completely new order and way of life, to which not a single existing institution, relationship, or old value applied. Every basic concept and value had to be re-examined. The thinking which had served a society dominated by shipping and agriculture did not meet the needs of the new industrial order. Manufacturers, who were forced to find their raw materials and their markets in all parts of the country, and the merchants and bankers, who marketed and financed both wheat and cotton, were bound to be nationalist in their outlook. And all of them would see the advantages in a strong and active central government to give aid both to industry and transportation. Their hostility to slavery, like that of the farmers of the Northwest, would increase with time and with their advance into the Modern Age.

Here, then, were two rapidly expanding sections whose ways had been strangely widened by the Industrial Revolution. Yet even in a shrinking, interdependent nation, their *economic differences* did not necessarily imply hostility. A region producing raw materials and one engaged in industry may be complements as well as rivals. Slavery, however, was a different matter. It represented two entirely different understandings of the demands of Christianity, of democracy, and of progress. It had to do with things which cannot be compromised. It was not only an integral part of southern social and economic life, but what was far more important, it symbolized the fact that South and North were moving in absolutely opposite directions. The one was holding firmly to the values of the past; the other was rushing madly into the Modern World.

Now the tragedy in this situation lay in the fact that, in the normal struggles for power in a government ruled by majorities, sectional interests became gradually tangled with basic differences and values. Conflicts were thereby lifted to the level of ideologies and civilizations. Men could compromise tariffs, internal improvements, and land programs; they must die for the preservation of their way of life, their ideals, and what they believed to be a civilization.

Said Professor Austin Phelps of Andover Theological Seminary: "Two opposing civilizations are in conflict here, and have been from the infancy of our Union." This was due, as Theodore Parker said, to the fact that:

> The South, in the main, had a very different origin from the North. I think few if any persons settled there for religion's sake; or for the sake of the freedom of the state. It was not a *moral idea* which sent men to Virginia, Georgia, or Carolina. "Men do not gather grapes of thorns." The difference in the seed will appear in the difference of the crop. In the character of the people of North, and South, it appears at this day. . . . Here, now, is the great cause of the difference in the material results, represented in towns and villages, by farms and factories, ships and shops. Here is the cause of differences in the schools and colleges, churches, and in literature; the cause of differences in men. The South with its despotic idea, dishonors labor, but wishes to compromise between its idleness and its appetite, and so kidnaps men to do its work.

The Charleston *Mercury* spoke for the South:

> The North and South are two nations, made by their institutions, customs and habits of thought, as distinct as the English and French; and our annual meetings at Washington are not Congresses to discuss the common interests, but conventions, to contest antagonistic opinions and to proclaim mutual grievances and utter hostile threats.

"No two nations on earth are, or ever were, more distinctly separated and hostile than we are," said Senator J. H. Hammond. "Not Carthage & Rome, England & France at any period." And when war came, the Reverend James H. Thornwell of South Carolina declared:

> The parties in this conflict are not merely abolitionists and slaveholders; they are atheists, socialists, communists, red republicans, jacobins on the one side, and the friends of order and regulated freedom on the other. In one word, the world is the battleground, Christianity and atheism the combatants, and the progress of humanity, the stake.

Coexistence had evidently become a problem. Yet coexistence was rendered difficult if not impossible by the assumption on the part of each that it represented the true American expression as envisaged by the founding fathers and embodied in the Constitution. Neither thought of itself as struggling for something new. Each was defending the old. Each was innocent of wrong; each was confident of virtue. Each firmly believed that the civilization which *it* represented was not only the finest fruit of the American experiment, but the pattern toward which the whole civilized world would one day come.

Northerners were confident that they were in step with progress. They pointed to their cities, their factories, their commerce, their schools, and their literary output, and ascribed them all to the system of free labor. Theirs was a land, as Wendell Phillips boasted, where every man was the founder of his own fortune, where families were reared by the Bible, where education lifted up not only the state but the nation as well, and where industry used every drop of water ten times over before it allowed it to fall into the sea. Statistics were on the northern side; wealth and growth proved the case.

Then with more of vehemence than a desire for accuracy, they pictured the South as they thought it ought to be—backward, tumbledown, ignorant, and immoral. Southern labor was starved and abused. Without the incentive for personal gain, it was inefficient and discontented. Only by force and imposed ignorance was the social-economic system maintained over its own people.

Southerners were just as confident of the superiority of *their* social-economic system. They praised the wholesome agricultural life where a man lived ten hours a day in the open air, rode his high-spirited horse as though he were part of it, followed the foxhounds in spite of fences and ditches, brought down a partridge with each barrel, and, at the close of day, returned to a home "characterized by comfort without luxury, and simplicity without meanness." They boasted of its stability—of the absence of labor conflict, race riots, and wild-eyed "isms." Religion and politics were not mixed there; spirit rappings were not heard; women did not wear bloomers. A boy might go to college there and "never learn, or read a word in school or out of school, inconsistent with orthodox Christianity, pure morality, the right of property, the sacredness of marriage, the obligations of law, the duty of obedience to government." As George

Fitzhugh wrote: "Society has been so quiet and contented in the South,—it has suffered so little from crime or extreme poverty, that its attention has not been awakened to the revolutionary tumults, uproars, mendicity and crime of free society."

As to their much-criticized labor system, they bluntly noted that its workers knew nothing of the ills of unemployment, neglect in time of sickness, and abandonment in old age. They insisted that the worker who always had a plenty of food, clothing, and shelter received a larger share of production than did the average worker elsewhere. Their condemnation of free society was expressed in their boasting. Like the communists and democrats of a later day, both assumed the perfection of their own system largely by pointing out the weaknesses in that of their opponents.

As stationary entities, these two civilizations might have lived together with only a minimum of friction, but in a world of shrinking space and increasing economic interdependence, a power struggle was inevitable. A clash of interests naturally suggested to each self-conscious civilization the desirability of allies and the advantages of expansion. It was this effort to extend political power by the formation of alliances and the creation of satellites that produced a state of fear and tension which, in fact, amounted to a cold war between the sections.

It began when the South attempted to draw the young and growing Northwest into its orbit. That region had received the majority of its early population from the upland South, and its great river system had thrown trade in that direction. Building on these early advantages, southern leaders, by concessions on lands and internal improvements, sought to develop these ties into a permanent political alliance. The famous Webster-Hayne debate was little more than a southern bid for western favor and a northern effort to counteract it. To the building of that alliance, John C. Calhoun gave as much attention as he did to the unification of the South itself, and on its foundations Stephen A. Douglas of Illinois built his political career. Its success gave the South control of the Democratic party and made the Democratic party the dominant political power in the nation.

That was why the Northeast so bitterly opposed the next steps in expansion—the annexation of Texas and the war with Mexico. The whole business, it said, was a proslavery move, an effort to secure more territory for the expansion of a rival system. Joshua Giddings spoke of the conflict "between the interests of free labor and slave labor, between the Northern and Southern states," and declared that the admission of Texas would give "the balance of power" to the southern states and thus enable them to "control the policy and destiny of the nation." Then with a magnificent tangling of material and spiritual values, he wanted to know whether the liberty-loving democrats of the North would be willing to give up their tariffs and their internal improvements in order to profit those who raised children for sale and dealt in the bodies of women.

Quickly the move to admit Texas as a state was countered by a demand for the admission of Oregon. How much this had become a power struggle between hostile systems was shown by the assumption, widely made, that this was a kind of bargain between rivals—a balancing of interests. So when Texas was admitted and Oregon delayed, the cry of betrayal was loud and long. The North, said one, had been "politically bound, hand and foot, and surrendered to the rule and government of a slaveholding oligarchy."

Northern bitterness over the Mexican War was even more intense. Many viewed it as a war of aggression fought to "lug new slave states in." Senator Thomas Corwin of Ohio called it "wanton, unprovoked, unnecessary, and therefore, unjust." Charles Sumner referred to the American army as "a legalized band of brigands, marauders, and banditti [fighting] against the sanctions of civilization, justice, and humanity." He hoped it would be defeated and be forced "to pass submissively through the Claudine Forks of Mexican power,—to perish . . . like the legions of Varus."

The abrupt ending of the Mexican War and the acquiring of a vast new empire to the southwest only widened the terrain on which the cold war was being fought. The North made its move even before the war ended, to bar the extension of slavery from any territory acquired from Mexico. The South answered with threats of secession if denied equal rights in territory won by common blood. Tempers grew short; reasonableness even shorter. Congress became the meeting place of angry, defiant partisans. The press was given over to abuse and distortion. Each charged the other with aggression. Each insisted that its opponent was carrying forward a program of encirclement aimed at the ultimate destruction of its civilization. Vishinsky or Molotov or Dulles could not have conjured up a darker picture!

Fortunately, in 1850 such old master politicians as Henry Clay, Daniel Webster, Alexander H. Stephens, and Stephen A. Douglas were able to push abstractions aside and get back to the concrete problems of California, Texas, and fugitive slaves. They found that men could still deal with concrete problems in a rational way and that compromise was possible. They kept the democratic process working.

The larger result, however, was only to increase distrust and to turn Congress, the only common meeting ground, into a place where more bitterness and hostility could be expressed. There, where "the windowless walls" shut out "all air, all light, all reality," personalities reacted to other personalities, and speakers labored under the illusion that they expressed the emotions and attitudes of the masses far removed and quite unconscious of the irritations and excitement produced by personal contacts. Thus, much that was artificial, immediate, and personal was translated into sectional hatred and impressions given of the masses that had only to do with individuals. Political parties meanwhile splintered and went to pieces. The old Whig party died. Moves toward the creation of strictly sectional parties began to appear. Only the weakened and slowly disintegrating Democratic party made any pretense of being national in its appeal.

To save and bolster this last political prop of the democratic process, Stephen A. Douglas attempted to revive the old Northwest-Southern alliance. He would win the Northwest with internal improvements based on railroad building and the South, by leaving the question of slavery in new territories to the settlers themselves. He succeeded only in revitalizing the cold war. Excited partisans accepted his proposal to leave the question of slavery to the settlers as an invitation to fight for control. "Come on, then, gentlemen of the slave states," cried William H. Seward. "I accept [your challenge] . . . in behalf of the cause of freedom. We will engage in competition for the virgin soil of Kansas, and God give the victory to the side which is stronger in numbers as it is in right." "We must send men to Kansas, ready . . . and able to meet abolitionism on its own issue, and with its own weapons," answered the Charleston *Mercury*. Like President Truman a century later in Korea, or the Russians in Egypt or Syria, both were ready "to assist free peoples to work out their own destinies in their own way."

The frightening thing about the national situation in the next few years, as Kansas bled and political parties disintegrated, was the steady growth of distrust and fears and hatred. Social and intellectual contacts between North and South were sharply curtailed, and a kind of iron curtain hung between them. Every northern traveler who crossed Mason and Dixon's line was viewed as a possible abolitionist. Northern teachers and northern peddlers were seized and driven out. Waves of panic swept the section as rumors of slave insurrections, stirred by outsiders, spread from neighborhood to neighborhood. Tar and feathers were applied indiscriminately, and suspicion was the same as conviction.

Then with equal zeal they turned on northern books, periodicals, and schools and set about creating a southern brand of each. Bitterly they denounced anyone who "preferred the trashy stuff of Boston, Cincinnati and New York, to the pure, healthful, home-made productions of Southern pens." In a few cases they actually engaged in "book burning." They called their sons home from northern schools where, they charged, young men imbibed "doctrines subversive to all old doctrines." They asked that only native teachers "born to the manor" should be employed and that they should be supplied with textbooks which inspired faith in southern institutions and inculcated southern patriotism. They urged Southerners to boycott northern summer resorts and to confine travel to places friendly to the South. They would, if you please, seal the southern mind against outside influences and mold it to an acceptance of the superiority of all things southern.

Witch hunting among their own people naturally followed. Persons with liberal opinions fell under suspicion. A few college professors lost their jobs; others chose to resign and cross the border to the north. One of them fired a parting shot that has a modern ring: "You may eliminate all the suspicious men from your institutions of learning, you may establish any number of new colleges which will relieve you of sending your sons to free institutions. But as long as people study, and read, and think among you, the absurdity of your system will be discovered and there will always be found some courageous intelligence to protest against your hateful tyranny." He was right, but the protests of the few did not save the section from that deadly intellectual miasma which comes from the irresponsible broadcasting of suspicion.

On the other side of this iron curtain it was not necessary to exercise caution. Few Northerners had ever read anything written in the South, and the works of Fitzhugh, Holmes, and Hughes were scarcely noticed. Few Northerners had traveled across Mason and Dixon's line, and the few who did, returned to give so dismal a picture that few cared to follow. The only slaves known to the North were runaways or a fictitious one by the name of Uncle Tom, who at least had a cabin. Some did go to the trouble of burning the Constitution because it protected southern interests, and there were a few cases of persecution for the defending of southern ways. But on the whole, men felt safe and confident that all was on their side.

With these developments, the idea of two civilizations locked in deadly conflict reached its climax. The struggle was now entirely on the high ground of principle. Each party thought of itself as struggling to preserve "the last best hope of mankind." Each was convinced that it stood on the defensive against unprincipled aggression. It was useless to argue with such people; it was impossible to reason. Armories began to be built, funds appropriated for arms, and military companies organized. Strength alone could give protection.

But making oneself strong did not, they said, mean war. The ability to use force was the surest guarantee of peace. "You have only to put the government in a position to make itself respected," said Senator Trumbull, "and it will command respect." Build up the nation's arms, urged the Chicago *Tribune*, and "thousands of bullies . . . [will] become as mild as so many sucking doves." "The national government may have to *show* its teeth," echoed the New York *Tribune*, "but it is not at all likely that it will have to *use* them." Sound preparation to use force was the best way to insure peace.

It was, therefore, inevitable in such an atmosphere that the extremist (perhaps we should call him the abstract idealist) should have appeared with his doctrine that the end justifies the necessary means. Bearing letters of marque from God, his patience exhausted by delay, he was ready to accept personal responsibility for a people's failure to meet their obligations to mankind. He was certain that the only language the opponent could understand was that of force. He was willing to risk war if that were the price for setting the world in order.

It seems strange that men who were convinced that the opposing civilization carried within itself the seeds of its own destruction should not have been willing to wait patiently for nature to do its work. Middle-of-the-road men were playing for time to compromise. Seward was convinced that the border states were, day by day, drawing away from the South and toward freedom. Fitzhugh was equally certain that the turmoil and strife inherent in a free society would soon destroy the whole edifice. "Towards slavery," he said, "the North and all Western Europe are unconsciously marching."

But patience is not a characteristic of the extremist. Innocence and virtue excuse him from obedience to objectionable laws and endow him with the privilege of righteous indignation. So when the democratic process ceased to function and moderate men stood helpless before the mounting fears and hatred and anger of both sides, the Yanceys, the Rhetts, the Charles Sumners, the John Browns, and their "fellow-travelers" had their chance. Their eyes had seen the glory of the coming of the Lord, and with their help He would trample out the vintage where the grapes of wrath were stored. Out in Kansas, on the floors of the Senate, at the party conventions, at Harper's Ferry, they translated the threats and challenges of a generation into action. They made war inevitable. They forced a nation to use the most undemocratic method known in order to save the democratic values. They caused the defenders of one social-economic system to strike with the air of righteous crusaders for independent existence so that they might preserve what they believed was the only sound democratic order. They caused the defenders of the rival social-economic system to fight for four long bitter years for the preservation of a Union which was worth saving, said its great spokesman, because it represented earth's great experiment in government of the people, by the people, for the people.

And besides, said a spokesman for the new business interests: "We cannot afford to have established on this continent the intolerable restrictions to commercial intercourse, which are fast dying out among the nations of Europe."

X

THE FATAL PREDICAMENT

"In any civil war the question of war guilt is of the deepest importance." A feeling of self-righteousness and a firm belief in the depravity of the enemy builds morale in war days and helps to justify the heavy cost when the struggle is ended. Thereafter the victor may glory in the triumph of truth and righteousness; the defeated may find consolation in having fought nobly for a noble cause.

Since both sides invariably call legality, morality, and tradition to their assistance, the historian, even a hundred years later, still feels the pressure of emotions generated. The debate seemingly never ends, and that calm objectivity which permits a feeling of sorrow for a whole people who drifted into a situation where only bloodshed would serve is long in coming. Yet when a united nation expects the descendants of both victor and vanquished to join in a centennial celebration of such a civil war, about the only permanent good that can be hoped for is the hastening of such an attitude. Little of national value can result from the re-enactment of battles as romantic episodes devoid of all the horrors of death and destruction or from the recounting of events cast in the pattern of good men facing bad men and truth opposing error. Nations do not learn wisdom from such things.

It is for this reason that the historian might better stress the blindness, the blundering, and the helplessness of men on the eve of the American Civil War and deal with it as a national tragedy, not as a romantic museum piece—as something to regret and to gain a lesson from, not as something to glorify.

If we must have a simple statement of how this civil war came about, we need only to remember that a sectional controversy changed from words to action when eleven southern states, one by

Reprinted from *Politics and the Crisis of 1860,* ed. Norman A. Graebner (Urbana: University of Illinois Press, 1961), pp. 122–41.

one, attempted to withdraw from the Union, and the administration in Washington refused to allow them to do so. Each side then revealed the depths of its feelings and the uncompromisable character of their disagreement by a willingness to go to war in defense of the position taken. That turned the struggle into one of preserving the Union on the one side, and of defending the legal rights of a state on the other. It simplified the complex differences which, for decades, had been driving the sections apart and reduced them to a conflict of principles. Each position had value in stirring men to fight for "the right" and in throwing war guilt onto the other.

But such an approach, although it served well the purposes of the moment, is of little value to the historian. Secession and northern resistance to it were merely the final stages in a situation that had long been developing. The really fundamental questions as to why the southern states insisted on leaving the Union and why the northern states would not permit them to go, are left unanswered. It does not tell why men who had so recently united in forming "a more perfect union" now thought of themselves as two distinct peoples, hating each other with "a Carthaginian hatred." Few men in either North or South could have answered those questions. Nor have the historians of succeeding years been able to do so in a satisfactory way.

In order to justify secession, most of the southern states did attempt statements of grievances. These were made as much to convince their own reluctant citizens as to satisfy the outside world. They, therefore, dealt primarily with those immediate abuses and threats which would have the greatest emotional appeal. Underlying factors were largely ignored. Yet these statements did reveal the final patterns into which all differences had been cast—the symbols which covered and took the place of details.

South Carolina led off with an elaborate assertion of the federal-compact character of the American government which permitted withdrawal when one party did not live up to its obligations. The stipulation to return fugitive slaves, they said, had been written into the Constitution and this compact would not have been made without it. Yet northern states had openly refused to live up to their obligations. They had passed laws which nullified the acts of Congress or "rendered useless any attempt to exercise them." Some states had refused to surrender to justice those who had incited servile insurrections. All of them had denounced the southern domestic institution of slavery as sinful and had now "united in the election of a man to the high office of President of the United States whose opinions and purposes were hostile to slavery" and to its future expansion. Public opinion "at the North" had thus "invested a great political error with the sanction of a more erroneous religious belief."

The other seceding states of the lower South followed this same line of defense. They varied their statements to fit local conditions but stressed the threat to domestic institutions and their inability to protect themselves longer. Georgians, for example, spoke of "the feeling of insecurity" among the people who had become a permanent minority and of the "imminent peril" of "being in the power of a majority reckless of Constitutional obligations and pledged to principles leading to our destruction." They, too, pointed as proof to the refusal to surrender fugitive slaves. Alabama saw Lincoln's election as the triumph of a sectional party "hostile to the domestic institutions and to the peace and security" of the state. It was "a political wrong of so insulting and menacing a character as to justify secession." Mississippi declared herself to be "so identified with the institution of slavery" that she had no choice left but submission to the mandates of abolition, or a dissolution of the Union. Hostility to slavery had trampled underfoot "the original equality of the South," denied her the right of expansion, nullified the Fugitive Slave Law, and destroyed the compact made by the Founding Fathers. Secession was "not a matter of choice but of necessity." Texas, somewhat more concerned with the way Southerners had been excluded from the territories, ascribed it all to a northern desire to gain control of "the common government, to use it as a means of destroying the institutions of Texas and her sister slave-holding states." She also complained of the lack of federal protection, of the acts against the returning of fugitives, and of the final reduction of the South "to a hopeless minority."

It is thus apparent that slavery, its protection, its expansion, and even its moral standing, had become the symbol of northern aggression and of southern rights. Even the reforms sometimes suggested by the conservative opposition in these states dealt almost exclusively with the protection of slavery.

The border states had additional reasons for action. The pathetic and indignant statements that came from their conventions carry a note of betrayal and of bitterness at Lincoln's call for troops to put down rebellion. They needed only to say that up until now they had remained in the Union "loyally discharging all their duties under the Constitution, in the hope that what was threatening in public affairs might yield to the united efforts of patriotic men from every part of the nation, and by these efforts such guarantees for the security of our rights might be obtained as should restore confidence, renew alienated ties, and finally reunite all the states in a common bond of fraternal union. . . ." They now found their ports blockaded, their soil threatened with invasion, and their help demanded in waging "a cruel war." They had no alternative to secession.

Now the interesting thing about the reasons given by the southern states for leaving the Union in 1860 and 1861 is the almost total absence of concrete and specific cases of injury other than those relating to fugitive slaves. Emphasis is almost exclusively on such intangibles as the violation of assumed constitutional rights, on unjust criticisms of southern institutions, and on apprehensions of dangers yet to come. Indignation, hurt pride, and stark fear are revealed in every line. The haunting prospect of inequality, perhaps even of inferiority, is strikingly apparent.

In other words, a careful appraisal of southern complaints offered in 1860 leaves much to be explained. There is too wide a gap between the emotional reactions and the actual damage done. Either the Southerners were not justified in taking the extreme step or, somehow, they had come to know that they stood helpless before an all-destroying force. Even in the matter of fugitive slaves the historian finds an element of uncertainty regarding the actual damage suffered. Only a very small percentage of those held in bondage ever became permanent runaways, and there is absolutely no way of knowing how many of these few crossed Mason and Dixon's line. Information in this field is scanty and much of it unreliable. Southerners exaggerated their losses for propaganda purposes, and abolitionists, in old age, remembered their aid to fugitives through the magnifying haze of time. At any rate, the United States Census found only 0.0003 per cent of all slaves to have been fugitives in 1850. Unquestionably the great majority of these never left the South. Few of them had run away because of Northern influence.

This figure is probably as unreliable as are others. But it does show that material losses did not disturb the South half as much as did the clearly revealed fact that neither the Constitution nor the laws of Congress could longer protect the South in its right to the return of fugitive slaves. There were limits beyond which northern consciences would not go.

A closer look at the territorial issue is also revealing. Ever since the late 1840's the chief southern complaints against the North had been the denial of equal access to the territories. This had brought threats of secession and had precipitated a serious national crisis in 1850. "Wilmot Proviso" and "California" had become fighting words, as had "Kansas" and "Lecompton Constitution" a few years later. Yet in the statements made in 1860 there were only vague and scattered references to the territories. Even in these, the emphasis was on the fact that the South had been denied equality and not on the loss of territory. The reasons for this were simple. There had not been, in the first place, any particular need for the expansion of slavery, and few intelligent Southerners had thought the existing territories fitted for it anyway. They had fought for a principle. Now, in 1860, it was perfectly clear that the people themselves in both California and Kansas, by the normal process of permanent settlement, had made the decision for freedom. It had not been the work of any administration or of any one politician or any one party. Time had taken care of the issue.

In the case of Kansas, for instance, editors all over the South, by 1858, were declaring themselves "heartily tired of seeing the word Kansas" and were convinced that "the question of slavery had been settled by the parties in that territory." As one conservative Southerner wrote: "It is certainly a small matter of gain to the South to have Kansas come in with a slave Constitution, & so to remain *only* until the Legislature can convene & call a Convention that will immediately assemble and, infuriated with a slavery constitution being forced on them, will abolish slavery without reference to the interests of slave owners. . . ." "We have long looked upon the fate of Kansas as sealed," wrote a South Carolina editor, "and have been frequently amused at the strenuous efforts which Southern politicians make, not to secure the territory to the South, but to be cheated out of it according to the letter of the law." He even defended Douglas because Douglas had done only what he had to do if he were to continue in public office. "The South," he added, "is too ready to find solace for her misfortunes in abusing those who will not cut their throats to save her."

The very use of the term "misfortunes" as well as the fair understanding of Douglas' situation shows that one South Carolinian, at least, understood that both the men of the North and of the South were in a sad predicament—the victims of circumstances. Evidently, he understood that the territorial issue was only a surface expression of a more fundamental clash.

Nor is the southern charge of a northern conspiracy in the triumph of a sectional party very convincing. It is true, of course, that the Republican party was a sectional party and that it had achieved formal organization with the passage of the Kansas-Nebraska Act. Its immediate stated purpose was to resist the spread of slavery into the territories, but powerful political parties are not born on the spur of the moment. The Republican party had been long in the making, and Kansas was only the immediate occasion for its emergence.

The same forces which had destroyed the Whig party and which had brought the Liberty and the Free Soil parties into being; the same conditions which had created the notion that there was a slave power operating in political life and that southern policies stood across the path of progress and the realization of the material possibilities of both Northeast and Northwest—these were the real forces that created the unfounded fear that Kansas might become a slave state and hurried forward the formation of the Republican party. Back of this, however, lay the perfectly apparent need for a new political party representing the interests of the expanding North as an industrial society and as a land of freedom.

We are not questioning the sincerity of northern attitudes regarding the moral weaknesses of slavery when we insist that industrial capitalism and consolidated nationalism were not compatible with southern political dominance; we are not denying the ingrained democratic values of northern men when we say that they also wanted tariffs, sound credit policies, river and harbor improvements, and homesteads. We are not saying that men live by bread alone when we point to the simple truth that the Republican party was the carrier not only of men's values, but of their interests as well. As such, it had to be a sectional party, but it was not less so than southern demands at Charleston in 1860 would have made the

Democratic party. Southerners could justly grumble against the working of fate, but they could not fairly ascribe Lincoln's election to northern intrigue.

William A. Graham of North Carolina saw the situation clearly:

> Our government is not an elected monarchy but a representative republic. High as this office [the presidency] may be supposed to exalt the man, he is at last but the servant of the people, and clothed only with powers to do good. If these powers are perverted to our injury and oppression, resistance will be made with united hearts, and with the hope of success; but who can prepare a declaration of independence, appealing to a candid world for its approbation and sympathy, upon the ground that we have been outvoted in an election, in which we took the chance of success, and a candidate has been elected, who, however obnoxious, we did not deem unworthy to compete with for votes? . . . Let us not injure a cause capable of the best defense, and admitted to be imperiled, by taking council of passion, not of wisdom.

But regardless of the soundness or the unsoundness of other southern complaints, the attack on slavery as a sin to be confessed and abandoned at once was an entirely different matter. Slavery had been an integral part of Southern life for at least two hundred years. Its people had often viewed it as a misfortune but never as a sin. Their clergy had defended it, and the scriptures had been a favorite source for defense. Southerners were not ready to confess moral inferiority. So to hear a United States senator speak of "the whole slave-holding class as a combination of ruffianism and bluster, whiskey-drinking and tobacco-chewing" and to be "held up to the gaze of an eager world as slave drivers, lost to humanity and accursed of God" was adding insult to injury.

Nor could Southerners view the sudden abandonment of slavery as so simple a matter as did the northern reformers. The Negro slave constituted the laboring force of the plantation and the domestic servant in the home. As property, he represented millions of dollars of invested capital, and Professor Thomas R. Dew had long ago warned the section that emancipation would wreck its economy and plunge it into bankruptcy.

The social threat was even greater. The presence of three and a half million Negroes held in bondage presented, at all times, a serious race question. Agitation, even without action, was a danger. The immediate ending of all slavery controls, even for moral reasons, meant social chaos. As the Charleston *Mercury* said, the Southerner was not left to speculate in order to know "the fate of white men in a community of liberated negroes." "Where are the white non-slaveholders of Haiti?" he asked, and then answered, "Slaughtered or driven out of that grand paradise of abolitionism."

> Suppose the object of the Northern abolitionists then accomplished . . . a strife will arise between the white men who remain . . . and the negroes, compared to which the atrocities and crimes of ordinary wars, are peace itself. The midnight glare of the incendiary's torch will illuminate the country from one end to the other; while pillage, violence, murder, poisons and rape will fill the air with the demoniac revelry of all the passions of an ignorant, semi-barbarous race, urged to madness by the licentious teachings of our Northern brethren. A war of races—a war of extirmination—must arise, like that which took place in St. Domingo. . . . The people of the Northern states cannot, or will not, understand this state of things. . . . The doom they are ready to visit upon the poor white man of the South, they would not dare propose to the white laborers of the North.

All this, of course, had to do mainly with anticipated troubles, not always with aggressions already committed. It does, however, confirm the truth of Judah P. Benjamin's statement that it was not so much what the Republicans and abolitionists had done or might do that counted as it was "the things they said" and the assumption of moral superiority with which they were said. Because they were "sinners," Southerners were being asked to accept a violent socioeconomic revolution by men who assumed that "the Earth belongs to the Saints and that they are the Saints of the Lord" and who would in no way be inconvenienced by the violence.

The good clergyman who offered prayer at the opening of the Mississippi convention added a deeper reason for southern action. After jogging the Lord's memory of "the maligned and mighty agencies which many of the sister states of this great national family have employed for our annoyance, reproach and overthrow, as equals in the Confederated Union," he called attention especially to the purpose pursued "of depriving us of our just rights, and destroying in our midst the institution which Thy Providence has solemnly bound us to uphold, defend, and protect." They too had moral obligations!

With Lincoln's election, the southern states, one after the other, held their conventions and declared themselves out of the Union. They talked of "submission or secession" as an effort to escape further northern aggression, but as a matter of cold fact, they were protesting against the loss of status. Their equality as a section was gone. Economically, they had been reduced to colonial dependence. Socially, their domestic institutions, once accepted, were under condemnation throughout the Western world. Politically, they were a permanent minority.

They were right when they charged that their way of life was no longer safe in the Union. Even their constitutional rights were no longer secure where men talked of a "higher law." They were wrong only in placing the blame too largely in the wrong place. Northerners had provided the irritations; they had flung the bitter facts into southern faces, they had waged an unceasing war on slavery and condemned it to ultimate extinction, but their real offense was that they had become the allies of the true culprit—the Modern World of nationalism, the Industrial Revolution, and freedom.

In this latter fact also lay the basic reasons for northern refusal to allow the southern states to break up the Union and to depart in peace. It was this which gave them the unwarranted feeling of self-righteousness. They themselves had not always been such ardent nationalists. There had been among them many who had been openly disloyal during both the War of 1812 and the Mexican War. These had hoped for American defeat and had talked of secession. Thirteen northern members of Congress had signed a declaration saying that the annexation of Texas would justify a dissolution of the Union. State after state had passed their personal-liberty laws in open defiance of the Constitution and the laws of Congress, and a few had made a bonfire out of that document. The Wisconsin legislature, in 1859, had gone so far as to resolve that the federal government was not the final judge of the powers delegated to it.

Even in 1860, there were men in almost every northern state who defended the right of secession. A Rhode Island editor declared that "even a single state . . . may with dignity gather her full robes of majesty about her and leave the confederacy which has already left her." He asserted that the "right of secession" was "the right [of a state] to keep itself intact from encroachment or annihilation." An Ohio editor bluntly stated that "if South Carolina wants to go out of the Union, she has a right to do so," and another frankly expressed the opinion "that any state of the confederation has, or at least ought to have, a perfect and undoubted right to withdraw from the Union. . . ." It was "one of the 'reserved rights' of the States." A New Hampshire editor went so far as to say that northern Democrats would not aid the Republicans in conquering the South. "If they have courage to undertake the task, they will have to undertake it alone, and when they march down to subdue the South, they will have a fire in the rear which will not add either to the pleasure or the success of their enterprise." In other words, northern love of the Union, like the southern distrust of it, had been a growth under changing conditions. They had only recently been ready to fight for its preservation.

There were, of course, some sound economic reasons for opposing secession. Men of the Northwest saw a threat to their trade. "Are these men fools?" asked Edward Bates. "Do they flatter themselves with the foolish thought that we of the upper Mississippi will ever submit to have the mouth of our river held by a foreign power, whether friend or foe? Do they not know that that is a fighting question, and not fit to be debated?"

Other Westerners saw their section "hemmed in, isolated, cut off from the seaboard on every side," and gradually sinking "into a pastoral state." Peaceful secession was out of the question.

Industrial and commercial centers also understood clearly that they were dependent on the nation as a whole both for markets and for raw materials in this day of mass production. As a northern businessman said: "We cannot afford to have established on this continent the intolerable restrictions to commercial intercourse, which are fast dying out among the nations of Europe."

Economic interests, however, do not adequately explain northern attitudes. A few, at first, talked of letting the erring sisters go, but when the reality of a divided nation had to be faced, a quick reaction followed. They discovered that they had become nationalists; that there had grown up among them a firm conviction that the United States was indivisible and that it had a manifest destiny to fulfill; that something which belonged to all Americans, North and South alike, was being threatened—an intangible, spiritual something, which gave America its meaning and in which God himself had an interest. They owed it to mankind to resist the destruction of democratic government, man's last best hope.

Such sentiments, however, needed a firm foundation on which to rest. The census gave swaggering evidence of wide material growth and of the superiority of a society where cities, factories, and commerce held sway. The North was in step with progress. It might have taken even more rapid strides had not the South opposed. But what they had accomplished was enough to silence the criticism only recently hurled at their new industrial capitalists, and to quiet the fears which machinery had stirred.

A feeling of moral superiority was also justified by the near-unanimous opposition to the further spread of slavery. Even the politician was calling slavery a relic of the Dark Ages and a blot on the national escutcheon. The contempt for the abolitionist, once almost as common, had given way to the conviction that slavery must be put on the road to ultimate extinction. The nation could not endure half free and half slave. Republicans, at least, had enlisted for the duration. They had no olive branches to offer the South. As one wrote:

> We cannot tell Mr. Yancy that we do not believe slavery wrong, for the reverse is the profound conviction of three fourths of the whole North, all parties included. This conviction takes its birth in the best instincts of our nature and is fortified by the principles of Christianity, the chief preachers of all ages and countries, by the teachings of legal writers, by the inspirations of poetry, by the laws of civilization. The belief that slavery is wrong is as firmly settled in the minds and hearts of the people as any article of their religious creed. It would be dishonest to say that this conviction will not remain and grow stronger every day.

Nor could he truthfully say that fugitive slaves would ever be returned. Even if the personal-liberty laws should be repealed, "the sentiments, movements, tendencies, principles and moral and economic laws" would remain unchanged. The South was asking for "an impossible revolution in the moral and political convictions" of northern men, and to say that slavery could live without such a revolution was to tell another falsehood.

"Then," he continued, "if these things are so, to assure the secessionists that slavery shall be protected and made perpetual, and that it shall be extended and recognized as a controlling power in the Union, and that all opposition to it shall cease, would be to tell a base lie and a very foolish lie. As well promise them that water shall run uphill and two and two shall make five."

Thus nationalism, progress, and a truer democracy had united in what was becoming a sectional crusade, a consciousness of a mission. One day it would find its battle song in a strange tangling of "the coming of the Lord" and the body of poor old John Brown.

Thus, in 1860–61, men of the North and of the South, each clothed in the armor of a just cause, saw no alternative to civil war. Differences had been reduced to the merits or the lack of them in Negro slavery and lifted to the level of a conflict between civilizations. Yet neither section had come to its present position through deliberate choice. The South had been reduced to the sad necessity of breaking up what Robert E. Lee called "a government inaugurated by the blood & wisdom of our patriotic fathers," and the North had been forced into the necessity of fighting to prevent it, by the despotic decrees of the emerging Modern World.

This was the culprit which had steadily pushed the sections apart and given them conflicting values. It had been responsible for the supposed injustices on the one side and the equally unjustified self-righteousness on the other. It had led the one slowly to accept consolidated nationalism, the other to fall back on states' rights; the one to accept the superiority of industrial capitalism, the other to extol the virtues of things rural-agricultural; the one to become the champion of freedom, the other to cling to slavery.

The North had only gradually and reluctantly accepted its new capitalists, its factories, its cities, and its new communications based on steam. It had only slowly learned that the good outweighed the bad and to hail it all as progress. Only gradually had it brought its old social and moral values into line and to the support of the new day. The crusade against slavery both as an impediment to progress and as a moral blight belonged largely to the last two decades.

The South had more readily accepted the task of supplying the new age with its cotton, but it did not deliberately choose between free-white labor and Negro slaves for its cotton fields. It simply took what was at hand in the mad hurry to reap profits. Virgin soils and high cotton prices only gradually silenced the harsh criticism of slavery which, up until the mid-1830's, had found wide and open expression in the Old South. Not until then was slavery called "a positive good" and the idea evolved that it constituted the foundations of a superior society.

Under such circumstances, the average Southerner really never had a fair chance to compare the merits of the old order with those of the Modern World. He met that world only as a market for cotton produced by slave labor or as a hostile force to be resisted, not evaluated. Yet, throughout the 1850's southern men had shown enough interest in scientific agriculture, in the building of factories, and in "the mechanic arts as the arm of civilization" to suggest that, under normal conditions, they too, in time, might have known its transforming power.

Nor did those Southerners who loved the Union and were opposed to secession ever have a fair and equal chance. Three-fourths of all those who lived at the South held no slaves and had no part in plantation life. They had shamed the North in their support of the nation at war with Mexico. They unquestionably constituted a majority in 1860. Their votes indicated as much. Yet majorities amounted to little in a period when fears, injured pride, anger, threats, and self-righteousness were involved. Under such conditions, the rabid few with emotion on their side, and with the chance to charge disloyalty, timidity, and subservience, had all the advantage. Aided by the uncompromising and haughty attitudes of Northern radicals, they reduced the majority first to silence and then to impotence. Soon the moderates found themselves moving with the tide and accepting what they knew to be disaster. We may not excuse them for their failure to act, but we can, at least, understand their feeling of helplessness in the face of what seemed a driving force against which resistance had all along appeared hopeless. Any assurance offered them now would indeed have seemed to be what the honest Northerner had admitted—only "base and very foolish lies."

It thus would seem that those who live a hundred years later—when the bulldozers and the factories of the Modern World are threatening to wipe out the last vestiges of the Old South, when the release of a new energy is rendering extreme nationalism a bit obsolete, and when capitalism has been modified and socialized almost beyond recognition—might begin to see the sad predicament into which the Americans of 1860 had been cast by circumstances not of their own choosing or creation, and to feel sorrow for a whole people who could not avoid a bloody civil war. They might know the futility of seeking out war guilt, more clearly understand that "the world do move" and that those who do not catch stride with progress are in danger of being run over. They could then see that the old and ever present problem of a just balance between local freedom and central efficiency cannot be solved by force—even by civil war—but must be sought in a wise and tolerant statesmanship.

XI

THE PRICE OF UNION

The historian's job is to find order in a disorderly world.[1] He must seek out the threads, whether they exist or not, which tie events together in a somewhat meaningful way. He must show that there is some sense in what has occurred—some progress or some decline, some relationship between events which rescues them from mere chaos. In his hands well-arranged causes produce inevitable and, therefore, just results. The human mind requires this for its sanity, and the historian must assume the responsibility and provide the assurance that we live in a rational universe.

This is what is meant by the lessons which history teaches. This is what makes history a profession. This is why we must forever be rewriting and reinterpreting our history and why what one generation has done with history is inadequate for the needs of the next. One age may wish to see the hand of God in all that has happened; another that economic forces have determined the course of human affairs; a third may wish to be shown that society is forever evolving from patterns simple to those more complex. But whatever the demand, the historian has at all times been adequate. The past in his hands makes sense. When he has finished arranging and interpreting events, this is, in spite of all its confusion and contradictions, an orderly world. Men and nations have gotten their just deserts.

With this understanding of the historian's task in mind, it is not surprising that the American Civil War has been seen as an "irrepressible conflict." Some have viewed it, as did Abraham Lincoln, in terms of "the eternal struggle between *right* and *wrong*." It was waged to save the Union, and the Union was worth saving because it was man's great experiment in democracy and because human

Reprinted from the *Journal of Southern History,* XVIII (1952), 3–19.

[1] This paper was presented as the presidential address before the Southern Historical Association at Montgomery, Alabama, on November 9, 1951.

slavery had no place in such an undertaking. Others have described it as an inevitable struggle between agriculture and industry for the shaping of a nation's economic destiny. They have seen two opposing ways of life, amounting to civilizations, in a predestined struggle for existence. Still others, with states' rights in mind, have insisted that it primarily involved the emergence of nationalism over and against the hindering forces of provincialism. But regardless of differing interpretations, *all* have understood that *progress* was at stake, a more just and equitable social order in the balance, and that victory ultimately rested on the side of justice and soundness. In this way a nation's conscience has been soothed to accept four bloody years of battle and ten years of civil enslavement as necessary and beneficial steps towards a sounder future.

Yet regardless of what historians have thought and said about the causes of the Civil War, the fact remains that the victory of northern arms over the Confederate States of America meant the triumph of one section over another; of one set of economic forces over a rival set of economic forces; of one type of social values over another; and of one set of political ideas and one party organization over those which had been in opposition. Regardless of the part which slavery and states' rights may have played in *producing* the war, its most significant and lasting result was the free and unhampered emergence of a new America—an America with a strangely different temper and spirit from the old, with a new set of values and with new dominating interests. Freed from southern restraint, the nation rushed forward into the Gilded Age, the era of Robber Barons, the day of Big Business and bigger depressions. To put it more bluntly, the values and interests of the Northeast, as evolved under industry and finance on a Puritan background, took charge to shape and direct the course of the United States into the Modern World.

Against just such an outcome in values and interests, the South as a section had long contended and, in the end, had risked her very existence. She had been able until now to force something of economic balance in national life, to retain the respectability of certain rural social values, and to hold in check the drift towards consolidation in federal government. Unfortunately she permitted the slavery struggle to obscure these facts. That was a fatal blunder.

It is probably true that Negro slavery was the fundamental factor in producing the American Civil War, and it is probably safe to make the assertion that if there had been no such thing as slavery, civil war might have been avoided. But when one talks this way he must understand that, by 1860, slavery had become the symbol and carrier of *all* sectional differences and conflicts. Because of its moral and social implications, it supplied the emotional force necessary for both attack and defense. It produced those fighting terms, "The Abolition Crusade" and "The Slave Power." It colored every issue and often hid the more basic issues behind the words "right" and "rights." As William H. Seward said: "Every question, political, civil, or ecclesiastical, however foreign to the subject of slavery, brings up slavery as an incident, and the incident supplants the principal question. We hear of nothing but slavery, and we can talk of nothing but slavery."

To the Northeast and, after 1854, to the Northwest, slavery became the sole reason for southern opposition to tariffs, internal improvements at federal expense, homestead legislation, national banking, and freer foreign immigration laws. It symbolized the political dominance which the South was supposed to hold in the nation through control of the Democratic party. It explained the southern emphasis on states' rights and strict construction of constitutional powers. It came to signify what they called "backwardness" in things social and economic. It was thought to have reduced the Northeast to the status of a conscious minority after Federalist days and to have kept the Northwest from its fullest development following the Mexican War. The Republican party had been created to right these wrongs.

In the South, slavery was magnified into the cornerstone of a perfect society. It was supposed to have solved the labor problem and the far more difficult race problem. It was the source of southern stability and the wide acceptance of personal and social responsibility which characterized the section. Its right to exist where men desired it and to expand into the new territories became the symbol of a section's constitutional rights and its equality in national life. In the end, the southern states were willing to go to war in its defense.

Yet in spite of these facts, it is perfectly clear that the war was waged over antagonisms much broader than slavery and that the purposes back of the so-called Reconstruction program, inaugurated at the close of the war, had far more to do with reordering the South as a section than they had to do with the Negro as a human being. The nearly total abandonment of the Negro to the control of the southern states after 1876, the brazen political-economic bargaining or compromising in the disputed election of that year, and the quick turning of the Negro's Fourteenth Amendment almost exclusively to economic uses were, in fact, only the logical climax of steady developments which had, for a generation, been reducing the South, as a section, to a completely colonial status in relation to the finance-industrial areas.

Without ignoring the part which fear, vengeance, love of Union, and interest in the Negro played in Reconstruction, it must be perfectly clear to every scholar that the establishment of permanent Republican party control, the protection of the already exorbitant tariffs, and the securing of financial arrangements satisfactory to the bankers, the creditors, and the rising industrialists were basic factors in determining the treatment given the South. Many Northerners were perfectly frank about the matter. The Negro must be enfranchised, they said, to counteract southern white votes which would most certainly be given to the Democratic party. If this were not done, wrote a friend to Charles Sumner, it would produce evils "fearful to contemplate"—"a great reduction of the Tariff doing away with its protective features—perhaps Free Trade to culminate with Repudiation,—for neither Southerners nor Northern Democrats have any bonds or many greenbacks." The *Nation* opposed "the speedy readmission of the Southern States" because of the effect it would have on government securities, and the New York *Tribune* was equally certain that "the cotton-planters," educated by Calhoun "to the policy of keeping the Yankees from manufacturing," would "vote solid to destroy the wealth-producing industry of the Loyal States." No wonder Governor Horatio Seymour of New York insisted that the radical talk of making the South over into the likeness of New England simply meant an acceptance of its "ideas of business, industry, money making, spindles and looms."

The appearance of such attitudes in Reconstruction should not, however, be a matter for surprise. Southern interference with the emergence of modern America had, in fact, constituted the basic reason for northern complaint. It was not just opposition to specific measures, such as tariffs, homesteads, and internal improvements, but rather the continued insistence on *the locality* in an age when increasing interdependence and improved communication demanded a consolidated nationalism: it was the emphasis on agricultural values and the refusal of Southerners to change their minds as the physical world in more than half the nation altered. These were the things that mattered most. The mass production of goods, the widening of credit, the application of steam to transportation, and the greater mobility of ideas, persons, and things were all out of keeping with a restricted central government, with purely local financial agents, and with a leisurely way of life. Constitutional regulations and governmental agents made for a handful of agriculturists and traders in colonial days did not necessarily meet the requirements of thirty millions of people emerging into finance-industrial capitalism and spreading over half a vast continent. The enslavement of human beings did not jibe with the labor requirements of free enterprise or the ethical standards of a competitive society. A "backward" minority had no right to restrain a progressive majority. Men who were already economically dependent had no right to political dominance.

The subjugation of the rural-agricultural South was, therefore, a foregone conclusion long before the indignation against Negro slavery, however real it may have been, provided the moral force which produced an irrepressible conflict. Regions which supply raw materials and markets seem inevitably to be cast for the role of backward dependents in the modern industrial age. Southerners had early realized this fact and their changing status in national life. Their complaints against a growing dependence were as bitter as were those of the North against restraint. Robert J. Turnbull had declared in 1827 that "internal improvements are drawing off our resources to the North, and tariffs are driving us rapidly into Colonial vassalage." He was convinced that the interest of the North and West was "that the government should become more and more National," while that of the South was "that it should continue Federal." The South would, therefore, have to wage a constant fight for the "preservation" of the Constitution against the "usurpation" of northern "manufacturers." John C. Calhoun had seen the Wilmot Proviso as "a scheme, which aims to monopolize the powers of this Government and to obtain sole possession of its territories." This meant inequality, and rather than yield one inch of southern equality, he would "meet any extremity upon earth." "What! acknowledged inferiority!" he cried. "The surrender of life is nothing to sinking down into acknowledged inferiority!"

The protests against economic, social, and intellectual dependence gained added momentum after 1850. The drives for agricultural improvements, direct trade with Europe, the establishment of manufactures, the improvement of southern schools, the establishment of southern periodicals, and the boycotting of northern colleges and summer resorts all had back of them both the realization of dependence and the desire to make the section self-sufficing. Writers and speakers were constantly pointing with shame to the fact that from the rattle with which the nurse tickled the ears of the southern child to the shroud that covered the cold form of the dead or the marble slab that marked the final resting place, everything with which the Southerner worked and played came from the North. The senseless talk of making Kansas a slave state arose, not from any sound hope of slavery expansion, but from a determination to preserve southern equality. In fact, the danger of slavery expanding to any existing territory in 1860 was so slight that the Republican appeal was primarily to an abstract principle and its popularity due to the fact that it represented northern opposition to all that the South now symbolized. Its economic program, on the other hand, was emphatically concrete and meaningful. It pointed directly towards modern America.

The South also reacted to Republican success as a symbol of defeat in a long struggle. It is difficult to explain secession strictly in terms of the threat carried by Abraham Lincoln as a President. Secession in terms of thwarted slavery expansion per se does not make sense. States reacted to an accumulation, to emotion, to a discouraged feeling of helplessness, to a conviction that all they stood for and all they valued was endangered. They were trying to protect the ways of a minority against the power of a differing economic-social majority. A movement that took from November, 1860, to April, 1861, to reach its climax represented a reluctant drift, not precipitous action.

As the possibility of civil war became clear, however, patriotic and moral justification for resort to force necessarily pushed aside the material elements in sectional conflict and lifted the struggle to high and lofty levels. All wars are ultimately fought for things too sacred to be yielded. God does not lend his support to unworthy causes. Men are willing to give their lives only for *right* and *rights*. Yet in spite of high-sounding words, the material causes for sectional rivalry and conflict were not overlooked. A few Northerners early spoke of a peaceful acceptance of separation, but when faced with the social-economic consequences, drew back, and few "patriots" showed the slightest inclination to yield on a single interest item. As a northern historian has recently written:

> Throughout the secession winter, the Northern compromisers generally showed great enthusiasm for concessions on matters that seemed to have no direct bearing upon their particular interests, but they displayed an unfeeling obduracy toward concessions on subjects that touched them closely. In Congress nearly every type of sectional legislation came up for debate; and Northerners, whether radical or conservative, Republican or Democratic, refused to surrender any law which brought special benefits to their constituents. Southerners could cry out against discrimination and Northern tyranny, but Yankee congressmen were unmoved.[2]

More significant was the fact that southern congressmen had hardly left their seats in 1860–61 before the complete overturning of the old economic order began. A homestead act, the passage of which marked the final yielding of the nation's natural resources to private hands, was hurried through. The long-debated protective tariff was started on an upward swing that would ultimately carry it to heights surprising even to the industrialists themselves. The quick passage of a national banking law, soon to be followed by a whole series of fiscal measures favorable to investors and creditors, put an end to financial values that had held since the days of Andrew Jackson. A Pacific railroad bill, in turn, marked the end of a long controversy over the part which government should play in internal improvements and economic developments. Even the immigration laws, which Southerners had so ardently defended, were loosened to permit the importation of wage earners by contractors. The Fourteenth Amendment, with its restrictions on state action, climaxed a legislative program of near revolutionary proportions.

War needs furnished immediate justification for most of this legislation. Yet the whole program was one toward which the North had been driving and against which the South had stood firm for more than a generation. It was a program which embodied every essential ingredient necessary for the rise of the American businessman, his institutions, and his values. It would make possible wealth undreamed of by those who planted. It would build great cities, require transcontinental railway lines, and begin the production of

[2] Kenneth M. Stampp, *And the War Came: The North and the Secession Crisis, 1860–1861* (Baton Rouge, 1950), p. 160.

material things in quantity and quality such as mankind had never known. It would be called the Industrial Revolution.

With the exception of speed and degree, however, there was little basically new in the developments which followed in the United States. Much the same social-economic transformation had already taken place in western Europe. England and France had early felt the magic touch of steam power and factory production. These would soon do a more rapid and more thorough job in remaking Germany. The rise to strength and dominance of the city and the factory was a common phenomenon in the nineteenth century. What was unique and peculiar in the American story was its temper and its methods—both the product of the sectional struggle and Reconstruction.

What was done to the South, and how it was done, is a familiar story. It was from one angle the complete elimination of an economic and political rival guilty of thwarting Progress. From another, it was the completing of a glorious mission in the name of patriotism and morality—the wielding of the Lord's "terrible swift word." Either justified a perfectly ruthless procedure. And, what is equally important, the practical-interest end might be served under the banner of the piously abstract. It is therefore always difficult to say whether Thaddeus Stevens and Charles Sumner were motivated by a godlike indignation or by a plain, everyday hatred of a sectional rival. The results, however, were the same. The South, which was once so powerful that some charged it with ruling the nation, was turned over to the mercies of an army of occupation, its political action regulated and supervised, and its social values discredited by the assumption of backwardness. If the section had any contribution to make to a people blundering into the Gilded Age, in terms of rural-agricultural moderation of industrial and financial excesses or of living as against acquiring, it was neither asked for nor appreciated. Southern emphasis on good manners, on personal and social responsibility, or on the right of men and regions to be different, were old-fashioned in such an age. These things were not progressive. They did not yield profits. They belonged to an era and a section that had produced a Jefferson and a Madison, a Marshall and a Calhoun, a Lee and a Davis but which had been unable to produce a single Rockefeller, a Morgan, a Hill, or a Carnegie. Until it had been made over in the image of its conqueror, it could be ignored.

Thus for nearly two generations the South would play little part in the larger affairs of the nation. Wrapped up with its own problems of recovery and adjustment, it would share little either in the great economic prosperity of the age or in the shaping of national character. Thus to the already staggering cost involved in the physical and political destruction of an important segment of the nation must be added the equally staggering waste of talent and ability and culture. Balance was being sacrificed; human qualities and values, essential to national greatness, were being discredited and ignored. Southerners were being forced, like the peoples in any conquered and occupied country, to resort to deception, violence, and intrigue. Double standards and nonmoral attitudes were inevitable results.

The cost in northern values was even greater. Doing these things to the South damaged the aggressor more than they did the victim. It gave the leadership in national life to such twisted, unbalanced, vindictive men as Thaddeus Stevens, Edwin M. Stanton, Benjamin F. Butler, Zachariah Chandler, and Charles Sumner. It loosed an "age of hate" and social irresponsibility. Stevens would break up and re-lay the whole "political, municipal and social" fabric of southern society. Chandler thought that the only rights southern whites possessed were "the constitutional right to be hanged and the divine right to be damned." The good citizens of Boston, assembled in Faneuil Hall, asserted that the "defeated rebels" had "no civil nor political rights" which loyal men were bound to respect. A northern clergyman declared in a sermon: "I would try and condemn to be hung for treason, every rebel who has registered as Colonel, or as a higher rank in the Confederate army, or was of corresponding prominence in civil service." The few he would pardon he would let go under sentence with a rope around their necks with a clear understanding that if they ever touched "their accursed feet" upon "this soil of ours again . . . that postponed halter [would] swing them still."

Action, fortunately, never quite matched such talk. But the emotions stirred did silence conservative voices and permit an extreme course to be taken. Even in cases where public approval was uncertain, bold men who knew what they wanted were able to drive ahead amid the confusion and uncertainty of conflicting forces. A certain ruthlessness in dealing with opposition; a complete disregard of public opinion; a justification of corruption where deemed necessary to reach ends; a harsh indifference to the welfare of the helpless; a sham righteousness assumed in the interest of progress—these were the attitudes that were being woven into the temper of a people about to enter the industrial age. Already one could almost hear a Vanderbilt exclaim: "The public be damned."

The political cost was equally heavy. The Republican party had come out of the war with the reputation of having saved the Union. It was not a deserved reputation. War Democrats had given loyal support, and extreme Republicans had made no end of trouble. Professor William Archibald Dunning always bluntly insisted that the Republican party, as such, had ceased to exist by 1864, and that a Union party composed of War Republicans and War Democrats had taken its place. More than that, a goodly number of old Republicans of the liberal Lincoln tradition were soon in revolt against the party's conservative trend, while a considerable group of old Democrats of the John A. Logan and Ulysses S. Grant stamp were becoming the most ardent of Republicans. In the fight against President Andrew Johnson, however, Republicans had ignored the facts in the case, unfairly charged all Democrats with Copperhead leanings, and had returned to the old arrogant assumption that they were, and always had been, the only sound and loyal party.

This assumption, moreover, included loyalty to the Republican economic interests now magnified and adjusted to the needs of the emerging new day. Business thus shared in the luster of loyalty and the great moral benefits from having freed the slave. The Republican party became the party of business; business, in turn, became the heir to all the attitudes which the Republicans had developed in "reconstructing" the "disloyal South." To keep the party in power became an object of more importance than preserving democracy. The emoluments of public office were, of course, a consideration, but the avoidance of southern policies was more vital. Even the appropriation of a presidential election, clearly lost, was justifiable. Sound economic policies—meaning tariffs, payment of debts in gold, and free enterprise—were a part of the Republican faith. The party had an economic mission as well as a divine commission. Henry Wilson declared that in the Republican party there was more of moral and intellectual worth than was ever embodied in any political organization in any land. It had been "created by no man or set of men but brought into being by almighty God himself . . . and endowed by the creator with all political power and every office under Heaven." And its claim to rule rested on both moral and economic grounds. For, as said George F. Hoar, it contained "the best elements in our national life . . . the survivors and children of the men who put down the Rebellion and abolished slavery, saved the Union, and paid the debt and kept the faith, and achieved the manufacturing independence of the country, and passed the homestead laws." So, said another, in 1876, "Let your ballots protect the work so effectually done by your bayonets at Gettysburg and on so many a field of strife."

The Democratic party, on the other hand, was charged with having sympathized with treason. It had sided with "rebels." It had "no high aims, no patriotic intentions." It was "controlled by the foreign population and the criminal classes of our great cities, by Tammany Hall, and by the leaders of the solid South." "Every unregenerate rebel calls himself a Democrat," cried Oliver P. Morton of Indiana.

> Every bounty jumper, every deserter, every sneak who ran away from the draft, calls himself a Democrat. . . . Every man . . . who murdered Union prisoners . . . who invented dangerous compounds to burn steamboats and Northern cities, who contrived hellish schemes to introduce into Northern cities . . . yellow fever, calls himself a Democrat. Every dishonest contractor . . . every dishonest paymaster . . . every officer in the army who was dismissed for cowardice calls himself a Democrat. . . . In short, the Democratic party may be described as a common sewer and loathsome receptacle. . . .

The conclusion was obvious. As the Chicago *Tribune* put it: "The War of the Rebellion, on the surface a conflict between the North and the South, was in reality a conflict between the Republican and Democratic parties and principles." It would not be ended until "the Democratic party was dead and buried." *Harper's Weekly* was just as specific. "Reconciliation," it said, "will not result from taking the control of government from New England, the Middle States, and the Northwest and giving it to the Southern and border States. The power must remain where it is, because there the principles of the New Union are a living faith."

Such blunt acceptance of the basic significance of a long-existing power struggle, more than a decade after the abolition of slavery, which is supposed to have been the sole reason for sectional strife, is indeed revealing. It recalls to mind the words of Joshua R. Giddings, back in 1844, when he warned that the annexation of Texas would place "the policy and the destiny" of the nation in southern hands, and then asked:

Are the liberty-loving democrats of Pennsylvania ready to give up our tariff? Are the farmers of the West, of Ohio, Indiana, and Illinois, prepared to give up the sale of their beef, pork, and flour, in order to increase the profits of those who raise children for sale, and deal in the bodies of women? . . . I appeal to the whole population of the western States—of all classes and conditions, and political parties—to say whether they are willing to give up their harbor improvements, and the improvement of our river navigation, for the purpose of improving the southern slave trade, and of perpetuating slavery in Texas?

The basic nature of the conflict had evidently not changed. The only difference, seemingly, was that the sin of slaveholding carried the appeal in 1844, while the guilt of having attempted to break up the Union supplied the emotional force in 1874–76. Such appeals did infinite damage to the two-party system. They created a solid Democratic South and equally solid Republican blocs all over the North. Regardless of actual interests, men continued to vote their emotions. Reform of corruption became difficult; the honest facing of problems impossible. They magnified the service rendered by the soldier to the nation; brought men as unfitted as Ulysses S. Grant to the highest office in the land; and, with the organization of the GAR, thrust the military hand deep into the national treasury and made military service a prerequisite to the holding of every office from the presidency to the janitorship in the humblest county courthouse. What the resulting corruption and incompetency cost the United States no one will ever know.

Business, meanwhile, took its cue from politics. Ends justified dishonest means. Private conduct and the private conscience were one thing; what a man did in business was quite another. Men who later were to be called "Robber Barons" were as pious churchmen as were the politicians who waved the bloody shirt. Men who exploited labor as ruthlessly as they wasted a nation's natural resources or bribed a public official were even more honored and rewarded than were the politicians who, ten years after the close of war, were still saving the Union and freeing the slaves. One of the most brutal tricks history has ever played on blundering mankind was to shift the scenes so rapidly that these businessmen, who had so eminently succeeded by the accepted standards of their day, were scarcely permitted to leave the stage before they were being denounced as predatory capitalists. Evidently the application of

Reconstruction methods and values in business was not acceptable, even to the North.

The heaviest cost of Union, however, fell on agriculture. In a larger sense the economic struggle had been against the rural-agricultural interests and values united under southern leadership. The disintegration of the early alliance between the West and South, in the 1840's, had marked a turning point in national affairs. This agricultural combination until now had dominated national policy. Through the Democratic party, it had had its way with banks, tariffs, homesteads, and internal improvements. As the West grew and matured, however, differences arose, and the South more and more found herself standing alone on old issues. The question of slavery extension into the territories completed the break and pushed the strictly rural-agricultural issues into the background. Farmers, however much their interests remained the same, were now hopelessly divided.

War and Reconstruction only widened the gap while at the same time they actually increased farmers' common interests. Southern leadership, moreover, was now completely discredited. The nation's agriculturists, who justly laid claim to being gentlemen and who stressed the importance of culture, dignity, and good living in rural areas, were now broken and out of fashion. The Homestead Act and the heavy land grants to railroads, on the other hand, gave the northwestern farmer new and greater opportunities. Equipped with the new machinery which war necessities had popularized, he swept out across the vast prairie and plains regions to write in action one of the great epics of human history. Aided by the heavy flow of foreign immigrants, farmers and cattlemen literally flooded the Western world with food. In the three decades after 1870, one generation of men settled more land and turned it into farms than all their predecessors put together. In the same period, they added over 225 million acres to what the census called "improved lands"—an amount far in excess of all that improved since Jamestown.

Into the lap of the astonished world these farmers poured their yields. "Year after year came from widening acreage . . . torrents of wheat, of pork, of cattle, of corn, swelling the channels of trade. . . . Year after year, more and more freight cars creaked wearily with heavier and heavier loads to cities whose prosperity waxed higher and higher and higher." Dependent urban and industrial groups could go on expanding without worry about cheap food. Common men the Western world over could now eat roast beef and white bread, once the food of kings.

But there was another side to it. The farmer was selling in a world market and functioning in a society now dedicated to the proposition that the rise of cities and the spread of industry measure all progress, that governments are instituted among men for the purpose of aiding such developments, and that there is no difference between developing a nation's resources and exploiting them. Slowly, one by one, the European farmers accepted peasantry before the competition of cattle raised on the open range and produce raised on cheap homestead lands. In England this produced what W. H. R. Curtler calls "a minor social revolution" in the ruination "of the old landed aristocracy as a class." A Jena economist, meanwhile, warned the German farmer that he must "let go his hold on the traditions of the past; he must arouse his energies and adapt himself to the demands and circumstances of the time. Agriculture is now revolutionized." Scandinavian farmers suffered almost as much. Only industry, which was increasingly dependent on the outside world for food, raw materials, and markets, profited by what a Berlin writer called "the boundless blessings conferred upon the population of Europe by the shipments from transmarine sources." One day such dependence, phrased in a demand for an "equal place in the sun," would plunge the whole western world into war.

The western farmer himself fared little better in such an order. While he sold in an unprotected market, he bought behind the walls of a tariff that soon reached 50 per cent. He bore the brunt of the businessman's methods in railroads and finances. He overcrowded the range, and he glutted his markets. Without knowing it, he was depleting his soils and lowering his water levels. Soon he made the discovery that the new rulers of America no longer believed, as had Thomas Jefferson and John Taylor, that the farmers were "the chosen people of God." He even found out that the term "farmer" might be used to imply inferiority. When he attempted to strike back at the railroads and other corporations, he learned what Reconstruction had done to the American system of government. The attempt to impeach Andrew Johnson had weakened the presidential office itself and had struck a blow at executive independence. Soon, members of Congress would speak of the sweet reasonableness of a chief executive. The resfusal of the Supreme Court to test the validity of the Reconstruction program had amounted to virtual abdication. It had even permitted Congress to remove cases from its jurisdiction. It too had lost independence and was being overshadowed by the legislative department. Congress had grown all-powerful, and the welfare of business and finance seemed to be its chief concern. The Senate had become a millionaire's club. It was, charged James B. Weaver of Iowa, filled with men who represented "the corporations and the various phases of organized greed." "To an alarming extent," he went on, it could and did "control both the House and the Executive," with the result that while the war had destroyed a "slave holding aristocracy, restricted both as to locality and influence," it was "only to be succeeded by an infinitely more dangerous and powerful aristocracy of wealth, which now [pervaded] every State and [aspired] to universal dominion." The strictly sectional character of this new aristocracy was clearly indicated by Congressman George W. Morgan, who complained "of the tribute money which the shrewdness of New England politicians extorts from the people of the agricultural States for the benefit of certain Eastern monopolies. . . . So well established is the dominion of New England over the people of the other States," he continued, "that they humbly bow their necks to the yoke and meekly pay the tribute." "The lords of the loom" were, as Samuel S. Marshall of Illinois repeated, levying tribute "upon the people of the West at pleasure and without limit."

The real difficulty, of course, was that agriculture, under the new order of things, was not prospering. Another farming region was being reduced to a colonial status. The economic order was out of balance. As one writer said, the railroads had never been so prosperous; the banks had never done a better or a more profitable business; manufacturing enterprises never made more money; yet agriculture everywhere was in a languishing condition. It was a situation which Southerners had seen coming and had struggled to prevent. It was part of the price paid for Union. Spokesmen for the western farmer had simply taken over the role once played by Turnbull, Calhoun, and Davis. It was a leadership, however, vastly inferior. Ignatius Donnelly, James Baird Weaver, and William Jennings Bryan had little of the logic or the understanding of their predecessors. They too were doomed to defeat. Yet the problem they faced was the old familiar one; only the setting had changed. Farmers were battling to preserve their equality before the onrush of finance and industrial capitalism. Too late, they were discovering the tragic fact that slavery, in spite of its great importance, was only one phase of a far broader problem forced upon a people moving all too swiftly out of a simple past into the complexities of an industrial future.

And so the historian trying to find order in this disorderly world might, if his conscience permitted, suggest that the basic developments which took place in the United States in the nineteenth century, when stripped of their exaggerations, were the product of those great forces which were ushering in the modern world. He might even hint that the American tragedy lay in the way in which changes were brought about and in the ruthlessness, waste, and corruption which resulted. Looking for longer lines and a bit more sense in what happened, he might even argue that the greater interdependence of men and regions on each other which came with major technological, industrial, and financial changes rendered old political and social arrangements and ideas inadequate. Men's minds were left behind in one age, while their bodies were being thrust forward into another. The centers of power and influence had altered; population had shifted and concentrated; a new emphasis on nationalism and freedom for the individual had become necessary.

The historian might also suggest that under such conditions, developments everywhere overstressed the importance of industry and glorified the businessman and his values far above their worth. Fabulous returns in early days, moreover, tended to hide weaknesses and the all too apparent tendency to debase and exploit areas which supplied raw materials, food, and markets. Men failed to see the bitter rivalries that lay ahead as dependent industrial peoples reached out for necessary supplies and places in which to sell surplus goods. They could not know what would happen when the age of expansion neared its close, nor could they understand that the early conflicts on local stages were but a prelude to international wars which, in turn, would call for world organization and better means for using the democratic process and keeping world peace.

XII

THE "TURNER THEORIES" AND THE SOUTH

"Each age tries to form its own conception of the past."[1] According to its own standards, it selects and emphasizes. From what seems to be significant, it writes its history. But time alters historical values. That which impresses one generation as important may not seem so to the next. That which explains clearly to one group of men the course of events may appear to a later group to be entirely inadequate. History is, therefore, never fixed. It is never final.[2]

A generation ago (1893) Frederick Jackson Turner arose in emphatic protest against the interpretation of American history which predecessors had handed down and which his instructors at Johns Hopkins still accepted. It emphasized the germ theory of politics and held that American institutions were but a continuation of European beginnings. Turner, fresh from Wisconsin where he had seen the last stages of the frontier pass into modern complexity, felt that this did not explain facts as he knew them. He was confident that European institutions and practices, forced constantly to adjust themselves to new physical environments in the American West, were altered to some degree and became less European and more American.[3] Perhaps also he was lifting a western voice along with Populist and farmer, who in the early 1890's felt themselves neglected, the term "businessman" too narrowly defined, and the interest of those in power too much centered on eastern industrialists. The West, in general, was in a protesting mood.[4]

Reprinted from the *Journal of Southern History,* V, No. 3 (August, 1939), 291–314.

1 *The Early Writings of Frederick Jackson Turner* (Madison, Wis., 1938), p. 52.

2 This paper was read at the annual meeting of the Southern Historical Association in New Orleans, November 3, 1938. It was subtitled: "To what extent do the theories and studies of Frederick Jackson Turner constitute a true interpretation of the development of the South?"

3 Frederick J. Turner to Carl Becker, December 16, 1925 (Huntington Library).

4 Avery Craven, "Frederick Jackson Turner," in William T. Hutchinson (ed.), *Marcus W. Jernegan Essays in American Historiography* (Chicago, 1937), pp. 252–70.

At any rate, the Turner suggestion took hold. A few staid historians on the Atlantic coast went their way quite untouched. Turner never won more than footnote recognition from some of them. But in the West, where state universities were beginning to expand at an unheard of rate, the approach he offered carried conviction in line with things still to be observed. American history begin to be "reinterpreted and re-written because of him." For the next forty years, as one scholar has said, he "so completely dominated American historical writing that hardly a single production in all that time . . . failed to show the marks of his influence."[5]

But times have changed and with them our tastes in historical interpretation. The revisionists have fallen on Turner. One of them solemnly tells us that Turner's influence has been all to the bad; that he turned the eyes of the historians toward the frontier when they should have been fixed upon Europe and the international situations of which we were soon to be so much a part. Turner talked of *sectional* cleavage and interests when he should have emphasized the far more important *class* conflict, which is, as anyone should know, the really important division in American life. This critic speaks of Turner's work as an "extraordinary collection of learning . . . quite worthless."[6]

Most of these criticisms and of others which have been offered are based on the assumption that Turner intended to present a very clear and exact theory of American history and that this theory presumed to offer "a true and complete interpretation" of the development of the United States and of different sections in the United States. If the assumptions be correct, no one should be surprised that the modern historian, with his keener appreciation of the complexity of human affairs, has come to question the value of Turner's work. Most certainly in a field like that of the South, where most of the scholarly research has been done since Turner wrote and where revision is the order of the day, a careful restatement of the "frontier thesis" and a revaluation of its application is in order.

The best statement of Turner's "theories," I presume, is to be found in the essay entitled "The Significance of the Frontier in American History." Turner later made some slight alterations in

[5] Merle E. Curti, in Stuart A. Rice (ed.), *Methods in Social Science* (Chicago, 1931), p. 367; Louis M. Hacker, in the *Nation* (New York), CXXXVII (1933), 108.
[6] Hacker, in the *Nation,* CXXXVII, 108–10.

the views there expressed and changed the emphasis somewhat, but the original statement was the one seized upon and ever adhered to by "followers"—a breed of pest by which Turner was unusually cursed—and given wide application and wider currency by them.

The major assertions in this essay were to the effect that American history up to 1890 had been largely the history of the colonization of the West; that the "peculiarity of American institutions" was "the fact that they had been compelled to adapt themselves to the changes of an expanding people" who entered a succession of wildernesses and attempted to transform them into urban complexity.[7] Because the point of most pronounced change, through the interaction of men and institutions and environment on each other, was on the outer edge of advance, Turner centered attention there. He called it "the frontier" and said that the significant thing about it was the fact that it lay "at the hither edge of free land."[8] But he was evidently using the term very loosely, for he later spoke of an Indian and hunter stage, of traders and herdsmen, of exploitive single-crop farmers, and called the thing he was talking about "a process" not unlike that through which the human race had passed in its long journey upward from savagery to factories.[9]

He described the various types of frontiers and their modes of advance and then turned to the results produced by the process on men and institutions. What were the effects of being ever in motion, always readjusting to a new environment? What was added to or subtracted from the European peoples and practices by being planted on the eastern seaboard and then pushed steadily westward for three centuries?

Turner's answer was unquestionably intended to be both broad and general. Yet it had, unfortunately, to deal with specific qualities and characteristics. He believed that successive returns to the primitive and the forced readjustments to new environments caused men and institutions to be better fitted to the requirements of this continent. They were, in other words, *Americanized.*[10] That meant both the exaggeration of old traits and the addition of new ones. It might mean only a change in tone and temper.

The first change, developed in a somewhat confused and vague

[7] Frederick J. Turner, *The Frontier in American History* (New York, 1920), p. 2.
[8] *Ibid.,* p. 3.
[9] *Ibid.,* p. 11.
[10] *Ibid.,* p. 18.

fashion in Turner's essay, had to do with nationalism. As a mixing and melting pot, the West blended different European groups into a "composite nationality."[11] Local questions, such as slavery, became national through expansion. Trade became internal to a new degree, and domestic problems, such as land, internal improvements, and markets, tended to crowd aside those which dealt with foreign affairs. Even the Constitution was modified because Louisiana had to be purchased in the interests of western men.[12]

A second result had to do with that illusive thing called democracy. In this case it seems to have meant the increase of rugged individualism, as "fools" insisted on putting on their own coats for themselves, in the broadening of the franchise, and in a larger participation by common men in politics.[13]

Lastly, the frontier tended to change the fiber and mental attitudes of men themselves by adding a "coarseness and strength combined with acuteness and inquisitiveness," a "practical, inventive turn of mind," a "masterful grasp of material things," and "a buoyancy and exuberance" of spirit born of freedom and opportunity.[14]

In later writings something is said of the idealism engendered by the chance to begin over again in a constantly reshaping society. Much is made of the sectionalism which arose as different streams of population occupied differing physical basins and as a new and more native order arose to contend with older ones.

The general implication in this approach, as I see it, is that a new flavor, more American, was imparted to men and ways which experienced this constant retrial on a succession of frontiers. Yet on closer examination, this flavor proves to be a very uncertain thing. The emerging American qualities turn out to be only a bundle of contradictions. The West bred nationalism and sectionalism at the same time; it encouraged rugged individualism and yet forced a new degree of co-operation if men were to survive its dangers; it made its people coarse and material in mind and turned them into dreamers and idealists; it welcomed the innovator and forced a conservative conformity to existing practices upon those who would remain alive; it practiced democracy but tolerated slavery and set men to grasping for all the means to inequality.

What are we to conclude from such contradictions? Either that

11 *Ibid.*, p. 22.
12 *Ibid.*, p. 25.
13 *Ibid.*, p. 30.
14 *Ibid.*, p. 37.

Turner had only a very vague conception of his own contribution or that he considered these effects of the frontier, on which so many scholars have seized as the sum and substance of "the Turner thesis," as of no major importance. The conclusion is obvious. Turner believed that the *process* he was describing was the significant thing, not its effects on individuals and practices. Along that line it was only necessary to notice general drifts and to state them in general terms. Crosscurrents in the larger streams could be ignored. His emphasis was on *change*, not on *specific changes*. The *approach* was the important thing, not some exact pattern which might appear in its application. In fact, an exact pattern in all regions was not to be expected. The social and racial groups and the cultural patterns which moved out from old centers into the American Wests differed too greatly from each other. Those of New England or the Middle States differed as much from those of the South as did the environments into which they were thrust. The English groups carried different cultural patterns, such as home life or agricultural practices, from those of the German or Scotch-Irish who moved alongside of them. The West worked changes, sometimes great, sometimes small, on each of these. But it was primarily a change in flavor, not in form, save as all became gradually "Americanized." Frontiers differed. They did tend to develop a more or less common outlook and a few common practices, but differing cultural patterns still persisted. A Swedish settlement on the frontier differed from a German one; a timber frontier differed from a mining camp. Frontiers should be compared for greatest historical comprehension. In no other way could the influence of sectionalism in American history be properly understood.

The basic facts which Turner suggested for a better understanding of American history were, therefore, first: that throughout the formative period the new Wests, with something of common needs and outlook, were the most typical and the most influential portions of the nation; and second: that Wests in turn became Easts, leaving the future to sectional and class conflicts which might produce quite another America showing the traces of frontier experiences only as a landscape reveals the action of glaciers in ages long past.

That Turner thought that this approach—I call it an approach, not a theory or a thesis—applied to the South, there can be no question. That he considered it, in itself, "a true interpretation of the development of the South," or of any other section, for that matter, I seriously doubt. There was never anything final or dogmatic about Turner. He once said that "this paper makes no attempt to treat the subject exhaustively; its aim is to call attention to the frontier as a fertile field for investigation and to suggest some of the problems which arise in connection with it."[15] But within those limits he did include the southern advances into the West without reservations of any kind. He mentions the various frontier stages shown in Virginia and the Carolinas—trapper, herdsman, and exploitive farmer, and includes the fall line and the southern mountains among the natural frontier boundaries that are to be noted. It was at Cumberland Gap that he took his station to watch these stages moving, procession-like, into the interior. He notes the western influence on southern land legislation, religious developments, and slavery attitudes, and climaxes his political discussion by asserting that the West made Jefferson's democracy into the national republicanism of Monroe and the democracy of Jackson—all three southern men. He finds his best illustrations of sectionalism produced by expansion in the southern colonies and states.[16] The Regulator movements in the Carolinas and the constitutional struggles in Virginia and North Carolina stand out in his pages as significant evidences of both the sectional and the democratic force of the West.[17]

In a second essay entitled "The Old West,"[18] Turner enlarges on these southern applications. The western angles of Bacon's Rebellion and the early establishment up the James of Indian trading posts and forts, where "the warlike Christian man" was to be stationed, are a part of his picture of "the fighting frontier." The "cow-drovers" in the piedmont, wandering from range to range, followed by the Scotch-Irish, German, Welsh, and English farmers, each group with its own peculiar brand of evangelical faith, the grasping speculator and the ever present squatter help to form what he calls "the New Society"—more democratic, more self-sufficing, more primitive and individualistic than that which had evolved out of Old World beginnings on the Atlantic coast.

[15] Turner to Constance L. Skinner, March 18, 1922, "Notes Concerning my Correspondence with Frederick Jackson Turner," *Wisconsin Magazine of History,* XIX (1935), 91–103.

[16] Turner, *Frontier in American History,* p. 29.

[17] *Ibid.,* pp. 113–21.

[18] *Ibid.,* pp. 67–125.

This new order in the southern West created internal trade, raised the issues of nativism and lower standards of living, and set the old, on the coast, and the new, in the interior, in conflict over such questions as a broader franchise, a more equitable representation, a wider religious toleration, the use of slaves, and even the proper relations between the colonies and the mother country. Most certainly Turner found the southern frontier significant and the early southern Wests to reveal all the traits and to exercise all the influences which he had described as typical.

Here were Old World patterns set down in a wilderness—a country-gentleman ideal, peculiar forms of local government—including as essentials the county court, the sheriff, and the county lieutenant, an established church, and a tradition to aristocracy. Here also were German, Scotch-Irish, and other groups with cultural patterns quite distinct. All had come to America—the first great West. All had been changed to some degree. The interplay of environment and institutions had given something new in temper as well as in practice which in the end made harmony between England and the colonies impossible. Europeans had become Americans.

Further expansion into the interior had produced another social unit differing in turn from that on the coast. It too had found that the political ties which bound it to an older society gave less than satisfactory scope for development. The ending of primogeniture and entail, the broadening of religious freedom, the readjustment of representation and the franchise, and even the shifting of capitals to the westward, had all come in answer to demands of expansion. The new Wests of the South had demonstrated both their differing character and their increasing power. They had also altered old practices and old institutions to the more simple requirements of the small-farming economy which they practiced. The great piedmont region above the fall line, sweeping from Pennsylvania to middle Georgia, formed a unity in itself as against the separate entities into which the coastal region was divided. In characteristics and attitudes it met all the Turner requirements. In course of development and in influence it provided a satisfactory case study for his approach.

Up to this point, few would deny the value of the Turner theories and studies in making an approach to the development of the

South. The process of change from old to new, and the sectionalism produced by expansion and readjustment are fundamental to any clear understanding of the section. Even democracy, when understood as men of that day understood it—as a stirring for the recognition of new groups and rights—is clearly discernible; nationalism, in the sense of turning attention to native problems and seeking native answers to them, flavors the whole story. No historian, as far as I know, has questioned the value of the Turner approach to this period, or doubted the soundness of its conclusions. The real problem comes with the rise of the Cotton Kingdom. There conditions become so complex and tangled that even Turner himself seems to have been somewhat uncertain. Others have frankly denied the continuation of the western process and viewed the entire South as a unique entity in the national pattern.

Professor Frederic Logan Paxson is particularly emphatic on this point. He insists that because the plantation and Negro slavery played a part in the settlement of the Southwest, the region forfeited its western character and began "living in a new cycle." "In the generation that ends at Gettysburg and Vicksburg," he says, "the South ceased to be the West, and became enchained in a destiny of its own, in one of the great tragedies of social history." Because it did not reproduce the pattern which was being worked out in the Northwest of the day, it did not stay "true to the American standard."[19] Other scholars, while not directly denying the validity of the Turner approach, have laid emphasis on other things and found other central themes in the southern story. The late Ulrich Bonnell Phillips once argued that the race question gave unity to southern history and declared that the determination to keep the section a white man's country explained the larger course of developments.[20] Another writer, trying to explain what makes the South southern, has listed its weather, its English country-gentleman ideal, its Negroes, and its dominantly rural character as the essential ingredients. He has found its story from 1830 to 1861 to be shaped primarily by the constant necessity of defending itself against a northern crusade, launched first against slavery but later broadened out to include the whole southern way of life.[21] The in-

[19] Frederic L. Paxson, *When the West Is Gone* (New York, 1930), pp. 63–65.

[20] Ulrich B. Phillips, "The Central Theme of Southern History," *American Historical Review,* XXXIV (1929), 30–43.

[21] Avery Craven, *The Repressible Conflict, 1830–1861* (Baton Rouge: Louisiana State University Press, 1939), chap. i.

ference is that the frontier and the influences which it normally produced are lost in the struggle between North and South. True, these sections did come to conflict over the matter of slavery in the new territories, but the contest in Kansas in the fifties was more a manifestation of hostilities already engendered over other issues than a struggle over actual slavery expansion. There were only three slaves in Kansas in 1860.

What then of the frontier theory in this period? Did it cease to apply? Did a factor which had been of such great significance in an earlier period cease to influence the course of development in this? If so, the abolition charge that the ante-bellum South was thoroughly un-American had some foundation.

To begin with, it should be understood that expansion of far greater proportions than the Old South had ever experienced went on in the period from 1820 to 1860. The pressure from wasted lands, failing markets, and unsatisfactory political conditions in the eastern states was never so great. The lure of fresh lands, where cotton might grow and restore the failing fortunes of the section, was never quite so strong. Out of Virginia, the Carolinas, Georgia, and Tennessee settlers poured into the Gulf region to push back quickly the forest and to establish a new order. From 1820 to 1830 Virginia's rate of population increase fell from 37.5 to 13.5 per cent and in the next decade to less than 4 per cent. Speakers told of "Vast regions, once the abode of a numerous population, of plenty, and of social happiness" now "re-committed to the forest"; of "tide[s] of emigration . . . from all classes; as if the angel of desolation had cursed the land, and imbued the people with a hatred to the place of their nativity." By 1850 nearly one-third of the Virginia-born were living in other states.[22]

North Carolina suffered even more. Her rate of population increase fell from 15 per cent in 1830 to 2.1 per cent in 1840, and it still stood under 15 per cent in 1860. "The Alabama fever" raged with great violence and carried off "vast numbers . . . of citizens." "Anxiety and confusion" pervaded "all ranks of the people."[23] Lands lost their value and poverty became universal. Only

[22] *Seventh Census of the United States: 1850,* pp. 241 ff.; *Farmer's Register,* III (1836), 685–89; II (1835), 762–64.

[23] *Seventh Census . . . 1850,* pp. 297 ff.; J. G. de Roulhac Hamilton (ed.), *Papers of Thomas Ruffin* (4 vols.; Raleigh, 1918–20), I, 193–95, 197–99; Guion G. Johnson, "Social Characteristics of Ante-Bellum North Carolina," *North Carolina Historical Review,* VI (1929), 144–47.

Connecticut in this era and Iowa in a later one have matched the contributions to the West made by the Old North State.

The same story can be told for South Carolina and the older counties of Georgia and Tennessee. The first of these showed population gains of only 15 per cent in 1830 and of only 2.25 per cent in 1850. In 1860 there were 193,000 South Carolina–born persons living outside the parent state as against 276,000 remaining at home. Forty per cent of her people had sought homes in the West. Men spoke of "the wilderness regaining her empire"; of "the once thriving planter . . . tearing himself from the scenes of his childhood, and the bones of his ancestors, to seek in the wilderness" the things not to be found at home.[24]

The Southwest, meanwhile, grew in direct proportion to these losses. From 1830 to 1840 Alabama increased its whites by 76 per cent and its Negroes by 114; Mississippi, its whites by 154 per cent and its Negroes by 197. The actual gains in Alabama were ten times those of Virginia and twenty times those of South Carolina. And this was but the beginning of a great westward sweep that would follow the Gulf to the Mexican border and across it and reach north and west to Arkansas. The south central states, as a whole, grew three times as fast in the 1830's as did the Old South and by 1850 outnumbered the parent states by over 300,000, having added a million and a quarter in the last decade alone. As early as 1834 they were producing the bulk of the cotton crop and had begun their economic domination of the whole section.[25]

This advance had all the characteristics usually ascribed to the Westward movement. There were distinct stages which in turn conformed to the accepted patterns. Trappers and traders from the Old South had entered the Indian country well before the Revolution and had opened the ways through which others were to follow. Furs and skins became an essential part of the Southern surplus which went out from Richmond and Charleston to the world. Trade contacts altered Indian society, threw the tribes into international alliances, and produced a group of half-breed leaders hardly equaled for diplomatic ability in the American story.[26] The

[24] *Seventh Census . . . 1850,* pp. 333 ff., 353 ff., 533 ff.; *Congressional Debates,* 22 Cong., 1 sess., pp. 80–81 (January 16, 1832).

[25] Thomas P. Abernethy, *The Formative Period in Alabama, 1815–1828* (Montgomery, 1922); Frederick J. Turner, *The United States, 1830–1850* (New York, 1935), pp. 213–15; *id., The Rise of the New West, 1819–1829* (New York, 1906), p. 47.

[26] Verner W. Crane, *The Southern Frontier, 1670–1732* (Durham, 1928), pp. 108–36, 254–80.

frontier pressure against these tribes lifted military leaders like Andrew Jackson to national importance and forced the development of the nation's final Indian policy of removal and "permanent" reservations across the Mississippi River. It would be difficult to find a more typical frontier attitude and action against the red man than that revealed by the Georgians in the 1820's.[27]

There was also a southern pastoral stage. John G. W. de Brahm described it in the back country of the Carolinas just before the Revolution. He told of great herds of cattle sent down into Georgia, there to be herded and driven from range to range by cowpen keepers "like ancient Patriarchs or modern Bedowins." Roundups and brandings, expert horsemen, and the whole paraphernalia of the cattle trade![28] A generation later cowmen were all along the borders of the Indian country awaiting the departure of the tribes for the West but not hesitating, in the face of government agreements with the Indians, to pasture their cattle on the Indian lands.[29] The Oklahoma "Sooner" was in the making.

By the 1840's the cowboys had reached the piney-woods section of Mississippi, where, mounted on their "low built, shaggy, but muscular and hardy horses of that region, and armed with rawhide whips . . . and sometimes with a catching rope or lasso. . . . They scour[ed] the woods . . . sometimes driving a herd of a thousand heads to the pen."[30]

The cattle days in Louisiana and Texas are better known but somehow it has not occurred to the historian that this stage of frontier development had its best expression in the South, developed its important features there, and passed out of the South into the plains west, with which it is usually associated, with only slight changes in its character.[31]

The mining stage also had its place in the southern advance. A

[27] Ulrich B. Phillips, *Georgia and State Rights* (Washington, 1902), pp. 39–86.

[28] Plowdon C. J. Weston (ed.), *Documents Connected with the History of South Carolina* (London, 1856), p. 200.

[29] Franklin L. Riley (comp.), "Autobiography of Gideon Lincecum," *Mississippi Historical Society Publications,* VIII (1904), 443–65.

[30] J. F. H. Claiborne, "A Trip through the Piney Woods," *Mississippi Historical Society Publications,* IX (1906), 521.

[31] Little is said of Texas, the most "western" of the southern states, in this paper. She entered the picture rather late, but she was ready for secession with the other cotton states early in 1861. Texas was, therefore, southern by the final test. Her western character and spirit, on the other hand, were always so marked that writers on western history have given her ample recognition and space. In spite of both slavery and the plantation system, no one has dared to suggest that she ever "ceased to be western." The same holds for Arkansas. For that reason emphasis is here laid on the states east of the Mississippi.

recent writer has told of the gold fever which began to rage in North Carolina in 1825. Travelers reported hearing "scarce anything . . . except gold"; of "bankrupts . . . restored to affluence and paupers turned to nabobs." "The prospector" became "a distinct race" and the population 'round about "agonized under the increased and increasing fever for gold." Prospectors rushed about in quicksilver fashion from diggings to diggings, boom towns rose and fell, and the state of morals became "deplorably bad."[32] There is, in fact, little in the picture of the mining rushes which took place in North Carolina, Georgia, and Alabama in this period to distinguish them in temper or in character from those on other frontiers in other sections.

Nor did the early agricultural groups differ from those who in this period were pushing their way into the Old Northwest. The pioneering activities of Gideon Lincecum,[33] which began in Georgia just after the American Revolution and ended in Texas before the Civil War, might, with local variations, have been duplicated on the crest of any other frontier rolling westward. His grandfather had been killed by the Indians in North Carolina during the Revolution. His father, after a turn at Indian fighting, had spent some ten years farming about in different parts of the Georgia uplands, raising the first crop of cotton ever grown in that part of the state. He had accumulated property rapidly. Cotton brought high prices. But the West lured. Tennessee offered greater opportunities. Three times just after 1800 he started for that state with his family now augmented by a parcel of Negroes. Each time, however, after a stop on the way to raise a crop, he turned back and at last settled down on the Georgia frontier to await the removal of the Muskogee Indians and the opening of their lands to settlement.

In these years the boy Gideon had learned to gather cotton and had spent a few months in the rude frontier schools. He now left home, clerked and farmed, studied medicine by reading a few books, and then got married. He showed every prospect of becoming a successful farmer until the Alabama fever caught him. Then, not waiting even to harvest his crop, he set out again with his father to seek a new home in a new wilderness. He paused for a season with the cattle men on the Okmulgee and then made his way through

[32] Fletcher M. Green, "Gold Mining: A Forgotten Industry of Ante-Bellum North Carolina," *North Carolina Historical Review,* XIV (1937), 1–19, 135–55.

[33] Riley (comp.), "Autobiography of Gideon Lincecum," *loc. cit.,* pp. 443–519.

five hundred miles of forest to the little log town of Tuscaloosa. Two or three times later he moved on, keeping in the vanguard of settlement, sawing lumber, trading with the Indians, practicing medicine, and planting cotton. In 1834 he made a trip to Texas and after a few years longer in Mississippi moved there to end his days as a planter.

Gideon could hardly qualify as "the man of capital and enterprise" in the Turner picture, but he eminently fits the role of "the first agricultural pioneer." He presents sharp contrast to the wealthy and energetic Thomas Dabney,[34] who, finding his lands worn in old Virginia, picked up his whole plantation establishment and purchased four thousand acres of land from lesser men in Mississippi in the same year that Gideon was looking toward Texas. Gideon was the South's pioneer farmer—the exploiter of the soil's first wealth. Dabney represented the final purchaser—the man of wealth who brought "extensive" culture and permanent settlement. The two types taken together with the great body of farmers in between who were less restless than the one and less permanent than the other, complete an agricultural sequence which satisfies every requirement of the frontier process. The final pattern was not that reached in the Northwest but we should remember that Turner's emphasis was on *change*, not on some *fixed type of change*. Too long have scholars viewed the plantation as an anachronism in frontier development. It was, in fact, nothing more than the Southern expression of "capital and enterprise" in agriculture and it no more upset the normal frontier process than did the bonanza farmers of the Northwest or the capitalist on the timber, cattle, or mining frontiers.

It should also be noticed that the flavor and practice of this great southern West was thoroughly normal. Nor did they change any more rapidly than in any other West. "Flush days" in Alabama and Mississippi were the rule.[35] Speculation drove land prices up to as high as $70 an acre and pushed interest rates to from 40 to 50 per cent. Banking wrote new chapters even in frontier financial history and left debts unpaid even to this day.[36] Opportunity made

[34] Susan Dabney Smedes, *A Southern Planter: Social Life in the Old South* (New York, 1900), pp. 1–26.

[35] Joseph G. Baldwin, *The Flush Times of Alabama and Mississippi* (New York, 1853). For western flavor in humor, see Arthur P. Hudson, *Humor of the Old Deep South* (New York, 1936).

[36] Reginald C. McGrane, *Foreign Bondholders and American State Debts* (New York, 1935).

liars out of honest men. One of them wrote home to Virginia in July, 1835, declaring that the weather in central Alabama was never more than warm and that the nights were so cool that he always slept under a blanket.[37] A New Orleans newspaper described the period as one in which the people were "drunk with success." "The poor man of yesterday was worth his thousands today; and the beggar of the morning retired to his straw pallet at night, burdened with the cares of a fortune acquired between the rising and the setting of the sun."[38] A visitor to the Louisiana metropolis in 1833 wrote: "There is a hurry, a 'rush' among all classes of people here, that I have not seen in so great a degree, elsewhere. It looks almost like intrusion to detain any one upon matters unconnected with ordinary business-pursuits."[39]

A Natchez citizen unblushingly complained of a sprained wrist and a dislocated thumb resulting from "a hard fought battle with Mr. Daniel Hickey, whose Eyes by the Bye I completely closed."[40] In March, 1856, the editor of an Alabama paper wrote that guns and pistols were being "fired in and from the alleys and streets of the town . . . until it is hardly safe to go from house to house."[41] In the same year this paper carried a card for weeks offering a reward of $500 for the arrest of the "party" who on several occasions had shot at the signer through the Cahaba hotel window.[42] A city ordinance in Jacksonville, in the same state, prohibited the shooting of guns or pistols within two hundred yards of a dwelling. A schedule of fines for fights published in the Moulton *Democrat* in 1857 listed fist fights at from five to ten dollars, fights with sticks at twice as much, those with dirks at from twenty to thirty dollars, and those with bowie knives or pistols at from thirty to fifty dollars.[43] In twenty-three months of 1859–60 the New Orleans chief of police arrested 62 persons for murder; 146 for stabbing with intent to murder; 734 for assault with deadly weapons; 42 for arson; 44 for burglary; 53 for highway robbery; 2,148 for

[37] Benjamin Park to Lewis Hill, Sumter City, Alabama, July 8, 1853 (MS in private hands).

[38] New Orleans *Daily True Delta,* February 6, 1850.

[39] Dwight L. Dumond (ed.), *Letters of James Gillespie Birney, 1831–1857* (2 vols.; New York, 1938), I, p. 69.

[40] Charles S. Sydnor, *A Gentleman of the Old Natchez Region: Benjamin L. C. Wailes* (Durham, 1938), p. 6.

[41] Dallas *Gazette,* March 21, 1856. See, also, Frederick L. Olmsted, *A Journey in the Back Country* (New York, 1907), I, 143–44.

[42] Dallas *Gazette,* October 12, 1855.

[43] Minnie Clare Boyd, *Alabama in the Fifties* (New York, 1931), p. 197.

larceny; 232 for swindling; 2,110 as suspicious characters; 47,-403 for assault and battery, threats, and miscellaneous transgressions.[44]

Conduct along other lines revealed the same frontier temper. A visitor in Georgia just after the Revolution described the people as " 'the most prophane, blasphemous set . . . I ever heard of.' " She declared that she had seen groups of from fourteen to sixteen hundred assembled for public business " 'and perhaps not one in fifty but what we call fighting drunk.' "[45] Seargent Prentiss, writing of Mississippi in the early 1830's, said that "intemperance, skepticism, profaneness, [and] gambling" were "sadly prevalent."[46] An Alabama obituary praised the deceased for "honesty and integrity . . . when sober,"[47] and Ingraham declared that whiskey was the favorite beverage of the Mississippi yeoman, "present[ed] to the stranger with one hand, while they give him a chair with the other."[48] Reuben Davis admitted that his people "drank hard, swore freely, and were utterly reckless of consequences when their passions were aroused," but insisted that they were sober, reverent, and industrious. His version of the Mississippian's creed is as good a statement of the frontiersman's social attitudes as can be found:

> A man ought to fear God, and mind his business. He should be respectful and courteous to all women; he should love his friends and hate his enemies. He should eat when he was hungry, drink when he was thirsty, dance when he was merry, vote for the candidate he likes best, and knock down any man who questioned his right to these privileges.[49]

Religious expression in the early southern West was also of the frontier brand. The itinerant preacher usually pioneered the way for the different evangelical denominations. The wanderings and deeds of a Lorenzo Dow in Mississippi differ little in essential detail from those of a Peter Cartwright in Illinois.[50] Both of these

44 New Orleans *Daily Crescent,* June 18, 1860. On gambling and drinking in Mississippi, see [George L. Prentiss, ed.], *A Memoir of S. S. Prentiss* (2 vols.; New York, 1856), I, 129–36.

45 Ulrich B. Phillips, *The Life of Robert Toombs* (New York, 1913), p. 5.

46 [Prentiss, ed.], *Memoir of S. S. Prentiss,* I, 130–31.

47 Dallas *Gazette,* November 21, 1856.

48 [Joseph H. Ingraham], *The South-West* (2 vols.; New York, 1835), II, 172.

49 Reuben Davis, *Recollections of Mississippi and Mississippians* (Boston, 1891), pp. 18–19.

50 *The Life, Travels, Labors, and Writings of Lorenzo Dow* (New York, 1851), pp. 289–96; *History of Cosmopolite* (Philadelphia, 1815), pp. 184–86, 214–18.

men would have agreed with the Georgian, who a few years earlier insisted that "larnin" made the preachers "proud and worldly" and that frontiersmen wanted "none of your new-fangled, high-flying preaching."[51] Camp meetings flourished down to 1860 and men and women "got religion" after desperate struggles with the Lord and an undue amount of noise. A contemporary description of how Methodism won its way in the region would apply to all other denominations: "It lodged roughly, and it fared scantily. It tramped up muddy ridges, it swam or forded rivers to the waist; it slept on leaves or raw deer-skin, and pillowed its head on saddle-bags; it bivouacked among wolves or Indians . . . *but it throve.*"[52]

The same frontier flavor characterized other lines of activity. Robert J. Walker and his Mississippi colleagues openly checked the bidding on government lands in the interest of their speculations[53] and an auctioneer in Alabama would "frequently stop crying the land" to suggest that buyers compromise and "quit fooling away your money."[54] It was an Alabama senator who insisted that the squatters on the public domain were not "violators of the laws, and trespassers" but "meritorious individuals, because they have been the pioneers to all the new settlements in the West and Southwest."[55]

Nor was democracy lacking. Thomas Dabney met sharp resentment when he attended the house-raising with his slaves in Mississippi and when he used them to help get a sick neighbor's cotton out of the grass. He was told that if he "had taken hold of a plough and worked" by the side of the unfortunate man all would have been well but to sit on his horse and direct Negroes was offensive even to those whose fields were benefited.[56] The same democratic spirit was shown in the constitutions of these western states. In Alabama, Arkansas, and Texas all male white citizens were

[51] John D. Wade, *Augustus Baldwin Longstreet: A Study of the Development of Culture in the South* (New York, 1924), p. 64.

[52] William E. Wightman, *Life of William Capers, D. D.* (Nashville, 1858), pp. 471–72.

[53] *American State Papers, Public Lands,* VII, 495–96.

[54] *Ibid.,* pp. 479, 490, 496.

[55] *Cong. Debates,* 21 Cong., 1 sess., p. 415 (May 5, 1830). For claims associations, etc., see Clarence E. Carter (ed.), *The Territorial Papers of the United States,* VI, *The Territory of Mississippi, 1809–1817* (Washington, 1938), 598–600, 632. Note also the support given to homestead and pre-emption legislation by Alabama and Mississippi representatives in Congress.

[56] Smedes, *A Southern Planter* (London, 1889), p. 67. See, also, Wade, *Augustus Baldwin Longstreet,* pp. 5, 59, 61–64.

granted the right to vote and hold office without property or religious restrictions. In Mississippi where taxes or militia service was at first required for voting and the possession of property and religious faith for officeholding, a second constitution in 1832 wiped these out and added a most emphatic statement regarding the equality of all men.[57]

This democratic flavor did not disappear in the ante-bellum period. The coming of the plantation crowded it aside only to about the same degree that economic and social maturity weakened frontier democracy in the North. Even in 1849 Albert Gallatin Brown could still win wide approval in Mississippi by the boast of being " 'entirely a self-made man' " and by accepting "every respectable man as his equal." When the good Dr. Duncan threatened to leave the South in 1860 because he could not approve of secession, the Natchez *Free Trader* informed him that

> brains, not money; principles, not accidental position, rule the people of the South. England is the appropriate place for nabobs, where men bow humbly before Gessler's cap of money, and where lords are invested with every "virtue under heaven." But in the Southern States, men who make 4000 bales of cotton and own 500 negroes have not the influence on that account as the humblest mechanic who advocates correct principles.

A correspondent of this paper a decade earlier had insisted that the safety of the section lay with "her mechanics, her laborers, and her independence but not rich planters."[58] Evidently common men still believed in equality.

It might be possible also, I think, to show that slavery itself was affected by the move into the West. Just as the restless, nonconforming whites tended to get beyond the "hedge" and to drift ultimately to the West, so the rebellious, unsettled Negro found himself sold "down river." In early western states the runaway advertisements in the newspapers are more numerous, the number of Negroes whose backs are scarred, ears cropped, and breasts branded much greater, indicating, I suggest, not only harder tasks to be performed in the wilderness, and a greater amount of home-

[57] Francis N. Thorpe (comp.), *The Federal and State Constitutions . . .* (7 vols.; Washington, 1909), I, 89–114; IV, 2032–62. In speaking of social life in Alabama in the fifties, Miss Boyd says: "Social lines were indefinable then, as now. There was no perceptible division between slaveholders and non-slaveholders as classes. In marriage, in visiting, in professional or other employment no question was raised as to the ownership of slaves or interest in them." Boyd, *Alabama in the Fifties,* p. 214.

[58] James B. Ranck, *Albert Gallatin Brown, Radical Southern Nationalist* (New York, 1937), p. 60; Natchez *Free Trader,* September 19, 1860, August 20, 1850.

sickness, but also a habit of running away of long standing. Certainly there were more cases of assault on overseers and masters by slaves, more murders and, in turn, more lynchings of Negroes in the newer states than in the older ones. Slavery was less diffused, and the masters, as one slave complained, "more pushing." Paternalism weakened and the number of slaves whom the master had raised grew smaller. Talk of emancipation was seldom indulged in; the West gave the institution a new hold on the section.[59]

It has been assumed by historians that truly western conditions existed in the southern region only in a very early period and that they passed abruptly with the coming of the plantation system. From that time forward, they say, all that was western ceased to exist. "The South" came into being. In a recent textbook on the West in American history, Dan E. Clark insists that "the concentration on cotton production, with its accompaniment of slave labor, halted the process of frontier development that was normal in other sections." The "Old Southwest" knew the "backwoods pioneer" who "came and went as in other sections of the West," and the "small farmers" who enlarged the clearings. "But here the similarity ended. The cotton planters appeared upon the scene." Lands were exploited by a single crop and then abandoned while the planters moved on to newer regions, there to repeat the same process over and over again.[60] This procedure, says Professor Clark, prevented the completion of the cycle described by J. M. Peck in his *A New Guide for Emigrants to the West.* It missed the last stage in which "men of capital and enterprise" came, bought out the earlier settlers (who, by the way, had cleared the land) and begun the development of towns, substantial buildings, "extensive fields, orchards, gardens, colleges and churches" and indulged in "broadclothes, leghorns, crapes and all the refinements, luxuries, elegancies, frivolities and fashions . . . in vogue."

Such an interpretation, and Clark is only the last to repeat it, furnishes only another illustration of the matchless efficiency of abolition propaganda. Historians are still repeating its charges. As a matter of fact the planter and the order which he established meet every requirement of the Peck formula from men "of capital and enterprise" to the "frivolities and fashions." Wheat was as

[59] These conjectures are based on a rather comprehensive survey of Alabama, Mississippi, and Louisiana newspapers for the period.

[60] Dan E. Clark, *The West in American History* (New York, 1937), pp. 307–8.

much a single crop in the Northwest as cotton was in the Southwest and gave a depletion of soils which varied only as rainfall and character of sod formation differed. Every student of American agricultural history agrees on that point. Furthermore, the timber, mineral, or grass regions in the Northwest were treated in like fashion. There was nothing unique about what happened under cotton. Nor did the yeoman farmers cease to exist in the Lower South when a handful of planters settled among them. That class—and it did not differ in any essential way from the prosperous farming class of the Northwest—constituted an overwhelming majority in every southwestern state to 1860 and increased its acreage and ownership throughout the ante-bellum period.

Furthermore, as nearly as can be determined, the great majority of planters in any given "black belt" were self-made men who achieved their planter status in a single lifetime. In the few regions studied it appears that a majority developed on the spot or came from older western regions and did not migrate with plantations full-blown from the Atlantic seaboard. A more democratic story does not appear in American history than that offered by the rise of the planter and his large-scale effort in the Southwest. It is a story of hard-working pioneers who bought and sold land, moved along with population streams, and at last "made," as they described it, in some favorable corner. The number who had inherited capital and who brought "great resources" with them to the third stage of this West was no greater than that which came to the Northwest of the same period.

As to the rise of greater complexity in specialized services and in urban centers, it might be suggested that each plantation, something of a town in itself, supplied artisans, industrial laborers, and sometimes even "social workers," while Memphis, New Orleans, Mobile, and a sufficient number of inland towns furnished the commercial, financial, and professional groups. A closer study of the plantation system shows that planters often built their houses in village fashion and actually lived as urban dwellers. The plantation did not always scatter population. In fact, every significant feature of the third "normal western stage" was here to be found. It differed from that of the Northwest only as one West had a right to differ from another.

Thus both in detail and in flavor here was a new West. In essential qualities and temper it differed little from the other Wests of the day and offered the usual contrasts with the older areas from which it had sprung. It was southern; yet it was thoroughly western. Its institutions—political, economic, and social—were those of the Old South—the emphasis on county government and officials, the plantation and Negro slavery to a degree, the tradition to aristocracy. Yet the tone and outlook was as western as that of Illinois—a bit more of individualism and equality among men; more of waste and extravagance in the spending of Nature's gifts, more of optimism and more of resentment of privileges. Contemporaries recognized the differences and thought of the Cotton Kingdom as something quite distinct.

Furthermore the region early and late showed a mind of its own in regard to national policies. While the opposition to tariffs in principle and practice was general, the region staunchly supported Andrew Jackson in his stand against nullification. The offer of "treasure and blood" to "preserve inviolate our Constitution and our Union" made by an Alabama meeting, seems to have expressed the feelings of a great majority of the people.[61] On land legislation, representatives of the western Cotton Kingdom, such as Albert G. Brown, Clement Clay, Franklin Plummer, William R. Smith, Felix McConnell, and W. R. W. Cobb, were as staunch supporters of pre-emption and homestead bills as could be found in all the West. Most of them retained their liberal attitudes until well into the 1850's. And what is more significant, they were as sharply arrayed against the Old South in their land principles as they were against New England itself. For example: When a homestead bill came up for vote in the House, May 12, 1852, thirty-five representatives from the slaveholding states voted in its favor. Thirty of these were from the West. Of the thirty-four votes cast in opposition by the section, twenty-eight were from the seaboard. When the Senate refused to consider homestead legislation, February 21, 1853, twenty of the thirty-three senators who helped to block the bill were from the slaveholding states. Only three of them came from the new Southwest. Even in 1860, Brown of Mississippi could support homesteads with the declaration that he favored "land to the landless and homes to the homeless" regardless of whether they lived in the North or in the South.[62]

[61] Albert B. Moore, *History of Alabama* (University, Ala., 1934), pp. 219–20.

[62] Ranck, *Albert Gallatin Brown,* 59, 135, 190; *Cong. Debates,* 23 Cong., 2 sess., 1566–70 (Mar. 2, 1835); *Cong. Globe,* 32 Cong., 1 sess., Appendix, 514 (April 27, 1852);

East-West differences, moreover, were sometimes hidden by the growing North-South hostility. The expansionist attitude of the Southwest under the pressure for a united front quickly overcame a disposition on the part of the older southern states to think in terms of land and labor competition, and carried the section into the Texas-Mexican controversy almost as a unit. After a time another influence tended to obscure intra-southern differences. The increase of political strength and economic resources through cotton gave the Gulf states increasing influence in the slavery struggle and added something more of aggressiveness and self-confidence to the southern position. Then men talked of "The Cotton Kingdom" as though it constituted the whole South. They ignored dissenting voices. Only the Cotton Kingdom mattered. It thus came about that "King Cotton Diplomacy" was to have been the key to southern success under Jefferson Davis of Mississippi.

It might thus appear that the Turner approach has a considerably wider application to the ante-bellum South than has usually been supposed. The course of developments was so orthodox that one may well pause in wonderment at the almost total neglect of its story in volumes dealing with "The West in American History." Yet the reasons both for neglect and for the shifting of emphasis to other factors are not difficult to understand. In the first place, the process of evolution from simplicity to complexity which Turner described never went beyond the agricultural stage in the South. The country-gentleman ideal, the development of peculiar marketing arrangements, and the presence of Negro slavery on plantations, checked the development of towns, factories, and industrial captains. The Old South and the Lower South, in spite of efforts to alter the situation, formed a rural-agricultural interest to the outbreak of the War between the States.

Added to this, the slavery controversy emphasized likenesses, not differences, between the old and the new portions of the South. Faced by critics from the outside who called slaveholding a crime and slaveholders, criminals, the whole South moved from resentment to fear. The race question came to form a bond of unity be-

---

2 sess., 747 (Feb. 21, 1853); 33 Cong., 1 sess., 918 (April 14, 1854). For Brown's entire speech, see *ibid.,* 36 Cong., 1 sess., 2007 (May 9, 1860). I am indebted to Mr. John L. Harr, one of my graduate students, for assistance in studying the attitudes of southern congressmen on land legislation.

tween planter and poor white, between the man from Virginia and the man from Texas. The enormous variations, produced by major physical divisions, differing times and sources of settlement, competing economic interests, etc., were lost in a common fear of losing the white man's heritage. Sectionalism had characterized the early history of the South. Sectional differences of equal proportions now existed in Alabama, Mississippi, Louisiana, and Texas, and the foundations for sharp cleavage between the Old South and the Gulf states were ever present and often active. Yet in spite of this, the force of the urban-industrial aggressions, soon reinforced by the attack on slavery, pounded these divergent southern units into what appeared to be a great and distinct section. The normal working out of the western process was thus hidden under a whole set of artificial creations, and the great American West, North and South, bound together by the Mississippi River system, split unnaturally into two parts. East and West on both sides of Mason and Dixon's line were forced into combinations with units which would normally have been their rivals. The West, therefore, ceased to act as a distinct unit in balancing national life, and failed to make its usual contribution to nationalism and democracy. What that cost the nation and its future no one can say.

Civil war came and ended. Propaganda and bloodshed added their part to sectional hatred. Reconstruction deepened the courses already sharply cut between the sections. Yet the Confederacy, with its capital moved to Richmond, was scarcely able to hold together even in war days, and the so-called "Copperhead" movement in the Northwest constantly threatened the security of Lincoln's government. And when the war and its aftermath had been over long enough to again permit passion to yield to interest, the major truth which stared the American people in the face was that the urban-industrial Northeast had emerged triumphant over all rural-agricultural rivals, and had begun an alliance with the Bourbon elements in the older southern states for the expansion of their capital and influence to that region. Cotton and wheat farmers of the prewar Wests, North and South, might, hereafter, protest but the power to change things, as earlier Wests had done, had forever passed. That may some day be considered one of America's greatest tragedies.

XIII

WHY THE SOUTHERN STATES SECEDED

On December 14, 1860, a conservative Georgia editor stated in terms, which he evidently supposed everyone would understand and accept, the reasons why the southern states were seceding from the Union. "It is a mistake," he said, "to suppose that it is the mere election of Lincoln, without regard to anything else, that has driven the States of the South into their present resistance, and their present determination to seek that safety and security out of the Union which they have been unable to obtain within it."

What that "anything else" was, he then made clear. "The election of Lincoln," he said, "is merely the confirmation of a purpose which the South had hoped would be abandoned by the opponents of slavery in the North. It is a declaration that they mean to carry out their aggressive and destructive policy, weakening the institution at every point where it can be assailed either by legislation or by violence, until, in the brutal language of Charles Sumner, 'it dies like a poisoned rat in its hole.'"

The things to be noticed in this bald statement are that northern aggression consisted primarily in the determination to put the institution of Negro slavery on the road to ultimate extinction; that Lincoln's election made the carrying-out of that policy both possible and probable; and that the southern states, much against their wills, had been forced to seek "that safety and security" for their peculiar institution, outside the Union, which they had a perfectly good constitutional right to expect within it.

Most Southerners agreed that Republican hostility to slavery and the evidence of wide northern approval in Lincoln's election justified secession. They somehow felt that the real question before the people in the recent election had not been whether Breckinridge or Lincoln, Bell or Douglas, should be President but whether slavery be perpetuated or abolished. As one writer said: "No man of common sense, who is not prepared to surrender the institution of slavery with the safety and independence of the South can doubt that the time for action has come—now or never!" Some saw the economic danger ahead. "It was not safe," they said, "to trust eight hundred million dollars worth of negroes in the hands of a power that says we do not own the property, that the title under the Constitution is bad, and under the law of God still worse. . . . Slave property is the foundation of all property in the South. When security in this is shaken, all other property partakes of its instability."

Others objected to the Republican boast of moral superiority. They placed "honor" above "interest." They resented less what the Republicans had done or might do, than the things they said and the self-righteous way in which they said them. They could shrug off the material threats, but they could no longer endure the "untiring efforts" to degrade the South in the eyes of all who came within their reach—denying the piety of their clergy, and calling their congressmen "desperadoes" less worthy of trust than "the inmates of our penitentiaries." The question of honor was "paramount to all others."

But more than abstract honor was involved. Republican victory in 1860 was not just a temporary slip. The South had fallen steadily behind the North in population and, denied expansion, was losing political equality as well. The Republican threat to a way of life was bad enough. To lose all hope of an equal voice in national affairs was even worse. As one desperate Southerner said: "Rather than to surrender Southern equality in the Union, let our slaves be lost . . . our fields be desolated . . . our blood to flow," but "never, never should her people . . . yield this most precious of all earthly possessions—their feeling of self-respect."

The official statements made by the seceding conventions in their appeal to the rest of mankind for a sympathetic understanding of their "momentous step" also stressed first of all the threat to their "domestic institutions." The election of a sectional President, "pledged to principles and a policy which we regard as repugnant to the Constitution . . . beget[s] a feeling of insecurity which . . . alarm[s] a people jealous of their rights." The southern states were now a helpless minority "in imminent peril, being in the power of a majority, reckless of Constitutional obligations and pledged to principles leading to [their] destruction."

Some complained of the exclusion of their citizens from territories "owned in common by all the States" and of northern approval of John Brown's raid, but the one grievance above all others was the refusal to return fugitive slaves. This refusal proved beyond all doubt that neither the Constitution of the United States nor the Acts of Congress nor the decisions of the Supreme Court could longer be relied upon as protection for southern rights.

The final, and perhaps the most powerful emotional factor in the situation, was brought out by a speaker in the Alabama Convention.

> Mr. President, if pecuniary loss alone were involved in the abolition of slavery, I should hesitate long to give the vote I now intend to give. If the destruction of slavery entailed on us poverty alone, I could bear it, for I have seen poverty and felt its sting. But poverty, Mr. President, would be one of the least of evils that would befall us from the abolition of African slavery. There are now in the slaveholding states over four million slaves; dissolve the relation of master and slave, and what, I ask, would become of that race? To remove them from among us is impossible. History gives us no account of the exodus of such a number of persons. We neither have a place to which to remove them, nor the means of such removal. They, therefore, must remain with us; and if the relation of master and slave be dissolved, and our slaves be turned loose amongst us without restraint, they would either be destroyed by our own hands—the hands to which they look, and look with confidence for protection—or we ourselves would become demoralized and degraded.

Nor was there any reason to hope that the war on slavery would ever cease. As one editor put it:

> The settled hostility of the Northern people must become stronger with each year. The present dominant party in the Free States, based upon the single idea of opposition to the extension, spread, or existence of slavery, now numbering in its ranks nearly two million voters, will become more powerful as the sentiment upon which it is founded gains strength and intensity. It has now secured the President. In two years more, at most, it will have both Houses of Congress. Then the Supreme Court will be reorganized . . . and we shall have "no more Dred Scott decisions."

As the Reverend Benjamin M. Palmer told his people: "A whole generation has been educated to look upon the system of slavery with abhorrence as a national blot. They hope, and look, and pray for its extinction within a reasonable time, and cannot be satisfied unless things are seen drawing to that conclusion." It had thus become perfectly clear that the North either "could not let slavery alone," or "would not" or did not "intend to let it alone." It was just as clear, they said, that the "Black Republican victory of November [was] incontrovertible proof of a diseased and dangerous public opinion all over the North, and a certain forerunner of further and more atrocious aggression."

There had been serious crises in national affairs at other times, and Southerners had, more than once, threatened secession. But never before had there been such an atmosphere of desperation and finality, such intense realization of impending disaster, such a feeling of helplessness in the face of what seemed to be a driving force against which resistance had all along been hopeless. Lincoln's election did not present an immediate threat, but it did indicate that a new and final stage in the slavery struggle had been reached. Seemingly the nation had got itself into such a predicament that no one, however well meaning, could check the drift toward the use of force.

Up until the John Brown raid, there had been much southern protest and indignation because of northern criticism of slavery and because of denial of equality in the territories and in the distribution of governmental favors. But there had been little panic and much confidence in the southern politician's ability to protect his section, confidence in northern friends and in the Democratic party. Now all was changed. Talk of the "irrepressible conflict" and of "the higher law" now meant something. The Republican party, a strange mixture of moral values and sectional economic interests, had triumphed in a national election. Stephen A. Douglas had been forced to interpret his squatter-sovereignty doctrine in accordance with the views of his northern supporters, and the South's desperate gamble at Charleston to control the Democratic party, to secure federal protection of slavery in the territories, and to force the northern Democracy back under southern control, had failed. The game had been lost, and submission or secession were the only choices left.

For the first time the Southerner had to face the serious realities of life in a slaveholding society. He had to recognize the possibility of ultimate emancipation. He had to calculate the financial risk of having millions of dollars invested in slaves swept away; face the frightening possibility of bloody racial readjustment; be content with permanent political impotence if three-fifths of his slaves were no longer counted as population; and, above all, accept the harsh, cold fact that he stood alone in a world which insisted that slavery was both an economic burden and a moral outrage.

Other issues now lost their importance. Every decision had to be made according to the demands of slavery, and slavery alone. The only defense against economic, social, and political ruin lay in placing slavery beyond the reach of its enemies. The South had been driven into a corner. The choice between submission and secession would have to be made sooner or later.

Abraham Lincoln had understood the southern dilemma and had talked of solving the economic difficulty by compensated emancipation, and the social-racial problem by removing the Negro from the country. He had once framed a bill for these purposes. But nothing had come from his thinking, and the Republican threat, in southern eyes, was the old abolition threat to deal with slavery as a sin to be removed by the usual revival technique of conviction, repentance, and voluntary and immediate renunciation. The resulting problems were not to be taken into consideration.

The idea that some concessions or some plan such as Lincoln had suggested might have saved the day even at this late date overlooks two important considerations. At no time after the early 1830's is there a single shred of evidence to show that any number of planters, intoxicated by the notion that "Cotton was King," would have surrendered a single slave for any consideration ever suggested. It was now too late, even if it had once been possible—which is doubtful. Nor would the abolitionist at any time have considered such a proposal. As one editor put it: "The disease is too deep seated. The election of Mr. Lincoln to the Presidency, gives a tremendous onward impulse to anti-slavery sentiment. He rides a wave he cannot control or guide to conservative results, even if so disposed."

The historian attempting to answer the question as to why the southern states seceded must recognize the predicament into which the nation had fallen. He must understand that the southern states were right when they said that their domestic institutions were no longer safe in the Union. They erred only in not recognizing the more important fact that their institutions were not safe anywhere in the nineteenth century and the emerging Modern World. They were blind, also, in not realizing that secession was no remedy for their troubles in this age of growing national consolidation. They would find out, after four bloody years of heroic fighting, that in this age organization, efficiency, technology, and urban industrialism win wars regardless of individual courage and sacrifice.

The historian must also understand that Lincoln, in turn, was toying with the impossible when he said that slavery, where it existed, would be safe under his administration. He could not have checked the agitation against slavery, nor could he have guaranteed the return of fugitive slaves. He should have known that in the United States an institution which he himself had said was morally wrong could not longer be legally right. William H. Seward showed a far better understanding of the Republican party when he insisted that all human law "must be brought to the standard of the law of God . . . and must stand or fall by it." Charles Sumner saw the situation more clearly than either Lincoln or Seward when he said:

> They have proclaimed slavery to be *wrong,* and have pledged themselves with force against its extension. It is difficult to sense how they can longer sustain themselves *merely* on that grounds. Their promise sustains a broader conclusion, that is, the duty of no longer allowing the *continuance* of evil anywhere within our Constitutional action. They must become Abolitionists.

The abolitionists themselves had understood this and had resolved that the Republican position on "the folly and wrong of slavery," from which they drew "only the modest inference" that it ought not to be allowed to spread, really implied that "it ought not to be tolerated anywhere." It should also be recalled that both Seward and Lincoln had brought the moral issue into politics and used it to advance their political fortunes. Seward had talked of "the higher law" and "the irrepressible conflict," and Lincoln had insisted on the necessity of opposing Stephen A. Douglas, practical politician, because Douglas had been foolish enough to say that he did not care whether the people of a territory voted slavery up or down, even though he knew and Lincoln knew that they would vote it down. In so doing, they had lifted the issue to the abstract level of right versus wrong and had thereby created a situation with which the democratic process of toleration and compromise could not deal. Only force would answer.

With this much accepted, the historian must then remember that the final centering on antislavery aggression as the sum total of southern complaints was only the last stage in a long series of developments. Somewhere in the years after 1815, the South began taking over from the North the role of "the abused." In the emerging era when progress was beginning to be measured in terms of industry, cities, and complex finances, some southern spokesmen saw the inevitable growth of federal power and the corresponding decline of the agricultural South. They foresaw the day when the South would be reduced to that colonial status described, in 1860, as one in which "Yankees" monopolized "the carrying trade with its immense profits," "all the importing," and "most of the exporting business for the whole Union." "New York City, like a mighty queen of commerce, sits proudly upon her island throne, sparkling in jewels and waving an undisputed commercial scepter over the South. By means of her railways and navigable streams, she sends out her long arms to the extreme South, and with avidity rarely equaled, grasps our gains and transfers them to herself—taxing us at every step—and depleting us as extensively as possible without actually destroying us."

And the reason for this, they charged, was that "the whole policy of the Federal Government, from the beginning [had] been to build up and enrich the North at Southern expense. In this business, the monster engine, a high Protective Tariff, [had] been the chief instrument." And besides this, there had been the "fishing bounties, and the navigation laws, and the giving away the public lands, millions of acres at a time, all of which tend[ed] to aggrandise the Northern section of the Union." "On every living issue deemed vital to the South," said the Charleston *Mercury*, "the Northern members, as a body, [have been] against the South."

John Taylor of Caroline, in Virginia, had early talked this way, and Robert Turnbull, in South Carolina, had brought it to a climax in nullification days. Both denounced the tariff and the "consolidation" trends which permitted its passage. Both viewed it as a violation of the Constitution and as a conflict between economic interests. As Turnbull wrote in denouncing the tariff as "the recent exercise of powers never contemplated by the framers of the Constitution, . . . the more National and less Federal the Government becomes, the more certainly will the interests of the great majority of the states be promoted, but with the same certainty, will the interests of the South be depressed and destroyed." The interest of the North and West was "that the Government should become more and more

National," while the interest of the South was "that it should continue Federal."

For this reason northern statesmen were "not astute to enquire" as to whether an act was in keeping with "the clear intent and meaning of the Constitution." They did not tremble at such violations. Only the South had an interest in checking unconstitutional acts and in keeping the nation federal in character.

Thus for its interests and its safety, Turnbull insisted that the South must forever oppose the implied powers of Congress. The interests of the North and West would always lead them toward "usurpation" and departure from the social compact. They had no reason to quarrel with an expanding national government which was building *their* industry with unconstitutional tariffs, and *their* commerce with unconstitutional internal improvements. Bitterly Turnbull noted that "we hear of no projects in Congress to tax the manufactures of the North to support the agriculture of the South." It was all the other way around.

Alexis de Tocqueville, too, had seen such a situation as marking the end of our federal system. "States form confederations," he wrote, "in order to derive equal advantages from their union. . . . If one of the federated states acquire a preponderance sufficiently great to enable it to take exclusive possession of the central authority, it will . . . cause its own supremacy to be respected under the name of the sovereignty of the Union. Great things may then be done in the name of the Federal Government, but in reality that Government will have ceased to exist."

The tariff, however, in spite of its sectional character, poorly explained the growing inferiority and colonial status of the South as a section. Nor could southern unity be secured in opposition. Too many Southerners were longing for a diversified economic life, and too many saw other reasons for the South's plight. "Why are we so far behind in the great march of improvement?" asked one citizen. "Simply because we have failed to act in obedience to the dictates of sound policy. Simply because we have been almost criminally neglectful of our own interests." "You may nullify the tariff," said another, "but you cannot nullify the fertile soils of Alabama and Mississippi."

And so the tariff issue lost much of its appeal with the failure of nullification. South Carolina had stood alone. Her warning to the

South had been in vain. In time, the industrialists of the North and the planters of the South would join hands in shaping the nation's tariff schedules.

In the meantime, John C. Calhoun, unabashed and unenlightened by his nullification experience, had taken up where Turnbull left off. In the early 1830's he had come forward with the assertion that Negro slavery, as practiced in the South, was "a positive good." He followed this, in 1837, with what was ultimately to become the fatal southern orthodox platform. In a series of resolutions offered in the Senate, December 27, he insisted on the strictly federal character of the government in which the states had retained their sovereignty and "the exclusive and sole right over their own domestic institutions and police"; that "any meddling of any one or more States, or a combination of their citizens, with the domestic institutions and police of the others, on any grounds, or under any pretext whatever, political, moral or religious, with a view to their alteration or subversion, is an assumption of superiority, not warranted by the Constitution:—insulting to the States interfered with,—tending to endanger their domestic peace and tranquility."

This government, he said, had been founded to give increased stability and security to the domestic institutions of the states, and since slavery was such a southern institution, "no change of opinion or feeling, on the part of other states . . . in relation to it, can justify them or their citizens in open and systematic attacks thereon, with a view to its overthrow." He closed with the assertion that efforts to abolish slavery in the District of Columbia on the pretext "that it is immoral or sinful" would be an attack on the institutions of all slaveholding states, while the effort to check its expansion into the territories would be a denial of southern equality in the Union.

Here was an implied ultimatum to the effect that the permanence of the Union depended on the universal acceptance of the sovereignty of the states in a federal system and of the positive good of Negro slavery above criticism. It was a demand which men who had caught stride with the oncoming Modern World, even though not yet clearly conscious of its full meaning, could not possibly accept. It would, however, cause them to pause and to think, and instinctively to resist. Interests and morals were both involved.

Calhoun's extreme demands and his blindness or indifference to the nationalistic and democratic-humanitarian character of the age in which he lived had exactly the opposite effects from those he had intended. Already his short-sighted efforts to check antislavery petitions had enabled John Quincy Adams to bring a sacred American right to the support of the hitherto rather ineffective abolition movement. His next equally rash and short-sighted move to annex Texas solely on grounds of safety to southern institutions linked slavery and expansion, pushed the issue into politics, and created the impression that there was a "slave power" bent on spreading its peculiar institution by every means possible to every corner of the nation. Its ultimate purpose was just "to lug new slave states in" and thereby gain political control. A new and wider antislavery appeal was thus available; its political possibilities greatly expanded.

Calhoun and his supporters, it would seem, were bent on proving true all that the abolitionists had charged. By not understanding the fact that they were fighting an age, not just a group of fanatics, they had alarmed and aroused the whole North. Joshua Giddings in Congress was thereby enabled, with wide approval, to charge that the North was "politically bound, hand and foot, surrendered to the rule and government of a slave-holding oligarchy." He could insist, with equal support, that "Our tariff is as much an anti-slavery measure as the rejection of Texas. So is the subject of internal improvements and the distribution of the proceeds of the public lands. The advocates of perpetual slavery oppose all of them, they regard them as opposed to the interests of slavery." Blundering southern leadership had thus placed their section squarely across the path of what northern men had begun to think of as progress. They were demanding that the world stand still.

When James K. Polk, Democrat and slaveholder, accepted war with Mexico but compromised the Oregon boundary, fostered a lower tariff, and vetoed a river and harbor bill aimed primarily to aid the West, the North was ready with the Wilmot Proviso to check proslavery gains in the new territories. The sectional struggle shifted sharply from slavery per se to one of slavery expansion, and the bitter sectional crisis which quickly developed revealed the tragic condition into which the nation had fallen. A southern movement, impossible before, spontaneously developed, and the call went out for a southern convention. Talk of secession became common, and the charge of northern disregard for the Constitution and northern determination to monopolize the territories as a means of abolishing slavery accepted without question. On the other side, northern determination to check the spread of slavery and an awakened consciousness of slavery as a national disgrace were as marked and as positive.

The frantic efforts of patriots finally shifted the issues from abstractions to the concrete problems involved, and compromise became possible. But secession did not come until Calhoun had again proclaimed the sovereignty of the states; had restated his charge of northern aggression; and had made his demands for equal rights in the territories, the end of slavery agitation, the faithful observance of fugitive slave laws, and constitutional amendments to restore sectional equilibrium. He demonstrated again the fact that southern leadership had remained largely untouched and unchanged by the facts and thoughts of the onrushing nineteenth century.

William H. Seward, by contrast, seized the opportunity to announce the arrival of that century. Bluntly he told his colleagues that they lived in a "consolidated Union" in which the states had "surrendered their equality as States, and submitted themselves to the sway of the numerical majority without qualifications or checks." He also informed them that the issues before them were moral issues; that slavery was a sin; and that Americans could not "be either true Christians or real freemen if [they] impose[d] on another a chain [they] defi[ed] all human power to fasten on [themselves]." The demands for the return of fugitive slaves smacked of the Dark Ages, and our human laws must be brought "to the standards of the law of God. . . ."

Seward, in turn, was revealing the fact that the northern mind and conscience had kept pace with the industry, the cities, the finance, and the railroads of the onrushing nineteenth century. He was making it equally clear that a realization of the dignity of a human being and a deep feeling of guilt for its violation was as marked as the material changes.

The southern demand for a more efficient fugitive-slave law which came out of the Compromise of 1850 again showed how poorly informed southern leaders were and how inadequate was their understanding of the northern mind. Nothing could have contributed more toward rendering slavery obnoxious. Nothing could have convinced the North so completely of southern inhumanity and the calloused state of the southern conscience as did this act. Yet strict northern obedience was the condition on which the southern states accepted the Compromise, and northern refusal to comply with its enforcement constituted, in the end, almost the only concrete evidence offered in support of the charge of northern aggression and of northern lack of respect for the Constitution. As one Southerner said in 1860:

The only excuse for disunion, and the only reason that we deem the idea tolerable, is that the Constitution has been violated by the 'personal liberty acts' and negro-stealing mobs of the North, and that the election of a Black Republican will show that instead of fanaticism getting cool, it is growing worse, and, therefore, the sooner the South gets clear from them the better.

"The Constitution," said another,

affords no remedy for Southern grievances. To the Southern people the Constitution is as worthless as a piece of waste paper so far as protection to the slavery interest is concerned. The Constitution authorizes slavery; the same instrument declares that fugitives shall be returned to their masters; Congress has passed laws in accordance therewith; and the decisions of the Supreme Court affirm and maintain the mandates of the Constitution and the laws of the National Legislature.

Yet, as he said, if a master attempted to recover his servant in accord with his constitutional rights, he would be arrested, fined, and sent to prison in nine different northern states. No wonder that the Reverend J. Thornwell insisted that the original Constitution had been repealed and new terms of Union submitted for southern acceptance.

Yet, at this very moment, the Charleston *Mercury*, speaking for the only portion of the South eager for secession, was saying that the "Personal Liberty Laws" were not of the slightest consequence to the "Cotton States." "Few or none of our slaves are lost, by being carried away and protected from recapture in the Northern States." These laws only mattered "in the insult they conveyed to the South, and the evidence they offered of Northern faithlessness."

In the decade which followed the Compromise of 1850, the North as a whole moved rapidly forward into the Modern World. It was a period "when modern industrial capitalism was beginning to sink its roots deep into the American economy." Northern cities, both on the seaboard and far back in the interior, were reaching metropolitan proportions. Canals and railroads were bringing the Northeast and the Northwest closer together, and the coastal cities from Boston to Baltimore were competing for the western produce which once went largely to New Orleans. The "young industrial capitalism of textiles, iron, machinery, wood, and leather products" was no longer content to be held back by the restrictions on protection, banking, labor supply, and public works imposed by the Democratic party under southern influence. The hard, cold facts of economic and social interdependence were teaching them the value of national consolidation. The Union was an economic necessity.

Nor were the young capitalists willing to see slavery spread to the territories of the farther West. Rather, the territories should be homesteaded by free men and women and made more accessible by government aid to rivers and harbors and railroads. It took only the fictitious Uncle Tom and the unfortunate Kansas-Nebraska Bill to bring into being the sectional Republican party as the carrier of northern interests and values. These men did not clearly understand what they were doing, but they were in fact creating a political party which stood for the nationalism, the industrial capitalism, and the democratic-humanitarian impulses of the Modern World.

The southern states, meanwhile, followed their accustomed course. There were changes here as well as in the North, but they tended to strengthen old patterns, not to add new ones. More and more the Cotton Kingdom along the Gulf dominated the section. In spite of rather remarkable advances in the agriculture, industry, and transportation of the older states, "Cotton" increasingly spoke for the South. Its voice was more confident and more aggressive. Its planters had greater reasons for maintaining the status quo and more reason for fearing the attacks on slavery. The supreme confidence of its leaders in the power of Cotton to make or break the prosperity of the whole Western world provided most of the confidence with which the whole South ultimately accepted the risks in secession. It was the Cotton States' extreme demand for new guarantees for the protection of slavery in the territories which destroyed the Democratic party at Charleston.

Conservatives resented what they called "the fierce and eager instigations of the Cotton States," and border-state spokesmen insisted that the Cotton States should "bear with the few wrongs inflicted upon them, until those, who 'lose ten times as many negroes and suffer ten times as many inconveniences through the hostility of the Northern people to their institutions' " and "who stand between them and danger," should "feel it their duty and interest to act." Yet in the end those who had suffered most and would continue to suffer most, permitted those who had prospered most and suffered least to shape the section's destiny.

It was a University of Virginia professor who wrote at the time when secession was a reality:

> Indignation and alarm alternate in my breast when I think of wretched little South Carolina, like an insolent and enfeebled reactionary, plunging the whole country into strife and confusion of which others must bear the brunt. . . . And when I reflect that the mean desertion of the other Southern States compels us to make this the crisis of our destiny, whether we like it or not, I am oppressed at once with indignation and anxiety. And these feelings are aggravated by the consideration that while I think the conspirators of the cotton states deserve the condign punishment, our safety makes it necessary that we should interpose to screen them if need be. . . . They bluster and threaten, safe, as they imagine, behind the intervening tiers of quiet Commonwealths to whose chivalrous feelings and sympathy they design to appeal to support them in a course abhorrent to the principles of these States and destructive to their interests.

Yet when Lincoln called for troops, the good professor was convinced that "Nothing remains now to the Christian patriot but to strike strongly for the right, humbly invoking the aid and blessing of our fathers' God."

Thus under Cotton's rule and with able assistance from the northern abolitionists, from Seward, Sumner, and John Brown, the few who from the beginning had wished to break up the Union found the opportunity to shift the southern efforts from defense to aggression. They realized that it was not possible to dissolve the Union with "unanimity and without division." "Men having both nerve and self-sacrificing patriotism," said Barnwell Rhett, "must head the movement and shape its course, controlling and compelling their inferior contemporaries." Deliberately they turned their backs on the nineteenth century. Closing their eyes to the tattered realities about them and their minds to all the democratic-humanitarian demands of the age in which they lived, they proclaimed the perfection of their ways and values and their superiority over those of all the Western world.

It was the North, they said, which was deluded. What its leaders called progress was, in fact, the real backwardness. Its celebrated cities were breeders of crime and vice and social conflict. Its free labor system was nothing other than cruel, impersonal exploitation devoid of all responsibility. Its chaotic social-economic system was marked by periodic depressions, endless strife between capital and labor, and a constant threat of revolution. Its lack of stability had destroyed all respect for constitutional restrictions and had, at last, produced a sectional political party bent on national domination. It had produced an eroded people who would not fight even for their own interests.

In sharp contrast to all this, they pictured the South as a wholesome rural world, orthodox in religion and untroubled by the restless "isms" that beset the North. A peaceful world where capital and labor were one, and where the realities of inequality between individuals and races were accepted and adjusted to the benefit of all. The institution of slavery, instead of being a blight upon the region, was the very foundation on which a superior civilization rested. Instead of debasing the character of the master, as charged, it produced the highest type of leader and the man who accepted his responsibilities both to his slaves and to society. Only in a slave society, where all white men were equal, was a true democracy possible. Only where the Negro was enslaved was he happy, productive, and free from the worry and cares of a complex civilization for which he was ill-fitted by nature. On the mudsills of slavery a golden age was alone possible and all the world would one day accept the fact. The state, not the nation, should command first allegiance. The nineteenth century was moving in the wrong direction.

It is, indeed, difficult to believe that under normal conditions any considerable number of Southerners would have accepted either the absurd notion of northern decadence or of southern perfection. But nothing, in the 1850's, could long remain normal. In the North, change crowded on the heels of change and public reaction to events, whether economic or political, no longer took form from the events themselves but from the sectional slavery controversy. There might have been some question as to the actual danger of slavery expansion from the Kansas-Nebraska Act or the Dred Scott Decision, but that did not matter. The issue was one of right and wrong. What did matter was that the "slave power" had been given the legal right to expand and that brought a firm determination to see slavery confined to its present limits and set on the road to ultimate extinction. The day for compromise with slavery had ended.

This grim northern determination, when combined with the brutal fact that the South had become a permanent political minority, its social system under moral condemnation by the whole Western world, its economic life reduced to colonial status, gave the southern extremists a new lease on life. Critics stood almost helpless before the apprehensions, the fears, the indignation, and the self-respect to which the fanatics could appeal. "All that could be done by moderate, dispassionate, patriotic, and experienced men was to go with the current, endeavoring to subdue its boiling and seething energies. . . ."

By 1860, the extreme, self-appointed spokesmen for southern rights had all but silenced their critics and sealed the southern mind against all outside opinion. They were able to split the Democratic party with demands based on their assumptions of the rightness and perfection of the slavery system. With a curious psychopathic twist at the moment of decision in the Charleston Convention, William L. Yancey of Alabama indignantly upbraided his northern colleagues for treating slavery as an evil. They should have boldly pronounced it a positive good. If they had taken the position that slavery was right by the laws of nature and of God, they would have triumphed.

To this archaic demand, George E. Pugh of Ohio gave the only answer a modern man could give and the one that would be given over and over again: "Gentlemen of the South, you mistake us—you mistake us! We will not do it."

As the campaign of 1860 developed, a once-conservative southern editor impatiently brushed aside all projects for saving the Union. They were all "feeble and fruitless" because of "the absolute impossibility of revolutionizing Northern opinion in relation to slavery."

> Without a change of heart, radical and thorough, all guarantees which might be offered are not worth the paper on which they would be enscribed. As long as slavery is looked upon by the North with abhorrence; as long as the South is regarded as a mere slave-breeding and slave-driving community; as long as false and pernicious theories are cherished respecting the inherent equality and rights of every human being, there can be no satisfactory political union between the two sections.

Northern editors were just as realistic. "We cannot tell Mr. Yancey," said one, "that we do not believe slavery wrong, for the reverse is the profound conviction of three-fourths of the whole North. . . . It would be dishonest to say that this conviction will not remain and grow stronger every day." And to promise the "complete revolution in the moral and political convictions" which the South demanded, or to promise that all opposition to slavery would cease, was like promising that "water shall run up hill and two and two shall make five."

> The strife between freedom and slavery . . . is but a fragment of the great conflict of [the] ages, the ever raging war between those things which are just, virtuous, useful, and good, and those which are hurtful and vicious and wrong.

Had not the struggle between the sections rested on such foundations as these, there might have been some way out. But as things stood, the mere election of Lincoln was "only confirmation of a purpose which the South had hoped would be abandoned by the opponents of Slavery in the North" and, which failing, drove the states of the South into "their present resistance, and their present determination to seek that safety and security out of the Union which they have been unable to obtain within it."

"In no other way," said a contemporary, "can we account for the perfect whirlwind of public feeling which swept everything before it, either utterly annihilating conservatism and nationality, or reducing to impotence the few who still ventured to make a timid appeal on behalf of the Union. . . ."

But this, after all, answers our question only in terms of the day. It ignores the fact that while there is strife and hatred "men have eyes for nothing save the fact that the enemy is the cause of all the troubles; but long, long afterwards, when all passion has been spent, the historian often sees that it was a conflict between one-half that was perhaps too wilful, and another half-right that was perhaps too proud; and behind even this he discovers that it was a terrible predicament which had the effect of putting men at cross-purposes with one another."

The historian may still question the soundness of southern leadership, but he will remember that men, whose opportunity in the Modern World was one of producing its raw cotton, did not deliberately choose to do so on plantations with Negro slavery. They only went on with what was already at hand in their hurry to prosper. And having done so without the necessity of altering to any degree their social-economic patterns, they saw no reason for changing their traditional notions of the federal character of the national government, the benefits of Negro slavery, or the superiority of a rural-agricultural way of life. The social-intellectual side of the nineteenth century had not come their way. As a result, they were sometimes confused, sometimes reduced to rationalizing, sometimes overwhelmed by guilt.

Nor should the historian give too much moral credit to northern men, upon whom had been showered all the benefits of the advancing urban-industrial age, for advocating consolidated nationalism, free labor, and democratic-humanitarian reforms. These were the social-intellectual approaches which the new age demanded of those who shared its benefits. Northern men did not in all cases deliberately choose them. They merely accepted them as part of what they were soon calling "Progress."

And so the historian, having heard both sides, begins to understand the "fundamental human predicament . . . which would have led to a serious conflict of wills even if all men had been fairly intelligent and reasonably well-intended." He may, in historical perspective, even "learn to be a little more sorry for both parties" who came to believe that they had no alternative to war. Even the war itself might lose some of its romance, cease to be simply a struggle between good men and bad men, and begin to take on its true meaning as a nation's greatest tragedy. Yet, with all this later-day understanding, no historian can ignore the fact that the southern resort to secession for the protection of slavery reduced the whole matter, for northern men of that day, to one of saving the Union and destroying slavery as an obligation to the age in which they lived.

XIV

AN HISTORICAL ADVENTURE

Behind the oft-repeated statement that each generation must write its own history lies a tragic situation. It implies that there can be no *ultimate history,* and that the historian is doomed to be forever writing in the sand. He can say little of permanent value. He must expect his work to be superseded again and again, and that what he writes today will, by the next generation, be considered nonsense.

The enduring interest in history may, as he is told, "reflect a deep-rooted human need," but the honest historian knows that this need is not the same for all times and in all places. The past may be "intelligible only in the light of the present," but the hard fact remains that the same document, viewed at different times by different historians for different purposes, has a strange way of telling a different story. As a result, those who were hailed as profound scholars in their own day become objects of pity in the next. They are either revised, rejected, or ignored. The young graduate students of the next generation marvel at their ignorance, at their mistaken interpretations, and at their abysmal lack of historical insight. They are amazed that Frederick Jackson Turner, who propagated such an absurd thesis regarding the frontier, ever secured a professorship at Harvard; that Charles A. Beard, with his unbalance and distortions, ever got to Columbia; or how Carl Becker, with his abstract thinking, ever made Cornell. So when the young historians of the new day have finished the "Reconstruction of American History" (I give the title of a recent paperback), these once respected scholars are fit only for a term paper in a class in historiography.

The introduction to the volume I have just mentioned states that the purpose of the book is to tell "how a standard topic in Ameri-

Presidential address delivered before the Mississippi Valley Historical Association, Cleveland, Ohio, April 30, 1964.

can History was understood a generation ago and how its interpretation has altered since that time." It then adds that "the 'orthodoxy' of a generation ago was itself a revision of preceding formulations . . . and to judge from the evidence presented in this volume the reconstruction of American history is vigorously underway" again.

Do you therefore wonder that a recent scholar writing on the subject, "What Is History?" begins by saying: "I hope that I am sufficiently up-to-date to recognize that anything written in the 1890's must be nonsense. But I am not yet advanced enough to be committed to the view that anything written in the 1950's necessarily makes sense."

Now if this is all that even the most prominent historians of one generation may expect from the next, what attraction does history offer to the great average majority? Why give your life to writing in the sand? Why seek elusive truth which changes its character at every turn? Is it really enough for an individual to be told that "history is profoundly important because it enriches life"; "that of all creation man alone has devised for himself the means of transcending space and time"? I have my doubts. Most certainly the pursuit of history must yield something more substantial to the individual—something more satisfying if one is to give his all in its pursuit.

As one who has revised and, in turn, been revised, I am more inclined to fall back on good old Thomas Fuller, who wrote, some two centuries ago:

> Now know, next Religion, there is nothing accomplisheth a man more than learning. Learning in a lord, is as a diamond in gold. And if you fear to hurt your tender hands with thornie school-questions, there is no danger in meddling with history, which is a velvet study, a recreation-work. What a pity it is to see a proper gentleman to have such a crick in his neck that he cannot look backward! Yet no better is he who cannot see behind him the actions which long since were performed. History maketh a young man to be old, without either wrinkles or grey hairs; privileging him with the experience of age without either the infirmities or inconvenience thereof. Yea, it not only maketh things past, present, but it ableth one to make rational conjecture of things to come. For this world affordeth no new accidents, but in the same sense wherein we call it a new Moon, which is the old one in another shape, and yet no other than hath been formerly, old actions return again, furnished over with some new and different circumstances.

In these more critical days, one might well question the historian's superior ability to "make rational conjecture of things to come," yet few would deny the handicap of a crick in the intellectual neck which prevents the backward glance; or deny the advantage in balance and perspective to be gained from such a look. Acquaintance with men and times long gone and a knowledge of what lies behind the present unquestionably gives a more spacious present and a better stage from which to plan for the future. But after all, the real pleasure comes from the quest.

In fact, I am inclined to think that history pays its way largely in the personal satisfaction of sitting on the fence and enjoying vicariously the trials and tribulations of men and times now ended; of enjoying the rare privilege of taking sides in their quarrels without in the least bearing responsibility; of sharing the good and the bad alike without the slightest feeling of guilt or a troubled conscience; of taking part in their victories and their defeats, without the vanity of the one or the pain of the other; of enjoying their secrets to a degree that few shared them in their own time; of associating with kings and peasants, saints and scoundrels, without anyone questioning the kind of company we have been keeping.

Best of all is the accumulation of what I call the historian's "attic friends." As David Donald says in the preface to his biography of Charles Sumner: "After living with Sumner for a decade, after learning more about him than I know about any other human being, alive or dead—a great deal more, in some respects, than he ever knew about himself—I think of him almost as I would a member of my own family."

And I, too, have my attic friends—an old Virginia gentleman who lived in the days when tobacco had weakened the soils of his plantation, when neighbors were abandoning their exhausted lands and turning their faces westward; when tired men and patient women plodded on with a persistance too mechanical to have been born of hope; a time when slaves were said to have been advertising for their runaway masters. A grim old man he was, bitter because of failure in public life and because the Southland he loved so deeply was falling behind the prosperous North. I toiled beside him as he lifted the agriculture of his state to new prosperity. I traced the steps by which he was transformed into a southern fire-eater, and I stood beside him as he pulled the lanyard which loosed the storm on Fort Sumter. I followed him to Bull Run and understood his reasons for not wishing to go on with life when his cause became the Lost Cause. I think I understand Edmund Ruffin far better than he understood himself or do those who still bear his name.

Then, in an attic in Louisiana, I met and came to know good Rachel O'Connor—a young widow who went on managing a plantation for her brother after the death of her husband. Rachel, who told of "sixteen little negro children arising . . . all very healthy . . . except my little favorite Isaac. He is subject to a cough, but seldom sick enough to lay up. The poor little fellow is lying at my feet sound asleep. I wish I did not love him as I do, but it is so, and I cannot help it." Rachel, who stayed up all night to sew on coats so that her Negro boys might not suffer from the cold when being sent to work on the neighboring plantation. Rachel, whose troubles with overseers would shame Job himself, and who denounced their running after the Negro women with a vigor and the language of a Sumner or a William Lloyd Garrison himself. But Rachel who, when faithful old Daniel died, let the weeds take her garden because whenever she entered the gate, thoughts of Daniel sent her away in tears.

Two years ago, for no reason other than the inability to resist the urge to explore a body of available documents (call it habit or a disease), I made the acquaintance of some new attic friends—the Manning-Chesnut family, who lived their days out in ante-bellum South Carolina. Through their papers, and with brazen and almost indecent effrontery, I poked my historical nose into their private affairs, entered their homes uninvited, checked over their business accounts, and forced them to tell me their innermost thought about their fellow men, about the events of the day, and about the institutions that influenced their everyday living.

I soon discovered that the Chesnuts and Mannings are people well worth going out of one's way to know. Not many families can boast of a member who was the niece of a governor, sister of a governor, wife of a governor, mother of a governor, aunt of a governor, and grandmother of a governor. Not many men in the ante-bellum South made a fortune of over two million dollars with slaves on plantations and yet found time for public service. Not many ante-bellum women kept a diary which would become a national classic. Yet the Chesnut-Manning family produced all three.

It is because of the wide and varied activities of this family, which touched so many facets of southern life, that on this occasion I have decided to share with you their friendship and their experiences. Here was a southern family which owned great plantations in both the Cotton Kingdom and the Sugar Bowl, and who employed numerous overseers who made regular and detailed reports in original spelling to the owners. Their slaves were numbered by the hundreds, and they experienced all the peculiar problems inherent in that institution. Their records reveal the striking differences between slavery in cotton fields or on sugar plantations or at domestic tasks in the city or country home.

Then, to round out their activities, the men folk took an active part in the political affairs, both of the state and of the nation. They sat in local and national legislative bodies, and two of them were elected to the governorship of South Carolina. Their womenfolk, meanwhile, enjoyed a social life so strenuous that at times, as one of them wrote, "the girls seem glad to rest from their labors of dissipation—for really since Mrs. Douglas's wedding there has been a constant round of parties." But there was much more than parties and dinners. There were servants to look after, and Mrs. Chesnut found time to read and to conclude that Thackeray's *Vanity Fair* was his best work although she preferred his *Henry Esmond.*

It is thus possible for the historian, reading these family papers, to share in a rather intimate way the personal and public life of another era. He may understand the problems of a planting world based on staple crops and slave labor. He may face the problem of whether to use valuable slaves for the unhealthy task of digging and clearing canals, or to hire cheap Irish labor for the job. He may share the terror when Old Man River went on a rampage, threatening all the levies, or when cholera came prowling up from New Orleans to carry off as many as forty slaves from a single plantation. He may even feel some responsibility for seeing that plantation supplies were bought at a fair price; that the slaves were well treated, the cotton and sugar sent to market when prices were right. He will soon realize that these men were engaged in big business with large capital invested in land and labor and equipment—that they were the counterpart of the new industrial capitalists then arising in the North.

In the same sense, they were the employers of labor—only here labor involved a far greater personal responsibility. For slavery could be as brutal and exploitative, or as paternal and considerate as a master chose to make it, or as public opinion demanded. The treatment of slaves, therefore, generally reflected both the master's personal qualities and the values of the day. And this ante-bellum South seems to have retained, through rural dominance, much of its frontier individualism and to have had an unusual bent toward physical violence. Early and late the papers of the South Carolina governors are literally crowded with petitions begging lenience for those convicted of assault and battery, theft and murder. And what is so revealing is that these petitions usually declare the convicted man to have been honest, upright, and highly regarded in his community—the member of a prominent family.

Gentlemen felt justified in publicly horse-whipping offenders who had, as one reported, "said and written diverse, scandalous, false, malicious, scurrilous, and abusive matters against me and my father." In one case, the gentleman involved insisted that he intended no cruelty, but "excited by passion, in the heat and confusion of the fray" he had used the butt of the whip on the head of his opponent.

Duels were common between gentlemen, who considered it an offense involving life and death for anyone even to hint that they were not the soul of honor and courage. Such an affair between Louis Wigfall and Preston Brooks, which constitutes one large section of the Manning papers, reveals a degree of adolescence that would be highly amusing if it did not involve so many persons of public importance. The question here, in the end, was simply one of whether Wigfall would accept Brooks as an equal and their affair be considered "an affair of honor." This Wigfall insisted could not be the case, because Brooks was "a published liar and his second a blackleg." He could, therefore, make no settlement with such a fellow. Reading these letters, one gets a new understanding of why the War between the States became inevitable.

In such an atmosphere of accepted violence, it is not surprising that Negro slavery exhibited its worst and its best. The early South Carolina black code was more extreme than that of any other southern state. It permitted not only branding on the face and body but mutilation as well—the cutting-off of ears, castration, and the slitting of noses. No penalties were imposed if a slave died under punishment, and even the intentional killing of a slave was punishable only by a fine. This code, always worse on paper than in practice, had been revised at different times but was still severe. James Vernor, in 1821, convicted of whipping a slave to death "in sudden heat and passion," was fined only $30 and sent to prison for five months. For the same crimes, a few years later, both John Neal and Henry Wimberly were each fined $500 and given six months in jail. The fines, I might add, were remitted and the jail sentences reduced to five months. On the other hand, in the same year, one Negro was sentenced to be hanged for stealing a few pounds of bacon; another for breaking into a smoke house; a Negro woman on suspicion of arson, and another for giving a child the wrong medicine. It is interesting to notice that the execution of the latter was delayed until she had given birth to and nursed a child.

But there was another side to the picture. On the death of Colonel John Chesnut, his executors "on behalf of ourselves and every member of his family . . . have as a testimony of our gratitude and friendship toward his faithful body servant, Richard, given him his freedom & we do hereby bind ourselves and our heirs to execute in proper and legal form a deed of emancipation. . . ." Nor is evidence of the human side of slavery to be found only in wills. Governor John L. Manning early discovered the musical talents of his little Negro slave Robin, and determined at once to cultivate whatever ability along that line the boy might possess. He sought out the best teachers of violin that could be found, permitted Robin to give his full time to study, and as he progressed sent him away to procure further instruction. Robin repaid these favors by teaching three other young slaves to play on different instruments and welded them into a quartet which Manning boasted could play "with more precision than most." Their services seemed to have been widely sought, and the mutual affection generated convinced the governor that "slavery itself is the most effective mode, as far as it concerns the African race, of creating among them the most effective civilization." He had demonstrated to *his* satisfaction that Southerners were the real philanthropists and that Northerners were only "mock philanthropists." Then to prove his sincerity, as governor of South Carolina, he saw to it that white men convicted of killing slaves were hanged even if it required the calling-out of the militia. Here, I suggest, was rationalization at its best. Here was guilt unrecognized.

Yet nowhere in abolition literature is to be found more scathing denunciations of slavery than those in the Chesnut diary. In March, 1861, Mrs. Chesnut wrote:

I wonder if it be a sin to think of slavery a curse to any land. Men and women are punished when their masters and mistresses are brutes, not when they do wrong. Under slavery, we live surrounded by prostitution, yet an abandoned woman is sent out of any decent house. Who thinks any worse of a negro or mulatto woman for being what we can't name? God forgive us, but ours is a monstrous system, a wrong and an iniquity! Like the patriarchs of old, our men live all in one house with their wives and their concubines; and the mulattoes one sees in every family, partly resemble the white children. . . . My disgust sometimes is boiling over. . . . Slavery has to go, of course, and joy go with it. . . . I hate slavery.

And if South Carolina's black code was harsh, it had its critics. Aroused over the questionable hanging of a Negro boy accused of arson, ex-Governor Thomas Bennett wrote to Governor Richard I. Manning:

It was one of those cases which unquestionably involve much doubt. A conviction, resting solely on the confession of a child, under restraint, if not torture, within view of the Engine, was, to say the least, not very judicious. If, from the terror of death, he had denied his guilt, on what grounds could he have been executed? I never could, and cannot at this hour, separate myself from the conviction that all the forms, proceedings, and solemnities of a trial affecting the life of a fellow being should be the same whether White or Black,—and under this I have been led to another, that the sovereignty of the state can no more shield its character abroad from aspersions and censure than can the sovereignty of Algeria from the detestation of the civilized world.

It is time, and our duty to unite in rescuing this people from the odious stain upon their jurisprudence, and obliterate forever the chilling enactments of our terrible code noir. I do most sacredly believe that there is a virtue in our fellow citizens which would hail with transport so auspicious a change, and whatever the Cavelier for its dreadful denunciations may say, it is not in the character, the disposition, and feelings of this people to reenact that law if once stricken from the statute books.

There is another poor wretch who will die this month should you refuse to interprose your privilege for his sake. His fate, I venture to assert, would not have been at your disposal had his skin been the same color as ours . . .

I am indeed grateful for having been introduced to Thomas Bennett and to John I. Manning.

But life in these bygone days had its pleasures and its public side as well as its personal problems. One can still sense the confusion and excitement of that March day, in 1825, when General Lafayette visited Columbia. The newspapers of the day tell of the horse troops which met him at the North Carolina border; of the procession which marched down Richardson Street to the State House where Governor Manning waited, and then on through a triumphal arch to his quarters on Gervais Street. They tell of a public dinner, and of a grand ball; of marching troops, and of the ladies who received "the good man's smile." But the affair really comes to life for the latter-day intruder only in the detailed expense accounts found in the Governor's papers. There one learns of the black and cream colored horses, borrowed from different owners, to draw the general's carriage; of the scarlet coats, and glazed and varnished hats provided for his escorts; of the bands and military companies whose expenses ran to $1,947.75. And besides, there was the $10.50 paid to Jim for beating the "base drum," and a like amount paid to his companions for playing the fife and beating the "common drum."

And what a banquet! Tables lighted with 431 candles in 68 dozen candle sticks and ten servants to keep them going; turkeys, both tame and wild; capons, beef, mutton, veal, fish, sheep's heads, and three barrels of Virginia oysters; asparagus, carrots, turnips, beets, radishes and lettuce; 1,400 oranges, quantities of pineapples, citrons, olives, raisins, limes, and nuts; tea and coffee, Madeira, Port, Claret, and Champagne, with a patent corkscrew and $22 worth of ice; 1,000 best Spanish cigars; knives, forks, spoons, dishes, glasses, and trays, borrowed along with the best servants in town, and only one dish broken—a water pitcher valued at $8!

Layfayette's visit ended, South Carolinians returned to their normal turbulent ways. From earliest colonial times, this people had been forced to look out for themselves. They had stood alone against the Spaniard in Florida, the Indian on their western border, and the stormy Atlantic at their front. They had developed a sturdy independence and a hypersensitive jealousy for their rights. And just now there was good reason to be on guard. The federal Congress was taking liberties with the Constitution by passing harmful tariffs, and no one else seemed inclined to resist. Ignoring the fact that some of her best people thought that the Supreme Court had been set up to pass on the constitutionality of laws, and that Andrew Jackson was President of the United States, South

Carolinians again took matters into their own hands. It was a dangerous move, but they were long used to danger.

The Manning papers clearly reveal the course of events. In the beginning, as Richard Manning wrote (1828):

> I find the Legislature almost seemingly, and I believe really, at a loss how to move up this grand and important affair. While some are moved by the strongest feelings to take the most positive and decisive steps, others seem to be impressed with the necessity of awaiting longer to see what will be the result of time. . . . Most of the highest talents of the Legislature are for the most violent and decisive steps. . . . The great mass of the Legislature, however, I think are prepared to go to no great length or to violence, but are disposed to wait longer.

Yet, he added, if the government does go further, we "will rise with arms in our hands and with the might and power of a brave but injured portion of the Union strike for liberty. . . ."

Unfortunately, the federal government did go further, and "the highest talent in the Legislature" had its way. South Carolina dared to defy both the federal government and the far more dangerous Andrew Jackson. By 1832, as one wrote :

> The pillars of our confederated republic are tottering. The Proclamation of the President . . . has nerved the arm of all who are not too cowardly to contest for their rights, or, too corrupt to desire that the purity of our Constitution should be preserved. . . .

"South Carolina," wrote another, "is fast approaching a decided military nation. We are arming and turning out in all quarters; the finest spirits pervade our party, nothing daunted or alarmed at the potent threats of our good King Andrew the 1st. Thank God the men of Carolina are no longer won by a name. She understands her rights, how they are secured, & nothing but principle & justice will turn them from their course. . . . There are now under arms and ready to march 15,000 men who will not be coerced into submission. And no United States blackguard soldiers can set foot on our soil. . . ."

The tread of hobnailed boots on the streets of Oxford and Birmingham were already in the offing.

But as behooved an independent people, there were those who opposed "the violent and decisive steps." Richard Manning, himself, saw the danger in the triumph of either the state or the general government—for the one would lead to chaos and the other to tyranny. In the end, all welcomed compromise, but the struggle left its scars. Even in the town of Camden opposing groups, meeting on the streets, were "courteous & polite to each other, but it is seldom you see familiarity between the nullifier and the Union man." The gulf between low country and up-country had also been widened and resentment against aristocratic rule in the state intensified. Because of the conflict with an outside foe, says the state's greatest historian, D. D. Wallace, the inevitable struggle for a more democratic order in the state itself had been postponed.

That, I suggest, was a situation which would occur over and over again in this unique commonwealth, or for that matter, all over the South, and which enabled a minority with emotion on its side to silence the conservative opposition.

South Carolina had thus again revealed her unique personality—confident, sensitive, explosive, and beautifully rationalized in terms of honor and not-to-be-questioned rights. Her protest had been against a stronger and more active central government, and against the tariff as a symbol of a rising urban-industrial age. She would have none of either. Holding such values, she would in the years ahead see John Quincy Adams, contending for the rights of petition, as "one of the most wicked old men in the world"; John C. Calhoun as "undoubtedly the most intellectual man in Congress—very far superior to Clay, and in most respects to Webster"; William H. Seward as "a gifted and talented leader, although a demagogue, but in spite of it, a gentleman"; and Abraham Lincoln as "a wretched backwoodsman, who has cleverness, indeed, but no cultivation."

By 1849, South Carolina again saw "alarming and imminent peril . . . hanging over the institutions and sovereign rights of the slave-holding states, caused by the unconstitutional and mischievous interference with our domestic slavery and the rights of slave-holders on the part of the people of the North. . . ." She again felt herself wronged and insulted, with no "alternative but abject and humiliating submission or a like concert and determination in maintaining our constitutional rights. . . ." She must again "resist at any hazard." Many were ready for immediate secession, but the majority held back for co-operation with the other southern states, which never developed. The southern movement collapsed, but in the struggle Negro slavery became the symbol of all southern values and the cornerstone of a superior civilization. It had also convinced the radical South Carolina leaders that if rights and honor and self-respect were to be preserved, she must take the lead and stand alone.

With the election of Abraham Lincoln as President of the United States in 1860, South Carolina brought to a logical climax the course which she had consciously and unconsciously been following from the beginning. One cannot read the letters in this collection without sensing the genuine enthusiasm and pleasure with which the majority of her citizens welcomed the opportunity to declare her independence from the Union. A gala atmosphere pervaded the secession convention. There was little of the feeling of "painful sadness" which widely existed in other southern states. As James L. Petigru wrote: "The most deplorable part of our case is the total absence of a minority, and the general contempt for consequences." "They seem all to be bitten by the same dog." Even Senator James H. Hammond, who had held back, denounced his fellows as "great asses for resigning," three days later did the same, with the comment: "It is an epidemic and very foolish."

Two things stand out in every statement made. First, a clear recognition on all sides that South Carolina's institutions, her way of life and her values, as symbolized by Negro slavery, were no longer safe in the Union. Perhaps, if the letters received by this family from friends abroad mean anything, they were not safe anywhere in the modern world. Writing from England in January, 1860, an old friend bluntly told Governor Manning that the South was wrong in seceding because of Lincoln's election, that he would have thought the North wrong had it done the same when Buchanan was elected. He urged the South as an independent nation to do something about slavery. It was based, he said, upon a wrong principle. "It cannot in the days in which we live remain unaltered as a permanent institution. The world moves on & those who do not progress with it, are crushed by it. You cannot do all at once, but for your own sake, be wise and do something in time, do it of your own free will & you will be supported by all the intelligence and worth of the world & by the kindly gratitude of the gentle, affectionate black race who have been so greatly wronged by us white men." Secondly, the thing that stands out is the clear and almost naïve acceptance on all sides of first obligations and loyalty to Mother Carolina, not to the Union. It is not without meaning that, having dissolved the connection "between this State and the other states of North America," her convention announced "that the State of South Carolina has resumed her position among the nations of the world." No other southern state said that with such assurance. Commenting on this local patriotism, one South Carolina historian has remarked that James L. Orr, who attempted to diversify the state's industry, establish public schools, and in general catch up with the modern world, was despised for his efforts and would have been entirely repudiated had not John C. Calhoun died in his apartment and Preston Brooks in his arms.

In the next weeks, one can share in the intense emotions and excitement of "a nation" at war and a people confident enough of their superior abilities to risk a cherished civilization against overwhelming odds. We can watch the organization of military companies, such as "the Manning guards," composed of "the clever and respectable young men of the district"; the women busy at making uniforms and haversacks (although the pant legs were all for one side); of a more careful watch on the slaves—" a strict police is kept up with no white man allowed to stay near the place"; a music teacher, sent out of the confederacy on suspicion of being a Yankee—" for that he could be hung, and I think," said Mrs. Chesnut, "he ought to have been."

Then the rumors of a great battle and the anguish of waiting for news and the fear of receiving it; and then one day a letter:

> Today we fought the greatest battle since the days of Napoleon the Great. With 10,000 men we have utterly routed 40,000 of the enemy. . . . But at what a sacrifice has this victory been purchased. Hampton's legion . . . nearly cut to pieces—whole regiments & companies mowed down by the scythe of death. The fields are covered with their dead; army supplies, etc. Nor have we suffered less. I cannot tell the extent—Until the enemy became demoralized they fought well. I understand the fields and woods are strewed with their bodies, arms, etc. I cannot write more tonight. My eyes close of themselves with weariness.

Then a letter in reply, with the good wife asking for two things from the field of battle—a pair of the handcuffs which she had been told the Union soldiers carried to bring back their southern prisoners, and a copy of the printed "bills of fare" which the Union Army was said to have had for their dinner that day. Propaganda had already begun to play its part.

Then, through the long years, the realities of war.

My new house had 35 cannon balls put through it, and my old house was pretty thoroughly pillaged. . . . Your friends suffered heavily. Mrs. Hayes lost her furniture and found in its place 300 muskets, a coffin & a dead Yankee in her parlor—as many as 14 dead Yankees lying in Mrs. Slaughter's yard and many in almost all the yards. . . . I trust you have not and will not experience the horrors of war as we have, the ruined houses, the desecrated grave yard, the pillaged furniture, the carcasses still unburned of horses & even of Yankees, the amputated limbs dragged about by dogs, the pale, emaciated refugees returning to look after their homes,—as mournful a spectacle as you can imagine. Fifty years will not restore the situation.

And in the end, defeat, the South's economic-social system destroyed, and life resumed under an army of occupation. Even worse, were the deserters and robbers who followed. In 1865, a good lady wrote from Camden:

I have passed through scenes such as I could not live through again. We have had Yankee deserters & robbers in and all over our house—at midnight ten devils or twelve in the house and others guarding outside. I have had their pistols at my head & listened to their foul oaths. I have seen them in my children's pretty room . . . everything in it pitched into the middle of the floor, the house covered with broken glass, china broken, ornaments of all kinds, furniture, and etc.

My precious little Mamie knocked down by the blow from the butt end of a pistol—and Evie, her cheeks red under blows from a dastard villain's hand, standing with her cheeks crimson, her eyes flashing, with a pistol pressed to her forehead, saying, "You may kill me, and you may kill her, but my sister you shall never touch."

I am glad to add such a girl to my group of attic friends.

So in 1870, when Sumner's Harvard friend, George S. Hilliard, wrote asking for information regarding race relations in the days ahead, he was told that "the animus, sentiments, emotions, call it what you may, would play a very prominent part in the future; that they would become more and more intensified and at no distant day culminate in fierce antagonism, should the races continue to be mixed up equally in the same civilization,—tied up as it were in the bundle of life by the same political and social bands." And as to Hilliard's startlingly significant question: "Are marriages likely to take place between the races?" the answer was that "it will be fusion under the present state of things, should it not be antagonism pressed to the point of displacement." To avert such an end, Americans both North and South would one day work together, not because of "the political criminality of the past four years, but, in fine, because humanity is there and within it the germs of counter revolution." "Government of white men by colored ex-slaves is the acutest form of moral torture which has ever been applied to a community." It would sooner or later disappear.

In conclusion I ask: What can the historian, sitting on his impartial fence and knowing these people better than they knew themselves, write in the sand for his own generation? He will, of course, living in this day, be inclined to keep the Negro and slavery in the forefront and to see the sectional struggle which ended in civil war as one involving conflicting values and ideologies. That much his age imposes on him.

Yet it seems to me that if he will take a firm grip on the top rail of his fence so as not to fall to either side, he will begin to suspect that his own age has, to some degree, misled him. The really important fact for this South, as well as for the North in the years before the Civil War, was that the Industrial Revolution with its opportunities and its spirit of enterprise was "shaking to pieces the simpler economy of 18th century America." The materialistic and exploitative spirit of the age had in varying degrees infiltrated the South, but the material advantages in cities and factories and new financial institutions had lagged far behind. In fact, in matters economic, the South had drifted steadily toward a colonial status. The commercial-agriculture of the Cotton Kingdom had set the tempo but it had not fixed the way of life. Something which had given quality to an earlier South had been lost, but the patterns and institutions of that older age had remained to a tragic degree. The Mannings and Chesnuts had not moved to the Lower South, but their capital and their slaves had. They had gone on with their old institutions and accustomed ways of living, guilt-ridden now and then, but enjoying the benefits of the new day as cotton fed the hungry machines of the Industrial Revolution. They could literally eat their cake and still have it.

Their political activities, wide as they were, had not, therefore, included the reshaping of their social-economic structure or the adjustment of their thinking to changing national demands. Their situation had not required it. They liked things as they were and the upsetting side of the emerging modern world had not come their way.

In the political realm their section had steadily lost ground.

Internal division had continued to be a feature of southern political life. Only a precarious hold on the National Democratic party had enabled the South to influence public affairs. But even here the gains were more apparent than real. The bitter protest which had been launched against the Wilmot Proviso, in 1850, had not produced a successful southern convention. California, of her own free will, had rejected slavery, and the Fugitive Slave Act, which she received as her major part of the Compromise of that year, could not be enforced. It served only to deepen northern abhorrence of the "peculiar institution."

Douglas' Nebraska Bill, denounced as a surrender to the South, produced instead of slave territory a new national party pledged to oppose any future slavery expansion. The desperate effort of an administration under southern pressure to force the proslavery Lecompton Constitution on Kansas resulted not only in producing a free state but a Republican state. In fact, by 1860, the political situation had become so desperate for the South that her radical leaders were willing to risk their all in an effort to keep control of a rebellious Democratic party. The gamble failed and political impotence was added to economic colonialism. Submission or secession were the choices left.

The historian, knowing the bitter outcome of it all and the bloody cost to the nation as a whole, may denounce them for their blindness, their selfishness, and their lack of respect for human rights. But I would like to suggest that the larger fact is one of tragedy—tragedy local and national. The sight of any people drifting toward civil war calls for much more than the distribution of blame. The failure of men's minds to keep up with their bodies in a day when a new energy had become available through science and technology reveals much more of human nature than of depravity. Steam in engines could be as confusing as atomic energy in missiles.

And so I insist that the southern story is basically a tragic one, not because of slavery as so many have said, but because of other factors which allowed slavery, like so much else in their lives, to outlive its right to exist in the United States in the nineteenth century. The real tragedy lies in the fact that these people remained socially and intellectually *comfortably* where they were, while the whole Western world, of which cotton made them a part, rushed headlong into the modern world of nationalism, industrial capitalism, democratic advancement, and a new respect for human rights.

So the historian on his fence must understand that the men who produced cotton and sugar on plantations with Negro slaves did not do so from deliberate choice but because that was the traditional way, in their region, for gratifying the normal American urge to get rich quick. They lost out in the end to other Americans who had found a far more efficient method, a far more democratic way, and a far more just system for doing exactly the same thing. But more important, both learned later from Abraham Lincoln that they could "not escape history"; that "no significance or insignificance" would "spare one or another," but would pass them "in honor or dishonor to the latest generation."